DANCE FOR A CITY

DANCE FOR

FIFTY YEARS OF THE NEW YORK CITY BALLET

EDITED BY LYNN GARAFOLA WITH ERIC FONER

Columbia University Press   New York

♛ COLUMBIA UNIVERSITY PRESS

Publishers Since 1893

New York   Chichester, West Sussex

Library of Congress Cataloging-in-Publication Data
Dance for a city : fifty years of the New York City Ballet /
edited by Lynn Garafola with Eric Foner.

          p. cm.

          Includes index.

          ISBN 0–231–11546–6

          1. New York City Ballet—History. 2. New York
City Ballet—Anniversaries, etc.   I. Garafola, Lynn.
II. Foner, Eric.
GV1786.N4D36 1999
792.8'09747'1—dc21   98–39377

⊗
Casebound editions of Columbia University Press books are
printed on permanent and durable acid-free paper.

Printed in the United States of America
c 10 9 8 7 6 5 4 3 2 1

Contents

Acknowledgments

MANY PEOPLE have made *Dance for a City: Fifty Years of the New York City Ballet* possible. First and foremost, we wish to acknowledge the New York City Ballet for their foresight in launching this initiative and their generosity and cooperation in realizing it. We are especially grateful to the company's Ballet Master in Chief, Peter Martins; Director of External Affairs, Christopher Ramsey; Director of Sponsorship Marketing and Institutional Support, Katherine C. Foster; and Education Director, Ellen Sorrin; and to the many staff members who went out of their way to help us. We are also deeply grateful to the New-York Historical Society, its President, Betsy Gotbaum; Director of Development, Paul Gunther; Director of the Museum, Jack Rutland; and Director of Public Affairs and Programs, Stewart Desmond for their enthusiasm and unwavering support of the project and for the excellent work of their dedicated staff. The fact that dance is a subject few historical institutions have had the wisdom or courage to treat seriously makes their commitment all the more unusual—and appreciated.

Numerous librarians, archivists, and curators came to our aid, especially Maja Keech, Prints and Photographs Division, Library of Congress; Rona Roob, Museum Archives, The Museum of Modern Art; Madeleine Nichols and Monica Moseley, Dance Collection, The New York Public Library for the Performing Arts; Margaret Norton, The San Francisco Performing Arts Library and Museum; Fredric W. Wilson, The Harvard Theatre Collection; Jennifer Pearson Yamashiro, The Kinsey Institute for Research in Sex, Gender, and Reproduction, Indiana University; Timothy Young, Beinecke Library, Yale University; Cliff Farrington, Harry Ransom Humanities Research Center, University of Texas at Austin; Betty Austin, Special Collections, University of Arkansas Libraries, Fayetteville; Julio González, Music Center Archives, Los Angeles; Diana Haskell, The Newberry Library; Doug Ekland, Department of Photographs, Metropolitan Museum of Art; Judith Johnson and Janét Jackson, Lincoln Center for the Performing Arts; Gene Gaddis, Wadsworth Atheneum, Hartford; Catherine Keim, The Rockefeller Center Archives; Janet Parks and Daniel Kany, Columbia University; Sarah Woodcock, Theatre Museum, London; Francesca Franchi, Archives, The Royal Opera House, Covent Garden; Pamela S. Johnson, The Dorothea Tanning Collection, New York. Nancy Lassalle opened the archives of Ballet Society to us, and Thomas W. Schoff guided us to material at the School of American Ballet; both also shared their recollections of Lincoln Kirstein, SAB, and NYCB history. Gillian Attfield, Kenneth Auchincloss, Randall Bourscheidt, Judith Chazin-Bennahum, Kristina Cordero, Kathleen S. Curry, Virginia Dodier, Mary E. Edsel, Annette Fern, Lynn Foster, Jonnie Greene, Robert Greskovic, Linda Hardberger, Gordon Hollis, Nicholas Jenkins, Vicki Levy, Francis Mason, L. Stephen Miller, Erik Naslund, Genevieve Oswald, Richard Philp, Giannandrea Poesio, Naima Prevots, Mara Purl, Rosaria Sinisi, Douglas Blair Turnbaugh, David Vaughan, Vincent Warren, and many others answered questions, led us to material, and helped us over all kinds of hurdles. To the dozens of New York City Ballet dancers, past and present, who shared their scrapbooks, pictures, and memories with us, we are forever indebted. Their generosity has made *Dance for a City: Fifty Years of the New York City Ballet* a genuinely collaborative undertaking, the expression of a spiritual and artistic community extending across time and space.

We are deeply grateful to the lenders to the exhibition and to the writers who contributed to this catalogue; all have been generous with their time, treasures, and ideas. We wish to thank Barbara Horgan of The George Balanchine Trust for her invaluable contributions to the project and George P. Lynes II for all but waiving the fee to use his uncle's pictures. We also thank the many photographers who contributed to the project, who spent hours helping us select photographs and generously reduced or waived their fees. Glenn Castellano of The New-York Historical Society did a splendid job photographing material both for the exhibition and for this catalogue. We are indebted to Kate Wittenberg, editor in chief of Columbia University Press, for rushing this catalogue into print without sacrificing quality, and to Leslie

Kriesel for her excellent copyediting. Exhibition designer Stephen Saitas created an installation that is not only beautiful to look at but imbued with the very spirit of the company whose history it traces. Finally, we thank the late Nancy Van Norman Baer, whose pioneering exhibitions at the Fine Arts Museums of San Francisco are a continuing inspiration to anyone who loves dance.

This catalogue was made possible through generous support from the New York State Council on the Arts, and Furthermore . . . , a publication program of The J. M. Kaplan Fund. The catalogue is based on the exhibition and program series entitled *Dance for a City: Fifty Years of the New York City Ballet* presented at The New-York Historical Society from April 20, 1999 to August 15, 1999. At the time of printing, major support for the exhibition and program series has come from The Geoffrey C. Hughes Foundation, The Brown Foundation, The Anne Hendricks Bass Foundation, The Harriet Ford Dickenson Foundation, The Irene Diamond Fund, Gordon B. and Dailey Pattee, New York City Ballet, The Morris S. and Florence H. Bender Foundation, and Mrs. Henry G. Walter, Jr. Additional support was provided by Mary Porter, The Alice Tully Foundation, The Harkness Foundation for Dance, The Mary Livingston Griggs and Mary Griggs Burke Foundation, The Evelyn Sharp Foundation, and the Jerome Robbins Foundation. All public programs at the Society are funded in part by the New York City Department of Cultural Affairs.

Lynn Garafola
Eric Foner

DANCE FOR A CITY

HOLIDAY, Nov. 1952. The teaser for John Kobler's story, "The Exciting Rise of Ballet in America," read: "The remarkable legs on our cover belong to Maria Tallchief, prima ballerina of the New York City Ballet Company, and are Photographer Bradley Smith's nomination for 'the ideal ballerina's legs—long, shapely, strong but not muscular.' "

Dance for a City
Fifty Years of the New York City Ballet

IN 1949, in a special issue on the city, *Holiday* magazine noted that New York was "on the way to becoming the artistic center of the world." Museum attendance was booming; several opera troupes were thriving in addition to the Metropolitan; of "considerable importance" too was jazz. But the great change since the First World War lay in public attitudes toward ballet. Thanks to the New York City Ballet, depicted in performance at the City Center for Music and Drama, "ballet," in the words of the author, Robert M. Coates, "has become firmly rooted in New York life."[1] Amazingly, the company that had brought about this renaissance was only six months old.

The New York City Ballet was the last of several companies founded by George Balanchine and Lincoln Kirstein in a partnership that spanned fifty years and, initially at least, experienced more failures than successes. The new company made its debut on October 11, 1948 at City Center, a barn of a theater on West Fifty-fifth Street known until only a few years before as the Masonic Temple; it was a Monday, not a promising day in terms of box office, but unavoidable because it was the only night, apart from Tuesday, the house was dark during the New York City Opera season. On the program were three remarkable ballets—*Concerto Barocco*, *Orpheus*, and *Symphony in C*. All were by Balanchine, and all became signature works of the new company: all remain in repertory to this day.

During NYCB's sixteen years at City Center, Balanchine created an extraordinary body of work, including many of his greatest ballets. He nursed to maturity a brilliant roster of ballerinas and extended the boundaries of ballet technique. And he gave definitive form to a synthesis of the classical legacy inherited from St. Petersburg's Imperial Ballet, where he had trained, and the experimental impetus of Diaghilev's Ballets Russes, where he had served his choreographic apprenticeship, infusing them both with an American energy, rhythm, and style. Although other choreographers made ballets for the company, it was Balanchine who forged its artistic identity and molded the dancers into a splendid creative body.

Balanchine was no stranger to New York in 1948 when NYCB became a constituent member of the City Center of Music and Drama. He had come to the city fifteen years earlier at the invitation of Lincoln Kirstein to found, as Kirstein wrote, "an American ballet."[2] He arrived with impressive credentials—nearly five years with the Ballets Russes, stints with the Royal Danish Ballet, the fledgling Ballet Russe de Monte Carlo, his own short-lived Les Ballets 1933. Only twenty-nine years old, he already had more than one hundred dances and ballets to his credit. However, with fascism on the rise and the European economy sunk in depression, the future there looked dim, especially for artists left stateless, as Balanchine had been, by the Russian Revolution. He accepted Kirstein's invitation with alacrity.

GEORGE BALANCHINE.
Photo by George Platt Lynes. Private collection.

LINCOLN KIRSTEIN
in a chair. Photo by George Platt Lynes.
The Metropolitan Museum of Art, Gift of Lincoln Kirstein, 1985.

Even younger than his protégé, Kirstein was equally prolific. In 1927, while still a college student, he had founded *The Hound & Horn*, a literary review dedicated to modernism, and in 1928, the Harvard Society for Contemporary Art. By 1930, he was on the junior advisory committee of New York's Museum of Modern Art, where he subsequently curated a controversial show on American mural art and organized a Soviet film archive and the country's first dance archive. And even before Balanchine's arrival, he had published his first book, the novel *Flesh Is Heir*, which described Diaghilev's funeral cortège gliding across the Venice lagoon to the island cemetery of San Michele—a prescient image, for Kirstein's career as a ballet director would be largely modeled on Diaghilev's.

BALANCHINE (*with briefcase*) arriving in New York with VLADIMIR DIMITRIEV (*far left*). At the dock to meet them were (*from left*) A. EVERETT AUSTIN, JR., EDWARD M.M. WARBURG, AND LINCOLN KIRSTEIN. According to the accompanying article, "Balanchine . . . has learned to talk what he believes is real 'American,' and proudly announces that it is 'swell' that they are here.'" *Photo by Ella Barnett. Hartford Times, Oct. 18, 1933. Courtesy Connecticut Historical Society.*

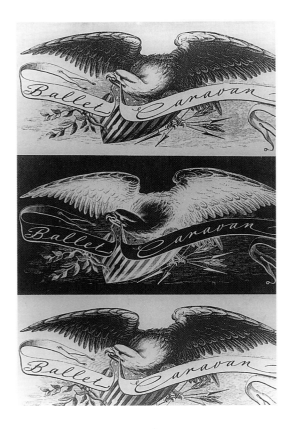

BALLET CARAVAN souvenir program.
Ballet Society Archives.

Between 1933, when Balanchine arrived in the United States, and 1948, when the New York City Ballet was founded, he and Kirstein created not one but several companies, in addition to the School of American Ballet (SAB), which soon became a ready source of dancers. Their first company, the American Ballet, made its debut in 1935 with *Serenade*, then, as resident ballet company of the Metropolitan Opera, mounted a haunting opera-ballet version of *Orpheus and Eurydice* (1936) and a Stravinsky Festival (1937), after which the Met terminated the engagement and the American Ballet collapsed. The second company, Ballet Caravan, which began as a summer touring group for the American Ballet's underemployed dancers, was really a Kirstein vehicle, an experiment in creating a repertory that was American in theme and modernist in form, a means of associating ballet with the country's emerging avant-garde. Balanchine was not directly involved. Instead, there was the collaboration of visual artists like Paul Cadmus (*Filling Station*, 1937) and Ben Shahn (*Tom*, unproduced); composers like Elliot Carter (*Pocahontas*, 1936), Paul Bowles (*Yankee Clipper*, 1937), and Aaron Copland (*Billy the Kid*, 1936); librettists like Glenway Wescott (*The Birds of Audubon*, unproduced) and e.e. cummings (*Tom*); and photographer George Platt Lynes. The choreographers—Lew Christensen, Eugene Loring, William Dollar, Erick Hawkins—were all young and American as well.

In 1941, as American Ballet Caravan, the Balanchine-Kirstein companies pooled their repertory and personnel for a goodwill tour of Latin America arranged by Kirstein's former MoMA colleague Nelson A. Rockefeller, an early supporter of SAB and now President Roosevelt's coordinator of Inter-American Affairs. For this tour Balanchine created two of his most enduring works, *Ballet Imperial* and *Concerto Barocco*; in its later "undressed" form, without scenery and elaborate costumes, *Barocco* became a NYCB signature work. Like its predecessors, American Ballet Caravan was short-lived. Kirstein was drafted into the army, as were some of the company's male dancers. Balanchine returned to Hollywood and to Broadway, where he had worked intermittently since the 1930s, adding to a string of hits that began with *On Your Toes* (1936). Commissions from Ballet Theatre and the Ballet Russe de Monte Carlo added to Balanchine's growing reputation while introducing him to future NYCB stars, including Maria Tallchief and Diana Adams.

In 1946, when he and Kirstein teamed up again, instead of a formal company they set up Ballet Society, a "non-profit educational organization for the advancement of the lyric theatre by the production of new works"[3] that was organized on a subscription basis and inspired by London's Camargo Society of the early 1930s. Most of the money came from Kirstein, who had received a substantial inheritance, and most of the new ballets were by Balanchine, including the seminal *Four Temperaments*. But the programming consisted of more than ballets. There were operas (Maurice Ravel's *L'Enfant et les Sortilèges*, Gian-Carlo Menotti's *The Medium* and *The Telephone*), films (Jean Cocteau's *Beauty and the Beast*), and both "ethnic" and modern dance works (among the latter, Merce Cunningham's *The Seasons*), all of

BETTY NICHOLS at the School of American Ballet, mid-1940s. Tuxedo Hall, 637 Madison Avenue, at Fifty-ninth Street, was the home of SAB from December 1933 until February 1956. Betty Nichols danced with Ballet Society from 1946 to 1948. *Ballet Society Archives.*

which suggests the breadth of Kirstein's interests as a producer and his continued faith in modernism. Other members of the Ballet Society team were conductor Leon Barzin, who became NYCB's longtime musical director, and lighting designer Jean Rosenthal, a veteran of the Mercury Theatre who lit the company's productions until the 1970s, while among the designers were a number of second-generation surrealists—Kurt Seligmann, Corrado Cagli, Joan Junyer, and Esteban Frances, a Catalan painter who did many NYCB productions. The subscribers included not only members of the city's artistic elite, but also many practicing artists and, among the dancers, a surprising number associated with modern dance.

Apart from offices on Fifty-sixth Street, Ballet Society had no home. Rehearsals took place at the School of American Ballet, and performances at rented venues, including Hunter College and the High School of Needle Trades, which had a modern dance series. It was at one such rented space, City Center, that Morton Baum, chairman of the Center's executive committee, happening to see an early performance of Balanchine's *Orpheus* (1948), experienced the *coup de foudre* that prompted him to invite the company to become a constituent of the theater, joining the New York City Opera and City Center Orchestra. The encounter was a fluke and a lifesaver that rescued the company from economic collapse. For all of Kirstein's largesse, subscriptions never covered more than a fraction of the operating costs.

Opened in 1943 by Mayor Fiorello La Guardia, City Center was owned by New York City and heavily supported by unions, then central to the city's political and cultural life. It had a popular-price ticket policy ("top" in 1948 was $2.50) and a large working-class and lower-middle-class audience. This audience NYCB tapped and in the early years partly catered to, even as it retained and built upon the knowledgeable public associated with Ballet Society. The result was an audience of unparalleled breadth and sophistication that eventually included most of the New York School of poets—Frank O'Hara, John Ashbery, Kenneth Koch, among others—and an eclectic group of visual artists, from Joseph Cornell and Edward Gorey to Willem de Kooning, Howard Kanovitz, and Eugene Berman.

This diversity helps explain the extraordinary richness of the NYCB repertory during the City Center years. Although the fledgling company had inherited a number of works from Ballet Society, new ones were needed to prosper and grow. Under Kirstein's dynamic leadership, the company embarked on an ambitious program of revivals and premieres that recalled Ballet Theatre (later American Ballet Theatre) during its most creative period of the early 1940s. Many were by choreographers other than Balanchine, including several Ballet Caravan or American Ballet veterans—Todd Bolender, who revived *Mother Goose Suite* (1948) and choreographed *The Miraculous Mandarin* (1951); Lew Christensen, who revived *Jinx* (1949) and *Filling Station* (1953); Ruthanna Boris, who choreographed *Cakewalk* (1951) and *Kaleidoscope* (1952); and William Dollar, who choreographed *Ondine* (1949) and *The Duel* (1950).[4] There were also Britons among the group— John Cranko, who choreographed *The Witch* (1950), which had designs by Dorothea Tanning and premiered during the company's first season at Covent Garden; Antony Tudor, who revived *Lilac Garden* (1951) and choreographed *Lady of the Camelias* (1951) and *La Gloire* (1952); and the great classicist Frederick Ashton. For many people, critic Anatole Chujoy would later write, Ashton's *Illuminations* (1950), a series of "danced pictures" suggested by Rimbaud, was one of the works that "justified the existence of the New York City Ballet."[5] Ashton also choreographed *Picnic at Tintagel*, which was designed by Cecil Beaton, as were *Illuminations*, *Lady of the Camelias*, and Balanchine's one-act version of *Swan Lake* (1951). Finally, there was Jerome Robbins, who in 1949, as Kirstein later wrote, "cast his lot with us."[6] As Associate Artistic Director, a position he held for the next decade, Robbins brought a distinctive note to the company's artistic identity. Indeed, aside from Balanchine, he was the only choreographer whose works during these years found a permanent place in the NYCB repertory.

As for Balanchine himself, he was at the height of his creative powers during the City Center years. In 1948 he had turned forty-four; he had gone from company to company, and seen most of his works—and most of the companies that had produced them—vanish. Now, for the first time, he had a company with a home and a future. True, at the beginning the company was small, the seasons short, and the finances strapped. But with the expansion of the school, which now had a full-fledged children's program and such outstanding teachers as Felia Doubrovska and Anatole Oboukhov, there was an ever-growing supply of well-trained talent. In time the seasons lengthened. There were tours—continental ones throughout the United States, with long stays in Chicago, Los Angeles, and San Francisco, and far-flung ones that took the company to Europe, the Far East and finally, in 1962, under the auspices of the State Department, to the Soviet Union, where Balanchine, after an absence of thirty-eight years, was welcomed like a returning prodigal. And very quickly, thanks to Kirstein's indefatigable proselytizing and personal stature, to say nothing of his deeply ingrained sense of civic service, the company acquired a public profile, a distinctive New York identity. There were gala occasions (the premiere of Ashton's

Picnic at Tintagel, for instance, took place before the British ambassador and other dignitaries) and fundraising benefits, *Time* and *Holiday* magazine cover stories, and pictures of NYCB dancers in Central Park.[7] And in 1953 Kirstein, now managing director of the whole of City Center, secured from the Rockefeller Foundation the first of the big foundation grants that would not only shore up the company financially but also give it a cachet enjoyed by no other American dance group.

With the company's newfound stability, Balanchine went into high gear. Like the chef he sometimes called himself, he cooked up something for everyone. The accent, to be sure, was on the modern. He streamlined ballets like *Concerto Barocco* and *The Four Temperaments*, eliminating the scenery (designed by Eugene Berman and Kurt Seligmann, respectively) and replacing the costumes (which they had also designed) with tunics and leotards that were stylized versions of ballet practice clothes. This dramatic transformation removed these works from their original neoromantic and surrealist contexts, relocating them in a timeless, anonymous present. With their spare, stripped-down look, they seemed as abstract as a Mondrian painting, as functional as a skyscraper of Mies van der Rohe; they belonged to the universe of "Broadway Boogie-Woogie" and the Seagram Building.

In *The Four Temperaments*, *Agon* (1957), and *Episodes* (1959), Balanchine's most celebrated "leotard" ballets of the time, that present was partly a metaphor for postwar New York. All three unfolded in a landscape of anxiety: they were anguished and sexually charged, with rhythms borrowed from jazz and percussive movements from modern dance, and matings fraught with loneliness, empty pleasure, and erotic tension. In the brilliantly inventive *Agon* pas de deux, the tension between the partners was magnified by the fact that Arthur Mitchell was black and Diana Adams white: this was the first duet by a major choreographer for a racially mixed couple. Other ballets invoked the city more directly. These included *Ivesiana* (1954), a darkly atmospheric work that hinted at rape ("Central Park in the Dark") and brilliantly depicted a young man's sexual humiliation ("The Unanswered Question"), and Robbins's *Age of Anxiety* (1950), which was inspired by Auden's poem of the same name, accompanied by Oliver Smith's blow-ups of the Flatiron Building, and "haunted," as critic Doris Hering wrote, "by the inspired melancholy and looming protectiveness of the big city."[8]

Race was a veiled presence in Robbins's first ballet for the company, *The Guests*. With a commissioned score by Marc Blitzstein, it began, as Robbins later explained, as a "ballet [about] competition among people who worked in a department store. It turned out that the winners [were] a black and a white. But the more we worked on it, the more we . . . [got] away from specifics."[9] Eventually, it became a semi-abstract study of what Doris Hering described as "the bitter problem of social stratification and snobbery and its effect upon two young people."[10] Other works too revealed an attentiveness to the era's characteristic social and psychological concerns. In *The Age of Anxiety*, there was a "Colossal Dad," represented, in critic John Martin's words, as "a gigantic figure from childhood imagination, a sort of wizard on stilts."[11] In *The Cage* (1951), which Robbins described as a "contemporary visualization" of the second act of *Giselle*, a community of barbarous Amazons strangled men in a frenzy of primal hate so shocking that the ballet was briefly banned in the Netherlands as "pornographic."[12] There were jazzy

---

Facing page: BALANCHINE rehearsing *Gounod Symphony* with MARIA TALLCHIEF at City Center, 1958. *Martha Swope/LIFE Magazine © TIME Inc.*

THE COMPANY AT THE GREEK THEATRE, Hollywood, 1956. Top row (*from left*): NICHOLAS MAGALLANES, TODD BOLENDER, JOHN MANDIA, BROOKS JACKSON, STANLEY ZOMPAKOS, GEORGE BALANCHINE, JIMMY DOOLITTLE, BETTY CAGE, JACQUES D'AMBOISE, ANDRÉ EGLEVSKY, [?]; third–fourth row (*beginning seventh from left*): TANAQUIL LECLERCQ, MARIA TALLCHIEF, FRANCISCO MONCIÓN, YVONNE MOUNSEY, HUGH LANG, DIANA ADAMS, HERBERT BLISS, VIDA BROWN, PATRICIA WILDE, ROBERT BARNETT, EDWINA FONTAINE (*second from right*), BARBARA HORGAN; second row (*beginning second from left*): EDWARD BIGELOW, IRENE LARSSON, CAROLYN GEORGE, JILLANA, KAYE SARGENT, MARIE-JEANNE, UNA KAI, CHARLOTTE RAY, ARLOUINE CASE, [?], BARBARA MILBERG, BARNEY NEWMAN, [?] ZORN; front row (*beginning second from left*): PATRICIA SAVOIA, ANN CROWELL, EDITH BROZAK, GLORIA VAUGES, JANET REED, ALLEGRA KENT, NORA KAYE, SALLY STREETS. *San Francisco Performing Arts Library and Museum.*

Facing page: MEMBERS OF THE NEW YORK CITY BALLET in front of Bethesda Fountain in Central Park, 1951. *New York World-Telegram and Sun Collection, Prints and Photographs Division, Library of Congress.*

ballets, such as *The Pied Piper* (1951) and *Interplay* (1952); there was *Afternoon of a Faun* (1953), a work of understated eroticism set in a contemporary ballet studio, and *The Concert* (1956), a hilarious spoof of culture seekers and their daydreams. And onstage was work by some of the best designers in the American theater—Boris Aronson, Oliver Smith, Irene Sharaff, and Jean Rosenthal.

In this period, Robbins was a riveting presence as a dancer. In *Bourrée Fantasque* (1949), where Balanchine first teamed him with Tanaquil LeClercq in what became a truly inspired partnership, Robbins was as "agile as a leprechaun and twice as mischievous," in the words of critic Walter Terry.[13] In 1950, when Balanchine revived *Prodigal Son* for the first time since its premiere in Paris twenty-one years before, he chose Robbins to be the biblical hero. "Here was a performance to wring your heart," wrote John Martin after the premiere. "It is dramatically true and it touches deep; there is not a movement that is not informed by feeling and colored by the dynamism of emotion."[14]

LeClercq was more than a partner for Robbins (and with her long legs and girlish build a prototypical Balanchine ballerina); she was also a muse. Robbins was fascinated by her coltishness and sense of fun, which he exploited to great effect in *The Pied Piper*, where she did a wild Charleston and even

chewed gum. He was intrigued by her banked sexuality, which he used in *Afternoon of a Faun*, pairing her with Francisco Moncíon, whose dark good looks added to the ballet's erotic tension. And he incorporated her zaniness into the role of the screwball ballerina in *The Concert*. After she was struck down with polio in 1956, Robbins made no more ballets for the company until the late 1960s. In 1957 he choreographed the Broadway musical *West Side Story*, and the following year formed his own company, Ballets: U.S.A., which mostly toured abroad. Only in 1969 did he return to NYCB.

At the same time that Balanchine was testing the aesthetic boundaries of ballet, he was also producing crowd-pleasers. One was *Swan Lake* (1951), which Morton Baum had suggested because, in Kirstein's words, it would "attract customers"[15]—which it did. But not even Baum could have anticipated the moneymaking potential of *The Nutcracker* (1954), the company's first full-length ballet, which premiered exactly two weeks after the twelve-tone *Opus 34* and has never gone out of repertory. Balanchine's was not the first American production of *The Nutcracker*. But it was the first to become popular Christmas entertainment and, as the company and innumerable imitators were to discover, a source of earned income that carried them through the entire year.

At the same time that Balanchine was remaking *Swan Lake* and *The Nutcracker*, he was also distilling the legacy of the past into works that were completely new. Innumerable ballets of the City Center years—*Symphony in*

AGE OF ANXIETY. The masked figure to the left of the
Flatiron Building is EDWARD BIGELOW as the "Colossal
Dad." *San Francisco Performing Arts Library and Museum.*

Facing page (left): JANET REED rehearsing children in *The
Nutcracker, 1950s. The Music Center Operating Company
Archives, Otto Rothschild Collection, Los Angeles.*

(right): TANAQUIL LECLERCQ and JEROME ROBBINS
in *Bourrée Fantasque. Dance Magazine, Feb. 1950 © Dance
Magazine, 1998.*

C (1948), *Sylvia Pas de Deux* (1950), *Scotch Symphony* (1952), *Valse Fantaisie* (1953), *Raymonda Pas de Dix* (1955), *Allegro Brillante* (1956), *Divertimento No. 15* (1956), *Gounod Symphony* (1958), *Donizetti Variations* (1960)—paid homage to the Russian, French, and Italian traditions he had imbibed as a youth. Updated by the speed, complexity, and plotlessness of the choreography, these traditions now shed their period identity, entering Balanchine's timeless paradise of the ideal. Here was grand ballet in a postnarrative mode, a magnificent display of the eloquence of the academic vocabulary, extended, technically refined, and rigorous to a degree previously unknown in this country—or anywhere else.

Another important vein that Balanchine mined during these years was neoromanticism, sometimes with a surrealist undercurrent. The combination first appeared in *Le Bal* (1929), left its perfume on *Cotillon* (1932), and reappeared in *La Valse* (1951), one of the most enchanting and mysterious of Balanchine's ballets, a work "permeated," as critic Anatole Chujoy wrote, "with the spirit of the romantic period of the 1830s and . . . with the sense of futility which pervaded Europe . . . when Ravel wrote the music."[16] Photographer George Platt Lynes caught some of the enchantment, and it lingers in Karinska's tulle-skirted ball gowns. Although by this time Balanchine was turning away from designers, his relationship with Karinska remained close. He loved her tutus, with their short, "powder-puff" skirts, masterful craftsmanship, and exquisite detail, and although his dancers were not the first to wear them, they became an NYCB signature. Like Pavel Tchelitchew, who designed several ballets for Balanchine in the 1930s and early 1940s, including *Orpheus and Eurydice*, and George Platt Lynes, who photographed

Balanchine's work for nearly twenty years, Karinska was one of very few artists who enjoyed his confidence and worked with him on a genuinely collaborative basis.

In *Liebeslieder Walzer* (1960), Balanchine did away with the surrealist trappings of *La Valse*. *Liebeslieder* was the most romantic of ballets, an homage to the waltz and a sign of the amazing fecundity of Balanchine's imagination, a ballet about passion and the myriad subtle ways it gets expressed—all told as pure dance. The work was in two parts: for the first, set in a nineteenth-century drawing room, Karinska designed long satin ball gowns; for the second, set under a galaxy of stars, dresses of shimmering tulle. Hailed, in critic Andrew Porter's words, as "one of the subtlest, most delicate, and most beautiful ballets of our age,"[17] the work occupies a very special place in the NYCB repertory.

In addition to these major veins, Balanchine cultivated a number of minor ones. There were remakes of twentieth-century classics such as *Firebird* (1949), which had scenery and costumes by Marc Chagall and catapulted Maria Tallchief to stardom; modern narratives such as *Orpheus* (1948), which had a commissioned score by Igor Stravinsky and designs by sculptor Isamu Noguchi; and revivals of Balanchine's Diaghilev-era ballets *Apollo* (1928) and *Prodigal Son* (1929). There were gay, lighthearted ballets such as *Bourrée Fantasque* (1949) and *Western Symphony* (1954) and high-stepping extravaganzas like *Stars and Stripes* (1958). And, as if this were not enough, Balanchine even choreographed an original full-length ballet, *A Midsummer Night's Dream* (1962). It was an record of unparalleled achievement.

Meanwhile, the company was rapidly expanding. In 1948, it was little more than a pick-up troupe with advanced students from SAB filling the corps; two years later, when it went to London (for a season that David Webster, General Administrator of Covent Garden, said would either "make" or "break" the company),[18] there were fifty-three dancers, all on payroll; by 1965, when it returned to the British capital, the number had jumped to about sixty-five. Equally dramatic was the lengthening of the company's home seasons. In 1949, the company performed at City Center for exactly four weeks; in 1955, for eleven; in 1960, for thirteen. Salaries had begun to rise, although even in the late 1950s a week's rehearsal pay was less than unemployment compensation. But rents were low, and neighborhoods like Yorkville abounded in cold-water flats that dancers could afford, once they came to New York. And come they did. Although New Yorkers dominated the corps (and the children's divisions at SAB) well into the 1960s, most of Balanchine's principal dancers of the 1950s were from elsewhere: Maria Tallchief from Oklahoma; Francisco Monción from the Dominican Republic; Nicholas Magallanes from Mexico; Melissa

TANAQUIL LECLERCQ and FRANCISCO MONCIÓN in *La Valse*. Photo by Walter E. Owen. *San Francisco Performing Arts Library and Museum.*

Hayden and Patricia Wilde from Canada; Diana Adams from Virginia; André Eglevsky from Moscow via Paris; Jacques d'Amboise from Massachusetts; Allegra Kent from California; Violette Verdy from France; Erik Bruhn from Denmark. What made NYCB so much a New York phenomenon was precisely this cosmopolitanism: NYCB belonged to the metropolis that was the cultural capital of the Western world.

Most of NYCB's first generation of principals came from Ballet Theatre and Ballet Russe de Monte Carlo. They were strong performers, but few were outstanding classicists. Under Balanchine's tutelage, the women, especially, were transformed, remade as speedy, athletic virtuosos with the best feet and turnout in the business and pointes like steel.

The NYCB ballerina of the 1950s was among Balanchine's greatest creations. Supple and long-limbed, she had the look of a greyhound. The city's energy infused her dancing, which was as fleet as New York's famously rushing crowds, as dramatically scaled as its skyline, as modern in line as its avant-garde. She had style as well as technique, and a personality that expressed itself through the clarity and articulation of the movement, rather than older conventions of self-presentation. When future NYCB principal Suki Schorer came to New York in 1959, she was "astonished at the way the New York City Ballet danced. That was how I wanted to move—that quickly, that slowly, that grandly, that clearly, and especially, that beautifully."[19] And much to Balanchine's astonishment, after much hard work she did.

By the early 1960s many changes were underway. In 1955 articles about a planned new music center in the Lincoln Square area were beginning to appear in *The New York Times*; it was a project in which, as Kirstein told the paper, he and Balanchine were "strongly interested." Soon Kirstein was appointed to the committee headed by John D. Rockefeller 3d to study the feasibility of what was now described as a "performing arts project" that "would take in ballet, concerts, chamber music, drama, light opera . . . as well as opera and symphony."[20] Four years later the Ford Foundation commissioned Ballet Society (which still existed as a legal entity) to conduct a survey assessing the professional standards of ballet schools throughout the country. At the same time, it awarded Ballet Society a grant of $150,000 for scholarships that would bring students from outside the New York region to the School of American Ballet.[21] The creation of Lincoln Center and the channeling of Ford Foundation largesse would have broad implications for the company in the decades to come.

In 1964 the New York City Ballet moved from the former Masonic Temple on Fifty-fifth Street to its present home at Lincoln Center. The move symbolized the company's coming of age as an institution and was a tribute to its international stature. Although still in its adolescence, NYCB stood across the plaza from the Metropolitan Opera and the New York Philharmonic, among the city's most august cultural institutions. After the cramped quarters at City Center, the New York State Theater, the first theater built specifically for dance, was like a palace. Designed by Kirstein's friend, architect Philip Johnson, to Balanchine's specifications, it had a huge stage, a practice room as big as the stage floor, comfortable dressing rooms, and state-of-the-art equipment. Conceived as a national arts showplace as well as an urban renewal project, Lincoln Center was backed by a broad coalition of banking, real estate, and political interests that met in the person of Nelson A. Rockefeller, governor of New York State from 1958 to 1973 and, in Kirstein's words at the NYCB tribute following his death, a "wonderful patron."[22]

"'TRASH CAN-CAN'": Don't ask us how it helps keep the city clean, but [a] trio of City Ballet dancers performed this pas de trois today atop the Empire State Building in cooperation with Citizens Committee to Keep New York City Clean. *From left*, ELLEN SHIRE, LESLIE RUCHALE, and GLORIA GOVRIN." The picture was published on December 6, 1960. Photo by Herman Hiller. *New York World-Telegram and Sun Collection, Prints and Photographs Division, Library of Congress.*

From the start the project was plagued with controversy. Although the neighborhood marked for demolition had more than its share of old-timers living on fixed incomes and a growing population of impoverished newcomers from Puerto Rico, it was far from the slum described in the Center's promotional literature. Painters lived there (including, at one point, Barnett Newman, Ellsworth Kelly, and Robert Indiana, who designed one of Lincoln Center's inaugural posters), and it was teeming with small businesses and even larger commercial establishments, such as the twelve-story Kennedy Building on the site of the New York State Theater. In a vain effort to stop the demolition, which threatened to oust some 6,000 families and hundreds of merchants in the city's biggest redevelopment project yet, lawsuits were filed, and demonstrators took to the streets with baby carriages and slogans like "Shelter Before Culture." But the U.S. Supreme Court gave the project a green light, and in June 1958 the city turned the thirteen-block site north and west of Columbus Circle over to Lincoln Center for the Performing Arts and the project's other "nonprofit" beneficiaries—Fordham University and the American Red Cross. While John D. Rockefeller 3d's blue-ribbon committee of architects struggled over plans for the performing arts complex, the bulldozers moved in, and on May 14, 1959, amid a crowd of 12,000, President Dwight D. Eisenhower broke ground for the Center on two square blocks of leveled plain.[23]

1958-59

Internally too the Center was riven by politics. From the start Kirstein, who had wanted a theater for years, supported the project. The Met had no objection to including NYCB in the complex (early on, in fact, it was suggested that the company "supply" the Met's "ballet requirements" instead of having "separate permanent ballet groups").[24] It did, however, have strong objections to the New York City Opera, City Center's other major constituent, demanding, at one stage of the negotiations, that NYCO "refrain from producing grand opera of the production magnitude [of] *Aïda*, *Faust*, [and] *Macbeth*," that it give priority to the Met in scheduling Italian operas "of modest production" and "smaller Mozart operas," and that it drop from its season repertory any contemporary opera in English the Met might chose to produce.[25] Kirstein, with his strong sense of loyalty and public service, refused to break ranks. "I was in at the start of the organization of Lincoln Center," he wrote to Newbold Morris, chairman of the City Center board, on March 27, 1961, "and only resigned from the Board of Directors when I realized that Messrs. [Anthony A.] Bliss and [Charles M.] Spofford

MRS. ELLEN LEVITT of 114 West Sixty–first Street led the picket line outside the Astor Hotel as Robert Moses out–lined plans for the Lincoln Square project, Oct. 29, 1956. Photo by Phil Stanziola. *New York World-Telegram and Sun Collection, Prints and Photographs Division, Library of Congress.*

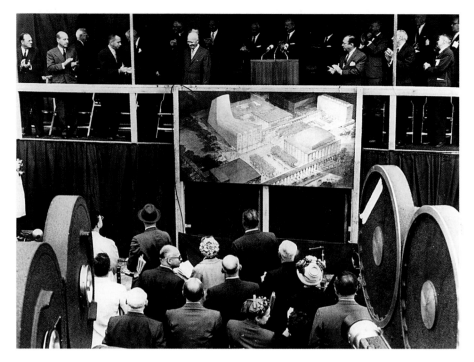

GROUNDBREAKING
CEREMONIES at Lincoln
Center, 1959, with one of
many architectural plans
for the complex. *New York
World-Telegram and Sun
Collection, Prints and
Photographs Division,
Library of Congress.*

were dedicated to the destruction of the City Center as the only possible com-
petitor for the Met at such a time as rising costs would mark the distinction
between the rich man's house and the poor man's house impossible for the
ultimate control of the Met." In a letter to Nelson Rockefeller, he struck a
similar populist chord, calling the project "a real-estate development handled
by able bankers, lawyers and insurance agents, in which art would only receive
a more hygienic facility." He warned that if City Center did not retain its independence as part of the new entity, he and Balanchine would "withdraw those
dancers who wish to stay with us and find funds to operate elsewhere."[26] He
never had to carry out his threat. In the end a deal was brokered, and City
Center received full control over the New York State Theater.

By the time this controversy reached the press, it was linked to another,
equally divisive issue. Who was to represent dance at Lincoln Center? For
Kirstein, the answer was obvious—the New York City Ballet. For others, including Martha Graham and Lucia Chase, who, with Kirstein, Doris Duke, William
Kolodney, and William Schuman (among others), met regularly in 1958 as members of the Center's Advisory Council for the Dance, this was far from self-evi-
dent. Indeed, much of the discussion in the Council's meetings centered on the
need to form a single, expanded Lincoln Center Ballet Company, which would
subsume existing companies and might include two subdivisions, one oriented
toward classical dance, the other toward modern dance:

A unified, overall organization for the Dance is, therefore, a subject the Council must consider. In this connection Miss Graham had pointed out that a ballet training foundation was important in the field of Contemporary Dance, and Mr. Kirstein had added that the techniques of the Ballet had expanded and absorbed much from Modern Dance. . . . The repertoire outlook will probably be a blend of the old and the new and must satisfy the public's demand for what Mr. Kirstein referred to as "invention."[27]

The Balanchine/Graham *Episodes*, which came to the stage the following year, may well have exemplified the kind of relationship the committee had in mind.

At the same time, as Philip Johnson's designs and Lincoln Center's promotional literature make clear, the new theater was intended to serve multiple functions. A full-page ad in a 1960 issue of *The New Yorker* described it as a place "you will come for operettas, music festivals and dance programs. And also to see great foreign companies like England's Old Vic, the *Comédie Française*, and the Kabuki Dancers of Japan."[28] Johnson's preliminary designs, now at Columbia University's Avery Library, made provision for blocs of seats to be removed or closed off in all parts of the house. Thus, the larger hall Kirstein wanted for ballet could also accommodate attractions best served by a smaller one.

In 1964, William Schuman, now president of Lincoln Center, turned the populist argument against City Center. As Allen Hughes reported in *The New York Times*:

Mr. Schuman, who truly wants the New York City Ballet at Lincoln Center very much, also wants the same kind of competition in dance as there is among orchestras and other musical media in Philharmonic Hall and as he says there will be among opera companies when the new theaters for these arts are opened. He said specifically . . . that he felt Lincoln Center should have both the New York City Ballet and a "more eclectic" company or companies . . . . For very nearly 15 years at City Center, there have been no appearances by any American dance company except the New York City Ballet.[29]

Hughes went on to contrast the situation at City Center with the varied attractions booked by Lincoln Center into the New York State Theater during 1964–65. In addition to NYCB, these included the Royal Danish Ballet, Chilean National Ballet, American Ballet Theatre, and two evenings of modern dance presented by the New York State Council on the Arts.

The controversy over the New York State Theater only deepened resentments in a dance world already divided over the Ford Foundation's decision in 1963 to award $7.7 million—the largest sum ever allocated to dance—to the New York City Ballet, the School of American Ballet, and six companies, including two in existence for less than a year, with close ties to NYCB. Modern dance was excluded, as well as ballet companies such as American Ballet Theatre and the Joffrey Ballet. Of the $5.9 million earmarked for NYCB and SAB, a little under half went to the company to strengthen its financial and administrative resources: similar "stabilization" grants would follow in the next fourteen years. The money for the School, actually two separate grants, was to enlarge the faculty, underwrite teacher training seminars, and increase the number of scholarships for advanced students living outside the New York area.[30] The scholarship program, which transformed SAB into a truly national institution, would in time alter the character of the company, transforming it from a microcosm of New York to a reflection of the country at large.

The New York State Theater opened on April 23, 1964. It was a star-studded occasion. Governor Nelson A. Rockefeller himself did the honors, telling Balanchine, "It's all yours, George. Take it from here."[31] In more ways than one, it was: as Kirstein's old friend, architect Philip Johnson, told *Newsweek*, "I did the house with Balanchine in mind. . . . It is really a theater for ballet. It is a sparkle in red and gold, with an old-fashioned lyre shape. It is both splendid and luxurious."[32] On the program was a scene from *Carousel* performed by the Music Theater of Lincoln Center (a short-lived company directed by Richard Rodgers), *Allegro Brillante* (led by Maria Tallchief and André Prokovsky), and *Stars and Stripes* (led by Jacques d'Amboise and Patricia McBride). A champagne reception followed on the Promenade. The second half of the program was broadcast live over CBS. Camelot had come to Lincoln Square.

The company itself had become high chic. Even before the move to Lincoln Center, Jacqueline Kennedy would drop in for an occasional performance, causing John Martin to remark: "Hardly a man is now alive who can recall another First Lady ever having gone to the ballet simply for the pleasure of it." Balanchine was invited to the White House, as were several of his dancers. They went to the Soviet Union under the auspices of the State Department, and on their return heard Mayor Robert F. Wagner proclaim "New York City Ballet Day." For all the glamour, they retained a link with the community around them. They danced for "slum children," Long Island schoolchildren, and maximum-security prisoners at the Clinton State Correctional Facility in Dannemora. They gave lecture-demonstrations at New York City junior and senior high schools, and a month after Martin Luther King, Jr. was killed in 1968, mourned his memory in Balanchine's *Requiem Canticles*.[33] They were chic, but with a sense of service and *noblesse oblige*.

"The Big Time," as Kirstein put it, tapped a new audience for NYCB. In 1966, at the behest of the Ford Foundation, a subscription system was introduced, the first by a major American dance company. With four tickets for the price of three, it was really a bargain, and the public was quick to respond; when the spring 1966 season opened, the company had a $500,000 box-office advance, the largest pre-sale of tickets it had ever enjoyed.[34] Critics were quick to note changes in the NYCB audience. Wrote Harris Green, the music critic of *Commonweal*:

When the City Center moved its ballet and opera to . . . the New York State Theater, it hurled itself into a subscription drive so desperate and indiscriminate in its search for large chunks of assured cash that it bombarded people who'd never had any interest in the arts with junk mail. . . . As a result, the New York City Ballet (the only Lincoln Center institution ever to be headed by a supreme creative genius) draws audiences so innocent they rarely bring Violette Verdy before the curtain for more than one bow.[35]

Dale Harris, writing in *Saturday Review*, put it a little differently: "The poets and painters whose support and critical judgments gave such excitement to the old days at City Center—not to mention a sense of artistic community—seem to have disappeared."[36]

Kirstein, for his part, reveled in the change. "For thirty-five years," he told Anna Kisselgoff in 1971, "I fought to be the Establishment. . . . Now we're the enemy and I'm delighted."[37] Still, the Big Time was expensive. In 1964, only months after moving into the New York State Theater, the dancers signed their first year-round contract. Sets had to be refurbished, and in some cases—such as *The Nutcracker*—

MIMI PAUL on the Promenade of the New York State Theater, 1967. Behind her is one of the Elie Nadelman sculptures enlarged and cast in marble for the site. *Prints and Photographs Division, Library of Congress.*

redesigned. Maintenance costs were higher at the new theater, and running expenses more than four times what they had been at City Center. A 1965 Ford Foundation grant defrayed some of these expenses.[38] But it could not contain the upward spiral set in motion by the move. It was not simply a matter of rising costs or the double-digit inflation of the 1970s, but of the breakdown of the old City Center financial structure and the failure of large amounts of federal funds—on which so much of the dance boom seemed to ride—to materialize on a sustained basis. The year 1966 witnessed the first of numerous strikes by the musicians of the NYCB orchestra. At stake, in addition to salaries (which in the early 1970s were still higher than the dancers') were employment issues—the size of the orchestra, the number of performances per week, the number of weeks guaranteed each year. Beginning in 1966, when the Joffrey Ballet became a constituent of City Center, performing at the Fifty-fifth Street house, the NYCB orchestra also played for the Joffrey. However, in 1973 City Center, now facing a $2 million deficit (partly because of NYCB's 1972 Stravinsky Festival), severely curtailed its support of the Joffrey, making the company's two six-week seasons financially untenable. (The Ford Foundation, which gave City Center two $500,000 interest-free loans to help deal with the crisis, specified that the money be used exclusively for the New York City Opera and the New York City Ballet.)

That fall, for the first time in NYCB history, the company's eighty-three dancers went on strike, demanding guaranteed work or pay for the full fourteen-week season, something management could not promise because the ballet orchestra, which was still without a contract after three months of negotiation, refused to give management a full no-strike pledge. Along with a substantial pay hike, the musicians wanted compensation for loss of work through the curtailment of the Joffrey's season. They struck again in 1976, this time demanding an increase from twenty-five to forty weeks of guaranteed work. After a month the musicians gave in. "The demise of the City Center is what all these strikes are about," NYCB's lawyer, Alan Jaffe, told *The New York Times*. "Until the mid-1960's, there was more musicians' work provided by the City Center. When that work died out, the musicians felt they had lost employment and they looked to the parent companies—the City Opera and City Ballet—to replace that." The situation was exacerbated by City Center's decision in 1975 to limit its sponsorship to those "parent" companies. Finally, there was the realization that federal monies would never amount to more than what Hilton Kramer called a "minor (if . . . crucial) role" in keeping NYCB and City Center functioning.[39]

"BALANCHINE Amid His New Breed." *From left:* SUSAN HENDL, LYNN BRYSON, DEBORAH FLOMINE, MARJORIE SPOHN, VIRGINIA STUART, SUSAN PILARRE, LINDA MERRILL, RENEE ESTÓPINAL, KATHLEEN HAIGNEY, GISELLE ROBERGE, DIANA BRADSHAW, MERRILL ASHLEY, GLORIANN HICKS, and GELSEY KIRKLAND. Photo by Bernard Gotfryd. *Newsweek,* Jan. 13, 1969.

Despite these financial crises, in other ways the company was flourishing. Thanks in large part to the Ford scholarships, a new generation of ballerinas had come to the fore, teens with the slim-hipped sexiness of a Pamela Tiffin or Twiggy. More than ever, the accent was on youth. Senior ballerinas left in a huff or found themselves warming the bench, while the youngsters— "rookies," *Newsweek* called them—got all the plum parts.[40] But for Balanchine, who celebrated his fiftieth birthday in 1964, the new breed kept his juices flowing. "I need dancers more than they need me," he acknowledged.[41] If few of the ballets created after the move to Lincoln Center measured up to the masterworks of the City Center years in terms of originality, his exploration of technique (something he claimed only to "apply") remained unparalleled: if anything, during the last fifteen years of his active choreographic life he took classical movement to dizzying heights of virtuosity, fantasy, and inventiveness that have never been matched.

The grandest tribute to this new generation of dancers was *Jewels* (1967), a plotless, full-length ballet inspired, so Balanchine said, by a visit to the Fifth Avenue jeweler Van Cleef and Arpels. Each "act" had a gem as the basis of its color and design scheme, as well as Karinska's magnificent costumes. But the real jewels of the work were its ballerinas—Violette Verdy, Mimi Paul, Sara Leland, and Suki Schorer in the haunting, mysterious *Emeralds*; Patricia McBride and Patricia Neary in the brashly sexy *Rubies*; Suzanne Farrell, partnered by Jacques d'Amboise, in the stately, imperial *Diamonds*, a summation of the great Russian tradition of *ballets blancs*. A meditation on the different faces of Eve, *Jewels* was testimony to Balanchine's absolute mastery of the most complex and varied forms of choreographic beauty.

It was Farrell, Balanchine's great muse of the 1960s and the Dulcinea for whom he revived the idea of *Don Quixote* (1965) nearly twenty years after he had first conceived and then discarded it, who came closest to expressing his ideal: she was swift, strong, musical, obedient, a virtuoso with the sensuality of a courtesan and the purity of a nun. More than any other ballerina, she embodied the "new" Balanchine style: her dancing had the speed and precise footwork of dancers of the 1950s, but also an expansiveness and amplitude that matched the larger scale of Lincoln Center. She loved taking risks; she would try anything, even the seemingly impossible, like off-pointe turns, thus becoming a collaborator in the fullest sense of the word in Balanchine's technical experiments. Onstage, she lived in the moment, tackling each phrase with a spontaneity that made it new no matter how often she danced it. She was Balanchine's spiritual daughter, as well as a child of the Sixties, and she left her mark on a generation of American dancers.

Farrell left the company in 1969. The action was precipitated by her marriage to NYCB soloist Paul Mejía, and although Balanchine allowed her to break her contract, her loss diminished his appetite for choreography. Indeed, in the next three years, apart from *Who Cares?* (1971), a lighthearted tribute to Broadway showgirls of yore, the quality of his work fell off, and critics were quick to pounce on his much revised *Firebird* (1970) and *PAMTGG* (1971) (whose music Clive Barnes dismissed as "almost too trivial for elevator music")[42] as evidence of his declining powers.

Implicit in the criticism, not all of which was fair, was a comparison with Jerome Robbins, who had rejoined NYCB in 1969 after an absence of more than ten years. *Dances at a Gathering* (1969), which premiered less than two weeks after Farrell's departure, was almost universally praised. Nancy Goldner called it a "masterpiece"; Barnes "a cross between *Liebeslieder Walzer* and Tudor's *Dark Elegies*."[43] Deborah Jowitt analyzed its air of naturalness:

The vocabulary is balletic, rich and immensely clever, but made to look simple by Robbins's beautiful way of shaping phrases. Preparations are never obtrusive; girls arise almost invisibly onto pointe, as if such an action were the natural consequence of drawing breath. Contemporary ideas about art have freed Robbins to be romantic in a way that choreographers contemporary with Chopin were not ready to be. Not for them the irregularities, asymmetries, open forms that give *Dances at a Gathering* its air of naturalness and inevitability.[44]

The works that followed *Dances*—*In the Night* (1970), *The Goldberg Variations* (1971), and *Watermill* (1971)—all ventured into new terrain. *In the Night* was an exploration of the pas de deux to four of Chopin's nocturnes. *Watermill*, which had music by Teiji Ito, was a daring experiment with stillness and arrested movement. *The Goldberg Variations* offered the challenge of a score that—at 100 minutes long and with thirty variations, all in the same key—almost defied realization. These works brought new life to the company at a critical moment.

By 1971, however, a project was in the offing that would usher in the final era of Balanchine's life—the 1972 Stravinsky Festival. This was not the first festival that Balanchine had dedicated to Stravinsky (in 1937 the American Ballet had offered one at the Metropolitan Opera), nor was it the only festival of the period to single out a composer (in 1975, Ravel was so honored; in 1981, Tchaikovsky). But Balanchine's relationship with Stravinsky was different. His music for *Apollo*, which Balanchine first encountered in 1928, was a turning point in the choreographer's life: it taught him to clarify, distill, and reduce; for the first time, as he later put it, he "dare[d] to not use all my ideas."[45] Over the years Balanchine choreographed numerous works to Stravinsky's music, from popular classics like *Firebird* and *Le Baiser de la Fée* (1937) to commissioned

Facing page: BALANCHINE as Don Quixote, with SUZANNE FARRELL as Dulcinea. Photo by Fred Fehl. *Ballet Society Archives.*

BALANCHINE as Don Quixote. Photo by Mel Finkelstein, *New York Journal-American, May 28, 1965. Harry Ransom Humanities Research Center, University of Texas at Austin.*

Below: JEROME ROBBINS rehearsing EDWARD VILLELLA in *Watermill,* 1971. *Martha Swope/LIFE Magazine © TIME Inc.*

Facing page: THE CORPS DE BALLET in *Symphony in Three Movements,* 1983. *Martha Swope/LIFE Magazine © TIME Inc.*

masterpieces such as *Orpheus* and *Agon.* No other composer was closer to him; with no other composer did he collaborate so willingly and with such happy results. The Stravinsky Festival opened just over a year after Stravinsky's death in 1971.

It was an extraordinary achievement, stretching the company to the limit, and, with a half-million-dollar price tag, risky as well. More than thirty works were given, including twenty new ones. Balanchine himself choreographed no fewer than nine of the premieres, of which three—*Violin Concerto,* a throwback to the angst-ridden "leotard" ballets of the 1950s, *Duo Concertant,* a duet that celebrated the union of music and dance, and *Symphony in Three Movements,* a paean to the new female athlete spawned by feminism—were major additions to the repertory. Robbins, John Taras, Todd Bolender, Richard Tanner, John Clifford, and Lorca Massine choreographed the rest. It was a truly magnificent tribute to the composer.

In the company's City Center days the house was seldom full. By the 1970s audiences were packing the New York State Theater. During the Stravinsky Festival nary a ticket was to be had. Balanchine had long rejected the star system (it was expensive and detracted from the choreography) and had turned a deaf ear to the pleas of Soviet defectors to create ballets for them. Still, by the 1970s, he was beefing up the company's roster of danseurs. All the new men came from abroad: Jean-Pierre Bonnefous (later Bonnefoux) from the Paris Opéra Ballet, Helgi Tomasson from Iceland (via the Harkness Ballet and Joffrey Ballet), and Peter Martins from the Royal Danish Ballet. Martins, who joined NYCB on a permanent basis in 1970, was tall and handsome, with the nobility of an Apollo—one of his most celebrated roles—and the technique of a cavalier. With Suzanne Farrell, who returned to NYCB in 1975, he formed an inspired partnership

that Balanchine nurtured in new works and by frequently casting them together in old ones. Two years later, Martins choreographed his first ballet, *Calcium Light Night*, and was teaching company class: by 1981, when he joined the roster of NYCB ballet masters, he was widely regarded as Balanchine's heir apparent.

Audience favorite though he may have been, Martins was never a box-office draw like Mikhail Baryshnikov, whose much-publicized defection from the Kirov Ballet in 1974 had made him an international superstar. Four years later, amid much fanfare, Baryshnikov left American Ballet Theatre, with its star salaries and repertory of nineteenth-century "classics," to join NYCB. He spent little more than a year with the company. He danced many new roles, but Balanchine, because of poor health, never created a ballet for him, although they worked closely on a revival of *Prodigal Son* that was subsequently televised. However disappointing the interlude may have been for Baryshnikov, for NYCB it was box-office magic; for the first and only time in its history, sold-out houses became a common occurrence.

Although NYCB audiences were never bigger than during the 1970s, when the dance boom was at its height and PBS was introducing the company into upscale living rooms across the country, the company's hometown was changing dramatically. Two decades of suburbanization and migration from Puerto Rico

PETER MARTINS taking class with the NYCB men at the Leningrad Choreographic Institute during the company's second Soviet tour, 1972. *Special Collections Division, University of Arkansas Libraries, Fayetteville.*

and the American South had brought about a great shift in the city's population and economic base. In 1975, New York City nearly went bankrupt. Crime was up, the Bronx was burning; Martin Scorsese's *Taxi Driver* and, a little later, Tom Wolfe's *Bonfire of the Vanities* captured the national imagination. New York had become Fort Apache, the symbol par excellence of the "inner city" and the ills afflicting urban America. Overnight, it seemed, the city's glamour had gone. Everywhere, that is, except at NYCB. "Everything is beautiful at the ballet," Cassie sang throughout the 1970s in Michael Bennett's long-running musical *A Chorus Line*. And so, to many New Yorkers the company became a kind of refuge from the city, a sanctuary that night after night expressed an ideal of urban culture under siege on the streets.

No work summed up this sense of glorious escapism more than *Vienna Waltzes* (1977). It was grand and glamorous, with seventy dancers and costumes that called for yards of Karinska's finest white silk. In the final tableau, mirrors multiplied the number of swirling couples until it seemed as if they would spill over into the real world, banishing its ugliness. The ballet was a tremendous hit (even *People* magazine did a spread on it!),[46] but it was not the only culminating work of Balanchine's last years. In *Ballo della Regina* (1978), he celebrated the consummate virtuosity of Merrill Ashley; in *Chaconne* (1976), the heavenly partnership of Suzanne Farrell and Peter Martins.

For all the glorious dancing, an era was drawing to a close. "I cannot wait," Balanchine had said in the 1960s, referring to the two years it allegedly took for a ballerina to get back into shape after childbirth.[47] Now, as he entered his seventies, the ticking of his own biological clock grew more insistent. He had always reveled in youth; now he pushed it to the breaking point, leading to devastating injuries that probably could have been avoided. Anorexia had

SUZANNE FARRELL and
PETER MARTINS in
Diamonds, 1977. Photo by
Paul Kolnik.

become a cause for concern, and feminists such as Suzanne Gordon, influenced by the women's health movement, singled out the cult of extreme
thinness associated with the ideal Balanchine physique as a cause of its rapid
spread among ballet dancers.[48] Education was also a problem: at a time when
increasing numbers of Americans were attending college, many NYCB
dancers, in a throwback to the 1940s and 1950s, didn't even have a high
school diploma. And by 1980 they were again threatening to strike: as dancer
Toni Bentley put it in her memoir *Winter Season*, "we only want enough
money to pay the rent."[49]

On April 30, 1983, after a long illness, Balanchine died at Roosevelt Hospital, only blocks from the New York State Theater. His death was front-page news; telegrams poured in from politicians and celebrities all over the world. The company performed as scheduled that afternoon and night, and the SAB annual workshop went on at the Juilliard Theater. But the dancers and many in the audience were in shock. With Balanchine's death, Jerome Robbins and Peter Martins became the company's joint artistic directors or, as they were called in NYCB parlance, "co-ballet masters in chief."

Together, they shepherded NYCB through the transitional period that followed Balanchine's death. It was not an easy time for the company. Many dancers left. Those who stayed found the change in management style unsettling: for years Balanchine had attended to every aspect of their lives, down to the color of their eyeshadow; now they had to make those decisions for themselves. "Balanchine was our father," Lourdes Lopez told Deborah Weisgall in 1996. "He taught you how to live. With Peter, you simply learn to dance."[50]

BALANCHINE WITH
PETER MARTINS, 1979.
*Martha Swope/LIFE
Magazine © TIME Inc.*

Facing page: SUZANNE
FARRELL and ADAM
LÜDERS in *Vienna Waltzes*,
1983. *Martha Swope/LIFE
Magazine © TIME Inc.*

Backstage, most of the old faces remained, but Martins, who took charge of the day-to-day running of the company, could hardly fill the void created by Balanchine's absence. Only thirty-six and still performing (he retired from the stage at the end of 1983), he was more of a peer than a boss to his fellow dancers. Moreover, despite his thirteen years in the company and the trust Balanchine had placed in him, not everyone viewed him as an unimpeachable authority on the master's works when differences of interpretation inevitably—and increasingly—arose.

Far graver was the question of who owned the Balanchine repertory. Although this was the core of NYCB's identity, the choreographer had willed it to fourteen legatees, including friends, dancers, and a former wife, without specifying its future relationship to the company. Already reeling from the impact of Balanchine's death, the NYCB board and administration now had to deal, as Bernard Taper wrote, with "the possible loss of the ballets that justified the company's existence. How could they program a season or plan for tours when at any moment their repertory could be pulled out from under them or extortionate fees demanded? And what might happen when the legatees passed their ballets on to others—to their heirs in turn, or possibly to exploitative entrepreneurs?"[51] Once the estate was settled, two of its three

DARCI KISTLER, 1981.
Martha Swope/LIFE
Magazine © TIME Inc.

principal legatees, Barbara Horgan, Balanchine's longtime personal assistant, and former principal dancer Karin von Aroldingen, established The George Balanchine Trust, into which they and several other legatees deposited their rights. There were threats of legal action on the part of the NYCB board, terrified of losing proprietory right to the ballets, and threats by Barbara Horgan of revealing to the world at large the board's exasperating shenanigans, of which the press, amazingly, was unaware. Strenuous negotiations followed, culminating in a five-year licensing agreement between the company and the trust. Under the terms of this 1987 agreement, the company, for a blanket fee, received the right to perform any or all ballets owned or represented by the trust. When the agreement expired in 1992, it was promptly renewed.[52]

Criticism of Martins's leadership did not surface immediately. Indeed, in the years just after Balanchine's death, he was treated by the press as the true, apostolic heir, a golden boy who could do no wrong: "Prince of the City Ballet" *Newsweek* called him in a 1983 cover story marking his retirement from the stage.[53] In some circles the backlash was as bitter as the honeymoon had been sweet. Balanchine had not only created a company and a repertory; he had also formed a generation of critics for whom the experience of his ballets as danced by the members of his company was a crucial source of intellectual identity and a basis for aesthetic judgment. For many of these critics, and the junior colleagues influenced by them, Martins was destroying—both willfully and inadvertently—Balanchine's priceless legacy.

Most of the criticisms had a grain of truth. His casting was often misguided; he sacrificed emotion to architecture, allowed the technical level of the company to slip, played favorites, and failed to develop the artistic potential of many dancers, especially women. As the decade progressed, however, the tone in the press grew sharper, the language more virulent, and the forecasts of doom more apocalyptic. NYCB was no longer Balanchine's company; it was no longer their company; under Martins, who assumed full artistic control when Robbins retired in 1990, a new aesthetic had entered the muscle memory of the dancers and transformed works full of vitality into museum pieces. Critics for whom Balanchine could do no wrong—and by the 1970s, they were legion—rushed to protest the betrayal. Like Peter, his biblical namesake, Martins had denied his Lord and must pay the price. The reviews do not always make for pleasant reading.

Whatever his flaws as an artistic director, Martins has kept the company going ("Basically, I've kept the ship from sinking," he once said).[54] In truth, his accomplishment is far greater than the holding action he describes. Simply put, he has succeeded in transforming what was basically a one-man operation—a company serving, in the manner of a classic modern dance ensemble, Balanchine's vision of dance—into a repertory organization closely associated with that vision but not identical to it. Few companies are able to make that transition. Many fold; others founder in the search for new direction; still others find the past a burden. "I'm interested in keeping Balanchine ballets as he would want them to be seen," he told Anna Kisselgoff in 1984, "not to make them look stylistically preposterous in 10 years. . . . Choreography has certain advantages. You can bring it right into your time and it will still be that choreography."[55] From the start, Martins had no interest in erecting a temple to Balanchine, in transforming the company into a museum of fossilized masterpieces.

Although Martins has certain choreographic preferences, he has largely subsumed his artistic identity to the needs of the company. He choreographs to schedule and, whether the result is good, bad, or indifferent, he delivers on time and close to budget. Whatever the slot, he manages to fill it: he has done big works and pas de deux, ballets to traditional music and "contemporary" pieces; he is a skilled composer of dances in the tradition of European ballet masters.[56] And he has kept the dancers coming. To be sure, SAB, since 1991 in magnificent new premises in Lincoln Center's Rose Building, continues to supply new blood. But it is Martins, as the company's artistic director, who must nurse it through the ranks. Although his way of doing this is certainly open to criticism, his accomplishments are also undeniable. He has presided over a distinguished roster of principals, from Suzanne Farrell, Merrill Ashley, Patricia McBride, Kyra Nichols, Heather Watts, and Darci Kistler, all largely if not entirely formed by Balanchine; to Wendy Whelan, Heléne Alexopoulos, Margaret Tracey, Jock Soto, Peter Boal, Damian Woetzel, and Albert Evans, all largely if not entirely formed by Martins. A dancer's life is notoriously short. Fifteen years after Balanchine's death, only a handful of the

PATRICIA MCBRIDE and DANIEL DUELL in *Donizetti Variations*, 1983. *Martha Swope/LIFE Magazine* © *TIME Inc.*

Facing page: MERRILL ASHLEY in *Ballo de la Regina*, 1978. Photo by Paul Kolnik.

company's dancers had ever worked with him. The rest had left, most quietly; others, like Suzanne Farrell and Merrill Ashley, with flowers and fanfare.

The New York City Ballet was not alone in undergoing a transformation in the 1980s. The city itself was in the throes of major changes. In midtown and around Wall Street a new generation of skyscrapers was springing up—huge, postmodern boxes attesting to the triumph of Reaganomics and the globalization of capital. Real estate was booming, and up and down Broadway luxury housing for singles and high-priced health clubs were swallowing up dance studios. (In 1993, the studios at Broadway and Eighty-second Street that had once housed the School of American Ballet were taken over by Barnes & Noble for one of its superstores.) A new generation of millionaires descended on New York, but dance, it turned out, was seldom high on their list of philanthropies. The dance boom had long ended. Audiences fell off and so did traditional gift-giving, as foundations poured money once earmarked for the arts into education and health, replacing government cutbacks. Public funding for the arts plummeted, and what

KYRA NICHOLS in *Pavane*, 1994. Photo by Paul Kolnik.

remained increasingly went to programs and institutions uncontaminated by the label of "high art." Meanwhile, Christian fundamentalists, boasting new political muscle and a hotline to the conservative wing of the Republican Party, crusaded against homosexuality, the National Endowment for the Arts, and other perceived cultural evils.

At the same time, in studios and galleries downtown, a new generation of artists had come to the fore. Most had started out in the 1960s or early 1970s, and by the 1980s had become hot items in the booming art market and at the Next Wave Festival held annually at the Brooklyn Academy of Music. In dance, critics bemoaned the dearth of ballet choreographers, and funders embraced "crossover" projects, which typically paired modern dance choreographers with ballet companies, as the solution. The 1980s also saw the invention of MTV, and the music videos that influenced not only a generation of teen viewers but also young concert choreographers. At the same time, in one or another of its various forms, postmodernism—ironic, conceptual, enamored of technology, pastiche, popular culture, and theory—emerged as the era's unifying stylistic tendency.

Balanchine's choreographic revolution was rooted in the modernism that swept the arts before and after the First World War. His favorite composer was Stravinsky, who, more than anyone except possibly Schoenberg, epitomized that movement in music. Balanchine had only limited interest in "serious" American composers, apart from Ives, and he tended to equate jazz with the show tunes he had encountered on Broadway. This was not the case of Martins. Beginning with his first ballet, *Calcium Light Night* (1977), which was set to Ives, he revealed a sympathy with the city's "downtown" energies—its street rhythms, punk styles, unsentimentality, and postmodernism. And beginning with Heather Watts, his first muse, he identified this "contemporary" style with dancers whose restless energy, high-voltage attack, athleticism, and quirky bodies and bearing struck him as profoundly American. Although he has staged a number of ballets to older music, his preference is for twentieth-century composers, especially Americans: Michael Torke, Charles Wuorinen, John Adams, Philip Glass, Wynton Marsalis. In the fifteen years after Balanchine died, more new ballet scores were commissioned by NYCB than in the preceding thirty-five. However different his taste, Martins has remained deeply loyal to a key tenet of Balanchine's artistic credo—the integral connection between contemporary music and dance.

The American Music Festival, which opened almost five years to the day after Balanchine's death, underscored the company's goals in a typically NYCB way. In the space of three weeks, no fewer than twenty-one world premieres were given, many to commissioned scores, several with guest conductors, and all to music by Americans. To drive home the company's identity as a creative enterprise, each of the festival's ten programs had a front curtain designed by a major contemporary artist: on the roster of painters were Keith Haring, Julian Schnabel, Susan Rothenberg, and Francesco Clemente. For the first time since the company's earliest years, the work of living artists—as opposed to the "specialist" scene painters favored by Balanchine in the 1960s and 1970s—shared the stage with NYCB dancers.

In addition to seven ballets by Martins, the festival presented works by nearly a dozen other choreographers, including several NYCB dancers and members of the company's extended family. More surprising was the decision to open the company's doors to "outsiders," such as William Forsythe, the controversial expatriate director of the Frankfurt Ballet, and three well-known modern dance choreographers: Paul

Taylor, Lar Lubovitch, and Laura Dean. "Everybody is talking about the big difference between modern dance and classical ballet," Martins told journalist Diane Solway. "It's ridiculous. It's all about music and dancing. It's the same language with a different dialect. I don't look down upon modern dance. . . . It has inspired me in many ways. If I didn't find it important and if I didn't feel it gave me something, I wouldn't have invited them." At the same time, he affirmed the continuing tradition of NYCB avant-gardism: "This company is about creation and experimentation. . . . Classical ballet will always be the basis [of our work], but it's important not to exclude everything else and become stifled. This festival is about going with the times and fitting in and finding your way."[57] Although only a handful of the new works entered the permanent NYCB repertory, the festival revealed that Martins was neither afraid of venturing onto new choreographic terrain nor intent on making the company his personal choreographic instrument. The biennial Diamond Projects, which he has used to encourage in-house talent as well as outsiders—John Alleyne, Ulysses Dove, and Kevin O'Day, among others—versed in both classical and modern dance, underscore his commitment to new work in a contemporary vein.

PETER MARTINS (*far left*) with the first Diamond Project choreographers (*clockwise, from top*), ALEXANDRE PROIA, ROBERT LAFOSSE, BART COOK, DAVID ALLAN, RICHARD TANNER, JOHN ALLEYNE, TONI PIMBLE, LYNNE TAYLOR-CORBETT, WILLIAM FORSYTHE, and MIRIAM MAHDAVIANI. Photo by Jack Mitchell.

Facing page: HEATHER WATTS and JOCK SOTO in *Ecstatic Orange*, 1987. Photo by Paul Kolnik.

Although Martins prefers to mine this vein himself, he is also adept at choreography in a traditional mode, as he first demonstrated in his 1981 remake of *The Magic Flute*, a hundred-year-old ballet by Lev Ivanov. Ten years later, he staged *The Sleeping Beauty*, thus bringing to fruition a dream long cherished by Kirstein no less than Balanchine, who had danced in the ballet as a child in Russia and even staged the Garland Waltz in 1981. With a $2.8 million price tag, the production was lush. The scenic designs by David Mitchell recalled Chenonceaux and other fairy-tale châteaux of the Loire Valley; the costume designs by Patricia Zipprodt were set in the seventeenth and eighteenth centuries, as was the original ballet. There were a half-dozen Auroras and as many Lilac Fairies and Princess Florines, revealing the depth of classical talent in the company, while as Carabosse, Merrill Ashley and Lourdes Lopez revealed an unexpected flair for character acting. As for the choreography, it was streamlined, "cut and trimmed," as critic Laura Shapiro wrote, "so skillfully it's now an efficient two acts, with Petipa's beloved choreography at the center of the action, looking fresh and handsome." Shapiro also contended, however, that in this pared-down version, "perhaps inevitably, Martins has sliced out the emotional core of the ballet."[58] For Kirstein, who conceived the overall style, closely supervised the designs, and wrote an essay for the gala program, the production was a throwback to his days as an impresario.

Although Martins has refrained from turning NYCB into a museum, he has paid ample tribute to its rich choreographic past. Works by Balanchine and Robbins (until the latter's death in 1998, new ones as well as existing ones) continue to form the lion's share of the company's active repertory. He has restored certain "lost" ballets, such as Balanchine's *Gounod Symphony*, and mounted the Robbins Festival that was a high point of the 1990 season. But Martins's greatest feat as custodian of the NYCB past was the 1993 Balanchine Celebration. "The Balanchine Celebration is more than big," wrote *Dance Magazine*:

With seventy-three ballets performed over an eight-week period, it is massive. It is also totally unprecedented. Although many companies have paid tribute to the chief architects of their repertoires, none have attempted festivals on as grand a scale. . . . Spanning more than fifty years of his career as a choreographer and including both acknowledged masterpieces and lesser works, the NYCB tribute is like the Picasso and Matisse megashows mounted in recent years by the Museum of Modern Art—a major retrospective of a twentieth-century creative giant.[59]

DARCI KISTLER and PETER MARTINS in *The Magic Flute*, 1982. *Martha Swope/LIFE Magazine* © *TIME Inc.*

Facing page: WENDY WHELAN and PETER BOAL in *Opus 19*, 1996. Photo by Paul Kolnik.

The Balanchine Celebration was an enormous success. Fans came from far and wide, as did the dancers who performed at the marathon closing night gala. Balanchine may have belonged to New York City, but the reach of his influence was international.

Under Martins, certain aspects of company life have changed dramatically. "It's a new world," he said in 1996. "You don't have to hide your boyfriends and girlfriends. The kids are getting married, they are going to college, they're having babies."[60] Where Balanchine discouraged his dancers from continuing their educations, more than half the members of today's NYCB are enrolled at Fordham University, whose downtown campus is across the street from the New York State Theater. Balanchine did not want his ballerinas having babies; by the mid-1990s the company had several ballerina mothers, including Martins's own wife, Darci Kistler. Today's NYCB dancers are more concerned about health-related issues, including nutrition and injury prevention, than their predecessors; more apt to grapple with the problem of career transition even before their dancing days are over; more likely to take charge of their careers and have lives outside the studio. The nunlike existence that Balanchine extolled in his later decades has become a thing of the past.

The packed houses of the late 1970s and early 1980s belong to the past as well. NYCB is not the only "high" art enterprise to find its audiences dwindling, nor the only one in search of solutions. According to the company's market research department, the average NYCB ticket buyer is white, female, well-to-do, has a successful career, decides on her own to make the ticket purchase (even when she is married), lives in Manhattan or Bergen County, and started seeing the company on a regular basis in the 1970s. She is a concerned citizen, who writes letters to the company about issues ranging from the use of fur to investments in South Africa. And like many supporters of the city's elite cultural institutions, she is aging. There are many reasons for this decline in the balletgoing public—the low birthrate of baby boomers, who failed in a sense to reproduce themselves; the migration of senior citizens to Florida and other sunny climes; the cultural philistinism pervasive in many quarters of the city's new elite; AIDS, which devastated the arts, media, and fashion worlds; what some perceive as the company's diminished social clout on the party circuit.[61] But there are other reasons as well. Partly because of cutbacks in government and foundation funding, ticket prices have risen steeply. In 1976, a seat in the orchestra cost $10.95; in 1983, $23; today, it goes for $60 (or $80 at a "peak" *Nutcracker* performance)—far outstripping the rise in consumer prices.[62] In fact, apart from the uppermost reaches of the house, there are no seats for the price of that 1983 orchestra ticket. The result has been to price much of the potential audience out of the market, identifying the company's public with the wealthiest segments of society. The fact that much of the company's advertising has been targeted to young white professionals only underscores this. Yet NYCB, like New York's other major cultural institutions, exists in a city that has become a magnet for immigrants, and is heavily nonwhite.

Fifty years after its founding, the New York City Ballet can look back to a half century of unparalleled accomplishment. In virtually every way it has transformed the landscape of American ballet. As the instrument of Balanchine's imagination, it has created a body of work of a magnitude and depth unparalleled in the history of twentieth-century dance. It has enhanced the stature of ballet as an art form and the status of dancers as artists. It has raised technique to dizzying heights of virtuosity and defined an American classical style. It has seeded innumerable companies, most prominently the San Francisco Ballet, Pacific Northwest Ballet, Miami City Ballet, and Pennsylvania Ballet, supplying them not only with distinguished repertory but also with gifted dancers, choreographers, and artistic directors. In all but name only NYCB is the country's national showcase for ballet.

Now, perhaps, as America rediscovers the virtues of its urban polities, it is time for this national company to come home, to renew its covenant with the city itself. For however much the New York City Ballet belongs to the country at large, it is above all a citizen of New York. The city birthed it and baptized it, gave it life, energy, and the means to realize its founders' vision. Who knows? The ever-changing social world that is New York may well hold the key to the company's future.

BART COOK, with DARLA HOOVER (*left*), ROMA SOSENKO, HEATHER WATTS, MIRIAM MAHDAVIANI, and STACEY CADDELL in *Episodes*, early 1980s. Photo by Paul Kolnik.

The final moments of SERENADE, 1981.
Photo by Paul Kolnik.

THOMAS BENDER

The New York City Ballet and the Worlds of New York Intellect

FOR A HALF CENTURY, the designation "New York Intellectuals" has been the property of a particular circle of writers associated with *Partisan Review*. This memory and lineage have been reinforced by a long shelf of autobiographies and histories. In 1998, these intellectuals were celebrated in *Arguing the World*, a rare instance of a serious documentary film that had a successful run in the theaters. Yet to ask about the place of the New York City Ballet in New York's intellectual history, we must raise questions about this widely shared memory. The worlds of intellect in New York City turn out to be far more diverse and complex than the version so assiduously cultivated by *the* New York Intellectuals would suggest.

Memory, whether personal or collective, is seldom straightforwardly false, but it often gets the proportions wrong. Such is the case in this instance; our memory mistakes a part for the whole. The rubric of New York Intellectuals has been construed too restrictively. There is no doubt that the *Partisan Review* group played a crucial role in challenging Stalinism in American intellectual life, in defining a liberal political ideology, and in sustaining the movement of literary modernism during the Cold War era. There were, however, other New York intellectuals working in a different key, exploring the worlds of music and the visual arts. They were not oblivious to politics, having worked in the WPA arts projects and collaborated, for example, with the great documentary director

Pare Lorentz when he made his classic thirties political films, *The Plow That Broke the Plains* and *The River*. But their attitude and their relation to politics were different, less exclusive, less tightly focused.

Virgil Thomson, one of the leaders of the second group of intellectuals, observed that between the 1930s and 1940s there was a shift in the sensibility of intellectuals in New York from politics (ideology) to art (aesthetics). He is right to see this in chronological terms, but the change was uneven, never completed, and the division persisted well into the 1960s. So I adapt and expand Thomson's fine phrasing of the two orientations. One group discussed "esthetics with intelligence and politics with passion," while the other, with whom he allied himself, were discussing "esthetics with passion and politics with intelligence."[1]

Irving Howe, one of the most distinguished of the *Partisan Review* writers, recognized and publicly acknowledged that there were other art forms and critics beyond the ken of the *Partisan Review* circle. Writing in *Harper's Magazine* in 1971, he explained that a few years before, after the New York City Ballet had moved to Lincoln Center, he "blundered onto a great artistic enterprise" and discovered "genius" in the person of George Balanchine. Self-consciously a literary man, one who "enjoys Wallace Stevens," Howe approached the company as an amateur. In time, however, he turned for further instruction to the dance writings of Edwin Denby, a "great critic" who, he declared, ought to be as well known as Edmund Wilson, the very incarnation of the ambition of the *Partisan Review* intellectuals.[2] Even as the literary culture to which Howe was so devoted was nudged aside by the burgeoning visual culture, he was generous in acknowledging the power of dance as an art form and the power of its critics, recognizing the possibility of an intellectual world beyond that familiar to him.

Howe here opened a door that I propose to pass through, seeking a fuller view of the intellectual world of New York and of the New York City Ballet's place in it. Intellectual historians have failed to grasp the full range of artistic and critical work that characterized the 1940s, partly because concerns of the Cold War era gave precedence to certain ideological themes and political trends. Scholars have pored over political magazines that discussed art, but they have overlooked arts magazines that were often politically alert. The attention given to *Partisan Review*, *The New Republic*, and *The Nation* is legitimate, but it has been too exclusive. The world of the arts disappears in this selection, particularly if, as is usually the case, one leaves out the back of *The Nation*, where in the 1940s Margaret Marshall brought together a remarkable and eclectic collection of cultural critics, including James Agee on film, B. H. Haggin on music and dance, Clement Greenberg on art, and Diana Trilling

KIRSTEIN'S essay on ELIE NADELMAN, published in the June 1948 issue of *Dance Index*, coincided with a major exhibition of the sculptor's work at the Museum of Modern Art.

on literature. Less regularly, but frequently enough to be noticed while paging through the magazine in the 1930s and 1940s, were essays by Lincoln Kirstein.

New York's stature as a capital of culture during the past half century has not been sustained by the contributions of its intellectuals to political ideology. Cultural achievement that can be identified with the city specifically has come from remarkable creativity and critical discourse in the fields of painting, sculpture, photography, architecture, music, and dance. Historical entry to these worlds is to be gained through magazines only infrequently consulted by general historians. Intellectual writings about the aesthetics and politics of a metropolitan democratic culture can be found in such journals as *Modern Music* (1924–46), *New Theatre* (1933–37), *Dance Index* (1942–49), and *View* (1942–46).

Edited by Minna Lederman, *Modern Music* was devoted to the advancement of modern music and critical writing about it. The magazine's range was broad, covering dance and set design, and its visual material was of high quality. The first issue, for example, had drawings by Picasso. Lederman published Virgil Thomson, Roger Sessions, Aaron Copland, and Elliot Carter, helping them to become writers as well as composers. They wrote both technical articles and more reflective ones that probed the relations of culture, society, and nationalism. Lincoln Kirstein and Edwin Denby, who credited Lederman with forming him into a serious critic, were provided with space to write about dance and musical theater.

Music, dance, and drama were covered by *New Theatre*, a self-consciously radical magazine exploring the relation of art to politics. It published articles by a wide variety of intellectuals—from Lincoln Kirstein to Robert Edmond Jones to Paul Robeson to quite obscure coterie and pseudonymous writers.

Dance Index, edited and funded by Kirstein, was

monographic in spirit but visually brilliant, with covers designed by Joseph Cornell. It was a compendium of dance forms and traditions, mostly classic but also folkloric, including popular American dance forms. It documented and thereby created a dance heritage upon which Americans could build. *Dance Index* published a remarkable article by Lederman on Stravinsky and the theater as well as two important ones by Balanchine, "The Dance Elements in Stravinsky's Music" and "Notes on Choreography," in which Balanchine summarized his choreographic principles.

The most wide-ranging and important of these magazines lost to conventional intellectual history was *View*, founded and edited by Charles Henri Ford, with the close collaboration of Parker Tyler, who wrote widely on film and art. Less portentous and more playful with ideas, politics, and aesthetics than *Partisan Review*, *View* addressed many of the same issues. Some writers identified with *Partisan Review* were regular contributors to *View*, including Harold Rosenberg, Lionel Abel, Paul Goodman, and Meyer Schapiro. But the focus on the arts was clear, with writers and artists not likely to be encountered in *Partisan Review*: Henry Miller, Paul Bowles, Alexander Calder, Max Ernst, Georgia O'Keefe, e.e. cummings, William Carlos Williams, Marianne Moore, and Joseph Cornell (on the actress Hedy Lamarr). Lincoln Kirstein translated Jean-Paul Sartre's "The Nationalization of Literature" for *View* in 1946, and in the same issue Lionel Abel published an article with a title reminiscent of our own time, "Georges Bataille and the Repetitions of Nietzsche." The work of the neoromantic artist Pavel Tchelitchew was probably overrepresented—he and Ford, the editor, were lovers, and Parker Tyler was later to write his biography. But Tchelitchew is an important, if mostly forgotten, figure in the art world I am describing. For example, it was Tchelitchew who introduced Kirstein to Balanchine, and he designed the sets for several Balanchine works of the 1930s and early 1940s. He also brought Joseph Cornell into the world of ballet, a domain of sexual fantasy that became an obsession for Cornell.[3]

The early issues of *View* took direct aim at *Partisan Review*. In the first number the editors of *View* accused the rival magazine of being still in the Stalinist camp, and in the second they attacked Clement Greenberg, closely associated with *Partisan Review*, for misunderstanding and disdaining surrealism, which Greenberg, declining instruction, later called a "spurious kind of modern art."[4] Greenberg had earlier offended by characterizing the neoromantic paintings of Tchelitchew, shown at the Museum of Modern Art in 1942, as having reached "a new high in vulgarity," and this no doubt invited response from the *View* editors.[5]

Many of the contributors to *View*—but not those to *Partisan Review*—were part of the circle of intellectuals with fairly direct ties to Lincoln Kirstein and the city's ballet world. There were, of course, a few intellectuals who moved between the different groups, most notably W. H. Auden, who was closely involved with Edmund Wilson and *Partisan Review* yet a longtime friend of Kirstein and an admirer of Balanchine. In 1939, Auden worked with Benjamin Britten to develop a libretto for Kirstein's Ballet Caravan, even though he always considered the ballet a "minor art."[6] James Agee, who had been Kirstein's roommate at Harvard and shared his interest in the photography of Walker Evans, was another. Willem de Kooning seems to have crossed nearly every group boundary there was in New York in the 1940s and 1950s. It was thus fitting that he remarked in 1951 that "there is no style of painting now . . . I don't need a movement."[7] Later, in the 1960s, Susan Sontag joined this list of crossovers. The poet Frank O'Hara, who, like his friend de Kooning, touched most of the city's intellectual affinity groups in the

Several of the artists in this group photograph, taken by George Platt Lynes in 1942 for the "Artists in Exile" show at the Pierre Matisse Gallery, had close ties to Balanchine during the 1930s and 1940s—MAX ERNST (*front row, third from right*), whose wife, DOROTHEA TANNING, designed *The Night Shadow* (1946) and *Bayou* (1952); MARC CHAGALL (*front row, second from right*), who designed the scenery and costumes used in *Firebird* (1949); PAVEL TCHELITCHEW (*standing, left*), who designed *Errante* (1933), *Orpheus and Eurydice* (1936), *Balustrade* (1941), and other ballets, including *The Cave of Sleep*, which was never produced; KURT SELIGMANN (*standing, with pipe*), who designed *The Four Temperaments* (1946); and EUGENE BERMAN (*second row, extreme right*), who designed *Concerto Barocco* (1941), *Danses Concertantes* (1944), and *Don Quixote*, which was never produced. Lynes had been photographing Balanchine's works since the 1930s. *The Museum of Modern Art, New York.*

1950s and early 1960s, felt strongly that the interesting people in New York "were in the artworld, not at the *Partisan Review*."[8]

The *Partisan Review* group formed a fairly well-bounded intellectual circle; the sociologist Daniel Bell, one of the central figures in the group, even developed a formal genealogy, with Elders, Younger Brothers, Second Generation (again with Younger Brothers), and Gentile Cousins identified for each generation.[9] Mapping the art world intellectuals is more difficult. There is no single focus or position to be argued. The best approach is to look for overlapping networks and linkages, rather than for bounded families or circles.

The originating networks date back to the 1910s and 1920s. There were, on the one hand, a series of interconnected salons that traced their lineage to prewar groups. On the other hand there were two student organizations at Harvard, both largely the work of Lincoln Kirstein: the Harvard Society for Contemporary Art and the literary magazine *Hound & Horn* (1927–34). By the 1930s these networks, never firmly bounded, became intertwined.

The movable salons emerged in the aftermath of the Armory Show in 1913, and Marcel Duchamp, who came to New York to place his controversial "Nude Descending a Staircase" in the show but who lived intermittently in the city throughout his life, was an important shadow and often real presence in these salons. This network of modernists had three principal meeting places: the Upper East Side home of Walter and Louise Arensberg, Muriel Draper's loft over a garage on East Fortieth Street, and the elegant Stettheimer residence at Alwyn Court, near Carnegie Hall, where the painter Florine Stettheimer, her mother, and her sisters lived. The Stettheimer salon continued into the 1930s, but the Arensberg and Draper gatherings were replaced by Constance and Kirk Askew's East Sixty-first Street salon. During the 1940s, Julien Levy's Gallery, which specialized in surrealist and neoromantic art, was a major link in the art world networks. Levy's artists included Joseph Cornell, Max Ernst, and Pavel Tchelitchew, and it also promoted photographers, giving Walker Evans, George Platt Lynes (who photographed Balanchine's work beginning in the 1930s), and Henri Cartier-Bresson their first New York shows.[10]

Muriel Draper's salon, characterized by Kirstein as "the High Bohemia of Manhattan," included Gurdjieff, Langston Hughes, Edmund Wilson, Gilbert Seldes, Paul Robeson, and Carl Van Vechten. It was there that Kirstein, while still a Harvard student, met Van Vechten, from whom he learned, as he put it, the "idiosyncratic authority of elegance." From Van Vechten too Kirstein learned about Harlem, and he began to think about it more as "an *arrondissement* of Paris than a battleground of Greater New York," a place of "high lowlife" that evoked Josephine Baker.[11] For Kirstein, who took seriously the moral legacy of his first name, African Americans were visible, part of the city, and in the first outline he drafted for a school of American ballet he proposed that half of the students be African American.[12]

Many of the regulars of the Stettheimer salon can be seen miniaturized *in situ* in the magnificent dollhouse made by Ettie Stettheuim, now in the Museum of the City of New York. The group included a number of painters and critics—Marsden Hartley, Charles Demuth, Duchamp, Albert Gleizes, Jo Davidson, Gaston Lachaise, Elie Nadelman, Van Vechten, Henry McBride. By the mid-1930s, it also included Pavel Tchelitchew, Charles Henri Ford, Parker Tyler, Kirk Askew, Glenway Wescott, Monroe Wheeler, and Virgil Thomson.

The Askew salon had a wider range of participants, but it also included Florine Stettheimer, Muriel Draper, Kirstein, and, of course, Van Vechten, who after 1930 had become a serious portrait photographer; Kirstein was one of his first subjects. Aaron Copland was a regular, as were John Houseman and Agnes de Mille. It was quite common for the Askew salon to adjourn to Harlem, and at least two African Americans, Taylor Gordon and Edna Philips, were regulars. Virgil Thomson and John Houseman were particularly interested in racially integrating artistic life in New York. As is well known, Thomson and Houseman recruited an African American cast for *Four Saints in Three Acts*. This remarkable collaboration, which had a libretto by Gertrude Stein, music by Virgil Thomson, stage direction by John Houseman, choreography by Frederick Ashton, and sets by Florine Stettheimer, cast African Americans in roles that were not race-typed. Later, Houseman and Thomson tried (without success) to stage a *Medea* following a translation by Countee Cullen, with African American Rose McClendon in the lead. During the New Deal, with Orson Welles, they staged a famous "Negro Macbeth" set in Haiti, and Houseman, under WPA auspices, organized the Negro Theatre in Harlem.[13]

These artists and intellectuals were notably ready to engage the whole panoply of the arts, aiming for collaboration at the personal level and the enrichment of particular art forms by mixing at the aesthetic level. Interarts collaboration of this sort found little encouragement in Balanchine's mature work. Yet he appealed to their equally strong commitment to the visualization of culture. Dance is, of course, an art at once of the eye and of the ear, but Balanchine rethought its presentation. He extruded the distractions of elaborate sets and costumes and isolated the dancing body, thus capturing the eye for the examination of the body in motion. Purified but not reduced, his ballets, made of fast and wonderfully complicated movements aided by brilliant lighting strategies, multiplied visual complexity. His ambition, one that appealed to these visually acute intellectuals, was to achieve a purification of the field but not the movement, to enhance the experience of the eye, enabling it to *see* music.

The Harvard Society for Contemporary Art and *Hound & Horn* brought together a group of talented Harvard students, only one of whom was a native New Yorker. Kirstein, the son of a Boston department store magnate, was the leader, but he was joined by Virgil Thomson, from Kansas City, later to become a composer and critic; Philip Johnson, from Cleveland, later to become an architect and critic; Edward Warburg, whose family home on Fifth Avenue is now the Jewish Museum and who became an early financial angel for the ballet enterprise; Kirk Askew, like Thomson from Kansas City, who later became a New York art dealer; and A. Everett "Chick" Austin, who went on to become director of the Wadsworth Atheneum, where *Four Saints* premiered and where the American Ballet, Balanchine's first U.S. company, made its debut. Alfred H. Barr, a graduate student at Harvard, shared their commitment to modern art and in some ways, along with Paul Sachs of Harvard's Fogg Museum, guided them. After he became the first director of the Museum of Modern Art in New York, MoMA became a base in the city for them.

While still in their twenties, these men had already accomplished much. *Hound & Horn* was a recognized venue for modernist literature, and the Harvard Society for Contemporary Art mounted a series of exhibitions that prefigured, perhaps not surprisingly given the personnel, the exhibition program of MoMA. All of them, save Austin, who was ensconced in Hartford, came to New York. Kirstein probably spoke for them all when he reminisced: "I wanted to repudiate Harvard. I wanted to repudiate Boston. I wanted to make myself a New Yorker or much more of a cosmopolitan."[14] In 1931, when MoMA established an "advisory committee" chaired by Nelson Rockefeller, the members included Warburg, Johnson, and Kirstein. A year later, Johnson collaborated with Henry Russell Hitchcock in creating at MoMA a show that named the International Style, perhaps the most influential architecture exhibition ever mounted.[15]

Remarkable resources were available to these talented and wealthy young men. When Kirstein met Balanchine (in the London home of Askew), he turned to Warburg for the financial means to offer Balanchine both a company and a school in America. Austin was able to promise a home for both in Hartford, at the Wadsworth Atheneum. Later, Nelson Rockefeller arranged a Latin American tour that provided the occasion for Balanchine to create two of his greatest plotless ballets, *Concerto Barocco* and *Ballet Imperial* (both 1941), the latter since reworked as *Tschaikovsky Piano Concerto No. 2*.

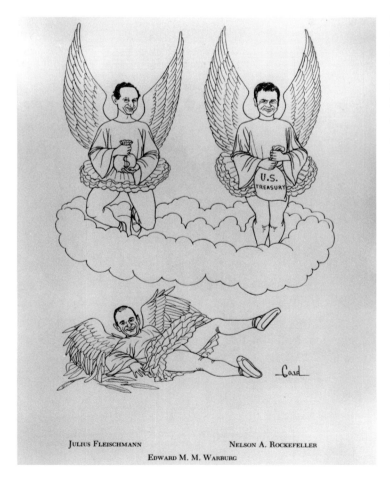

JULIUS FLEISCHMANN   NELSON A. ROCKEFELLER
EDWARD M. M. WARBURG

ALEX GARD's caricature of ballet "angels." JULIUS FLEISCHMANN (of Fleischmann's Yeast fame) was the financial mainstay of the Ballet Russe de Monte Carlo. Balanchine was the company's artistic director from 1944 to 1946. In Alex Gard, *More Ballet Laughs*, intro. *Walter Terry (New York: Scribner's, 1946).*

I'm Ike, you're Mamie.

I can't imagine now why this ever seemed so difficult.

After World War II, Uptown Bohemia became more difficult to place, but partly as a result the City Ballet may have become more of a focal point. Certainly, MoMA was no longer the clubhouse for this or any other group, and though Kirstein's ties to the museum were close through the 1940s, by the end of the decade he would turn against abstract art and MoMA's modernist agenda, accusing the movement and the museum of corrupting art. Stettheimer died in 1946, and the Askew salon ended. There was both a growth and a diffusion in the increasingly multinodal avant-garde, scattered throughout the city in a number of smaller networks. But nights at City Center, which in 1948 became the institutional base Kirstein and Balanchine had long desired, provided invaluable occasions, fleeting but repeated, when the arts networks could momentarily be one, visible, material. Thus, the informal network of Uptown Bohemians held together, sustaining both very personal ties and a certain aesthetic sensibility. At the same time, this community was extended to a number of arts networks downtown. When John Cage came to New York, MoMA provided not only an orientation to the art world, but also a performance space for him and for Merce Cunningham—as well as for events sponsored by Ballet Society, among others—thus linking uptown music and ballet with the experimental groups downtown.[16] In 1951, Frank O'Hara began working at MoMA, thus linking the downtown New York School poets with the world of the museum and the New York City Ballet, which he regularly attended, often with his Harvard roommate Edward Gorey. De Kooning and Joseph Cornell were also close in the 1940s and 1950s, thus linking the world of ballet, Julien Levy's surrealist gallery, and the downtown abstract expressionists, who owed more than is usually acknowledged to the surrealists.[17] Uptown now had entrée to the

fairly tough crowd of the Cedar Tavern. De Kooning, who was already personally very close to his
Chelsea neighbor, dance critic Edwin Denby
(often, like Gorey, O'Hara's companion to the ballet), was a regular at the Five Spot Cafe, a place for
jazz at Cooper Square, not far from Cedar Tavern.
The Five Spot, a base for Charles Mingus and
Thelonius Monk, connected de Kooning to the
interracial literary, musical, and theatrical world of
LeRoi Jones, who in turn could often be found at
the heavy drinking evenings at the Cedar Tavern.

Jones further extended the network to the
emerging Beat scene, which found a focus in
Yugen, a poetry magazine he edited in the Village
with his wife Hettie Cohen. The spirit of *Yugen*
was captured on the title page of the first issue:
"Yugen means elegance, beauty, grace, transcen-
dence of these things, and also nothing at all." It
was a rebel magazine, a point expressed by Diane
DiPrima in her short poem, "For Pound, Cocteau
& Picasso," also in the first number:

> So you sit
> robes and all
> you old ones
> and having broken every rule
> they ever made
> you now preach Order
> ain't you the cool ones.

Yugen was at the center of an arts community
that was distinctively interracial. The world Jones
created and that of the Five Spot Cafe was, in Dan
Wakefield's recollection, marked by a "bebop kind
of occasional, hopeful harmony."[18] Before it was
shattered in the early 1960s, an unraveling represented by LeRoi Jones's reincarnation as Amiri
Baraka and by his move to Harlem, it was possible
for Norman Mailer to feel a "marvelous sense of
optimism," saying that "blacks and whites were

Just once we could use the *Serenade* costumes and the backdrop from *Lilac Garden*.

EDWARD GOREY's whimsical drawings for *The Lavender Leotard: or, Going a Lot to the New York City Ballet* (New York: Gotham Book Mart, 1973) were an affectionate homage to the dances and fans of the company's City Center years. For the thirty years Gorey lived in New York, from 1953 to 1983, he seldom missed an NYCB performance. The ballets are *Stars and Stripes* (*opposite page, top*), *Agon*, and *The Cage* (*above*).

moving toward one another" in this downtown art world.[19] Even uptown, in 1957 Balanchine had made a striking interracial gesture in casting Arthur Mitchell and Diana Adams in the remarkable pas de deux of his plotless masterpiece, *Agon*. With no set and minimal costumes, who could miss the obvious fact that the ballet was raising the issue of race and sex? *Time* magazine noticed, calling attention to "a languorous, sensual *pas de deux* exquisitely danced by Virginia-born Diana Adams and Arthur Mitchell, a talented Negro member of the company."[20]

Jones published all the Beats in *Yugen*—and Frank O'Hara, whose aesthetics were closer to the conceptualism of Cage and Jasper Johns than to that of the Beats. O'Hara, motivated, as was often the case, by a combination of "sexual attraction, politics, and friendship," strongly supported Jones, and he introduced him to other people in the art world, including Kirstein and Balanchine.[21] "With Frank O'Hara," Jones recalled, "one spun and darted through the New York art scene, meeting Balanchine or Merce Cunningham or John Cage, or de Kooning, or Larry Rivers."[22]

DIANA ADAMS and ARTHUR MITCHELL in *Agon*, 1957–58. *Martha Swope/LIFE Magazine © TIME Inc.*

Although those in the overlapping arts networks I have described had serious political interests, mostly on the left, they identified with aesthetic, not political, commitments. What were the intellectual and aesthetic affinities that held this loose, complex, and crosshatched art world network together? It may be that we can clarify the allegiances at the center by investigating a contested border. I have already alluded to the tension that put the surrealists and neoromantics on one side of the border and the abstract expressionists—and especially their explicator, Clement Greenberg—on the other. Although I will focus on Greenberg and his ideas here, it is a broad and important division. With the exceptions of de Kooning, O'Hara, and perhaps Franz Kline, there was very little traffic between abstract expressionism and the other domains of the visual art world of the 1940s and early 1950s.

In fact, the territory of modern art in New York in that period was highly pluralized, more so than received history suggests.[23] But all was not peace and harmony. Clement Greenberg—and those for whom he spoke, with or without authorization—presumed to know the inherent logic of painting, and he was anxious to protect what he called the "mainstream" of Western art from contamination. A brilliant and combative art critic for *The Nation* and a sometime editor of *Partisan Review*, Greenberg demanded purity and autonomy for modern art. Contamination was a constant worry (no doubt a legacy of the sometimes crude intrusions of politics in the 1930s), but so was any notion of a big tent art world, something other New York arts intellectuals generally welcomed. Because they mixed media, opera and ballet could never be major art forms, however much one might enjoy them. Not only were surrealism and neoromanticism a wrong turn in art, but for him the whole idea of MoMA, which mixed a variety of media—film, photography, architecture, design, including commercially produced products, and, briefly, the theater arts, as well as painting and sculpture—seemed to misunderstand the nature of art.

Beginning with his famous *Partisan Review* article on "Avant-Garde and Kitsch" in 1939, Greenberg sought to protect high art from the contamination of commerce.[24] In "Towards a Newer Laocoon," published six months later, he insisted that there had been "a confusion of the arts" and that "purism is the terminus of a salutary reaction against the mistakes of painting and sculpture in the past several centuries which were due to such a confusion." To the avant-garde, he believed, had fallen the task of escaping from transgressive ideas and ideology that had contaminated art. He happily reported that the New York avant-garde had "achieved a purity and a radical delimitation of fields of activity for which there is no previous example in the history of culture." The arts, he assured his readers, "lie safe now, each within its 'legitimate' boundaries, and free trade has been replaced by autarchy."[25]

Greenberg, who like others in the *Partisan Review* circle relished polemic, possessed remarkable dialectical skills and, always assuming ultimate values were at stake, dominated critical discourse. Never afraid of controversy, Lincoln Kirstein challenged Greenberg, fairly ineffectually, in his famous attack on modern art.[26] But my point is not to recount and weigh a debate. Rather I aim to illustrate the existence of two versions of modernism: one singular, autonomous, and seeking purity within the discipline of a single field; the other polymorphic, less worried about contamination, even absorptive.

Irving Howe, who survived the ideological wars of his youth but later worried about the politics and culture of the 1960s, was less anxious about mixing than was Greenberg. He displayed greater sympathy and understanding of the virtues of absorption, at least as he witnessed it in the work of Balanchine. Howe observed that Balanchine effectively incorporated jazz, social dancing, Busby Berkeley-style razzmatazz, and vernacular movements like walking. For the choreographer and his audience, none of these assimilations threatened to undermine ballet. In Balanchine's hands and imagination, such alien materials enhanced rather than degraded art, for he insisted that they become ballet.[27]

In a different but related way, the extraordinary visual imagination of Joseph Cornell quite openly worked with ordinary materials and images, transforming "the quotidian and the overlooked into beguiling mysteries."[28] Certainly when de Kooning painted Marilyn Monroe he was, contra Greenberg, allowing the substantive concerns of the larger culture, even in popular form, onto his canvas, no less than Andy Warhol later did, and he too made powerful art of it. De Kooning, Cornell, Balanchine, and those intellectuals who followed their work were confident of the sufficiency of art's powers, and they were, therefore, quite comfortable with free trade.

So far my account of the intellectuals who were in the audience at City Center has emphasized the sociological, tracing lines of association and arguing that the "old" City Center crowd found an interarts perspective congenial in any number of forms ranging from ballet, movies, surrealism, and neoromantic painting to Beat and New York School poetry. They were not worried about boundaries, or at least not greatly so, and following Duchamp they were not anxious to separate art and life too definitively.

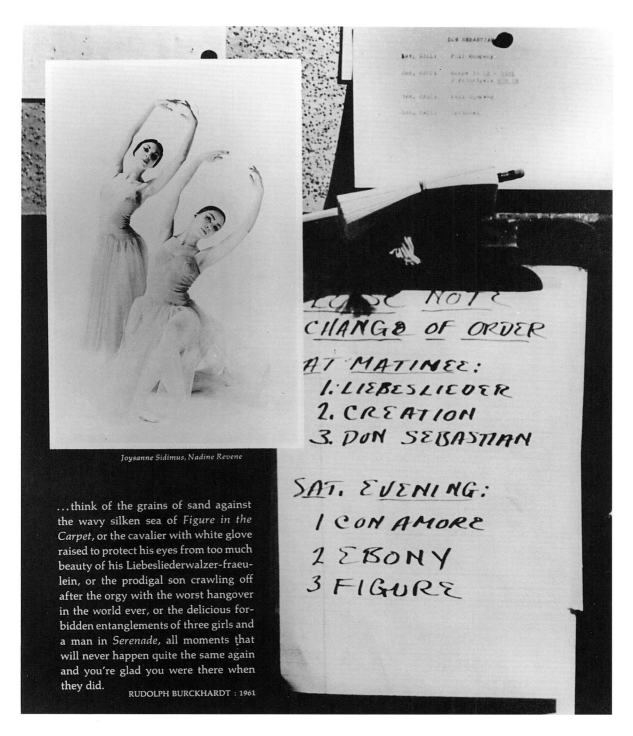

Joysanne Sidimus, Nadine Revene

...think of the grains of sand against the wavy silken sea of *Figure in the Carpet*, or the cavalier with white glove raised to protect his eyes from too much beauty of his Liebesliederwalzer-fraeulein, or the prodigal son crawling off after the orgy with the worst hangover in the world ever, or the delicious forbidden entanglements of three girls and a man in *Serenade*, all moments that will never happen quite the same again and you're glad you were there when they did.

RUDOLPH BURCKHARDT : 1961

A page from the 1962 New York City Ballet souvenir program, which had photography by WILLIAM VASILLOV, poetry by DARYL HINE, WILLIAM MEREDITH, DIANE DI PRIMA, LEROI JONES, KENNETH KOCH, CHESTER KALLMAN, ROBERT LOWELL, JAMES MERRILL, MARIANNE MOORE, and W. H. AUDEN, and prose tributes by RUDOLPH BURCKHARDT, JOSEPH LE SUEUR, BILL BERKSON, and FRANK O'HARA. *Ballet Society Archives.*

But there was in fact more substantive content, recognized today as a politics, embedded in their aesthetic commitments, and it animated much of the art. Of all unlikely people, Greenberg quite sympathetically noticed this preoccupation and drew public attention to it. The world of ballet, he insisted, was bringing a vital private matter, gender and sexuality, into the domain of public consideration. Writing in 1945, the only time, at least to my knowledge, that he wrote about dance, he complained that Ballet Theatre had dropped Antony Tudor's *Dim Luster* from its repertory for being too realistic in its treatment of contemporary sexuality. In Greenberg's view ballet was a bastardized art form. Still, he admitted, it did have important cultural work to do; it might valuably explore the increasingly troubled issue of sexual relations, examining the possibilities and impossibilities of modern romance and sex.[29] In fact, one of his essay's most perceptive insights was that Tudor had imposed "a homosexual pattern . . . on a heterosexual situation."[30]

NEW YORK CITY BALLET souvenir program, 1958–59. *Harvard Theatre Collection, The Houghton Library.*

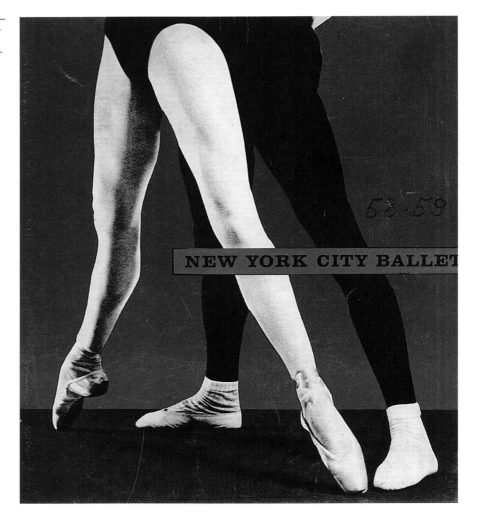

Sexuality is clearly central to the art, criticism, and lifestyles of the intellectuals who found work and pleasure with the arts of the eye and ear during this period. Sexuality, or, better, a complex relation to sexuality, was at the center of Duchamp's art, from his photograph of himself as Rrose Sélavy to his famous "Large Glass" and many of his ready-mades.[31] Stettheimer was forgotten in the 1950s precisely because her paintings, in the words of Elisabeth Sussman, "reveal a sexually ambiguous fantasy of the human body." But of course this is the reason for her reappearance in the 1980s and 1990s.[32] *View* had it right when it linked Stettheimer and Cornell in a special issue on "Americana Fantastica" (1943), for Cornell, like Stettheimer, was, in the words of Cornell's biographer, "a pioneer of sexual ambiguity."[33]

There was, of course, more to the art of Duchamp, Stettheimer, and Cornell, and not everyone I have named engaged in this public discourse of sexuality. Still, it is fair, I think, to offer this broad characterization of a diverse group of intellectuals. The blurring of boundaries between life and art, the mixing of art forms, and the focus on gender and sexuality point so clearly toward our own time as to invite further reflection. I am not sure whether anything is to be made of the fact that Cornell, Warhol, and the philosopher Ludwig Wittgenstein were all fascinated by the movie star Carmen Miranda. But surely it is revealing that Warhol and Jasper Johns were in the early 1960s among the first artists to rediscover Stettheimer.[34] Nor is it surprising that Charles Henri Ford and Parker Tyler, the latter of whom was Stettheimer's biographer as well as Tchelitchew's, were early interested in Warhol.[35] And it is by this point almost predictable that in 1962, the year it was created, Philip Johnson purchased and donated to MoMA Warhol's "Gold Marilyn Monroe."[36] In the 1980s, Frank O'Hara received official recognition in New York, winning equal public billing with Walt Whitman when the Battery Park City Authority inscribed lines from one of his city poems on the fence along the seawall in lower Manhattan. Cornell not only anticipated pop art, he became friendly with Warhol, who in the 1960s visited him in Queens.[37]

In pointing out these connections—and I could offer more—I do not mean to assert some kind of hidden but surely false continuity. I urge only a recognition that the other intellectuals of the 1940s may bear a closer, if still complicated, relation to our own time than the more celebrated "New York Intellectuals." Without pushing too far, I would also suggest that there were historical versions of modernism that are closer to current sensibilities than many postmodernists allow. But still we must acknowledge, even insist, that meanings and significance have changed with the passage of time. Not only postmodern but all appropriations and reappropriations distort. Elisabeth

ALLEGRA KENT and
EDWARD VILLELLA
in *Bugaku*. Photo by
Burt Stern.

Sussman, for example, points out that in Stettheimer's own time her work was "an epitome of modernist sophistication," but today it is recognized for presaging "the subjective, narrative, sexual, and decorative tendencies that are at the core of postmodernist art at the end of the century."[38]

The networks I have been describing largely dissolved in the 1960s. The dance historian Sally Banes has argued that 1963 was a year of transition and transformation in the New York art world, and certainly, if we can add a year to either side, it well dates the end of the world I have been describing.[39] But with that ending there are roots too, important anticipations of the culture we now call postmodern.

To begin with the larger global events that marked the moment as noted by Banes, during the period 1962–64 the United States almost started a nuclear war (the Cuban Missile Crisis) even as it signed the nuclear test ban treaty. Involvement in Vietnam began to deepen, and very soon, especially as it got entangled with cultural conflicts, including the wrenching crisis at Columbia University in 1968, it fractured the intellectual community into old and new left, to say nothing of invigorating a right in New York that came to power as neoconservatism in the Reagan years. Others responded by withdrawing from political engagement. In 1963, Martin Luther King, Jr. went to Washington seeking aid for the poor and proffering a dream of justice and integration. But other African Americans were already discouraged by continued white resistance to these efforts and acquiescence in injustice. Listening to Malcolm X, many turned to various forms of political and cultural nationalism. LeRoi Jones, a key figure of New York's downtown art world, became Amiri Baraka and moved to Harlem. Black Power and the Black Arts movement both marked and furthered the division in the city and its intellectual networks. In a stupid—possibly intentional—accident, Frank O'Hara, who from his curatorial position at MoMA (and in his seemingly endless partygoing) had connected so many people, died. *Partisan Review*, so closely identified with the intellectual life of New York, would soon move from the city to suburban New Jersey, subsidized by Rutgers University. Most important of all for this particular story was the creation of Lincoln Center, where the New York City Ballet moved in 1964. Lincoln Center meant a larger stage and a bigger audience for NYCB, but it also transformed the company. At about the same time, the Ford Foundation came through with much-needed funds to stabilize the company's always precarious finances, while awarding the School of American Ballet a series of grants that acknowledged it as the country's preeminent training academy. NYCB had not only joined the establishment but had become a national institution. It was the end of an era.

Rejecting the purity prescribed by Greenberg, multimedia happenings defined the agenda of a new avant-garde. What we today might call performance art found a particularly welcoming home in New York and came to define the city's avant-garde.[40] In 1963, Red Grooms founded Ruckus Productions as a "multimedia performance company." The new dance associated with Judson Church in Greenwich Village sought literally to *embody* contemporary, democratic, metropolitan culture.[41] The art world was transformed, but the past lingered on. In the early 1960s, Duchamp still lived in the Village, Denby watched the Judson performances with interest, and Warhol went to Judson Church with Charles Henri Ford.[42]

The intellectuals and artists who were part of the ballet world laid foundations that helped make this new avant-garde possible. Yet these newer movements, which today can easily seem middle-aged, have made the New York City Ballet appear old. Or perhaps the company, which had once stood on the cutting edge of New York modernism, allowed itself to be cut off from the 1960s avant-garde and its progeny. Either way, its place in the city's intellectual and artistic life is rather more peripheral than in the days when uptown met downtown at the old Mecca Temple on West Fifty-fifth Street.

Sibling Rivalry

The New York City Ballet and Modern Dance

THERE'S A CHERISHED DANCE WORLD MYTH THAT, at least in the United States, ballet and modern dance were quite separate entities—even adversaries—until very recently. Like most myths, this one contains an element of truth. Isadora Duncan, Ruth St. Denis, and other early modern dancers based their entire art on a deliberate refutation of ballet technique. Duncan abhorred the "unnatural contortions" of the *danse d'école* and proclaimed that, as opposed to the artifice prized in ballet dancers, her ideal, natural dancer "has never tried to walk on the end of her toes. Neither has she spent time practicing leaps in the air to see how many times she could clap her heels together before coming down again. She wears neither corset nor tights, and her bare feet rest freely in her sandals."[1]

At the same time, throughout the twentieth century, ballet dancers have recorded their scorn of modern dance. Of Duncan's 1922 performance in St. Petersburg, George Balanchine wrote, "To me it was absolutely unbelievable—a drunken, fat woman who for hours was rolling around like a pig. It was the most awful thing."[2] Agnes de Mille observed that in the 1930s "traditional ballet dancers . . . viewed modern dancers as amateur technicians; they could not turn pirouettes, therefore they were unskilled."[3] And as late as 1970, Lincoln Kirstein summarily dismissed modern dance as a mere succession of isolated artists with vivid personalities [who] have, by chance or choice, composed grammars of movement suitable to themselves, which they have briefly taught to companies of students who have supported them in public appearances. . . . Over the last seventy years they have neither provided a unified, legible method, a repertory that can be shared, nor a strong inheritance.[4]

It would seem from the constant sniping in the dance literature that the two primary idioms of high-art theatrical dancing have carried on a pitched battle ever since modern dance burst forth at the turn of this century, perhaps only reaching a truce in the very recent past—as the century draws to a close. In 1988, for instance, New York City Ballet ballet mistress Rosemary Dunleavy remarked, "It used to be that you were either in the ballet world or the modern-dance world. Now, there's much more of an exchange between us."[5]

Yet a closer look at the historical evidence suggests another story. The myth, perhaps, was more ideology than truth. The relationship between American modern dance and American ballet is far more tangled than we have come to believe. More like a sibling rivalry than the unadulterated hostility of enemy camps, it has been threaded through with similarities as well as sharp distinctions, love as well as envy, collaborations and incessant jostling for dominance.

Since at least the mid-1930s—that is, since the time when Balanchine and Kirstein founded the series of companies that led to the New York City Ballet—American ballet dancing in general has affiliated itself with and absorbed modern dance in a variety of ways. These include the borrowing of movements, structures, styles, themes, ideas, and values; the sharing of composers and designers; institutional formations; and the direct importation of modern-dance choreographers onto the ballet stage. And despite Kirstein's fulminations, the New York City Ballet in particular—and even Kirstein himself—participated at key moments in the periodic intermingling of the two forms.

Further, ballet and modern dancers, including dancers from NYCB, have repeatedly found themselves joined in performance spaces and situations—what might be called demilitarized zones—where the two putatively opposing camps have collaborated amicably on both artistic and administrative matters. One of these was the musical theater stage, where choreographers like de Mille and Hanya Holm put modern dancers and ballet dancers together in order to marry dramatic intensity with virtuosic spectacle, and where Balanchine worked with José Limón and collaborated with Katherine Dunham. Another was the summer resort, where revue enter-

tainments similarly mixed dancers trained in different idioms. At one—
Camp Tamiment, a meeting place for American leftists—Dorothy Bird
remembers that in 1939 she joined a group of "ten dancers, both modern
and ballet, [that] included Jerome Robbins, William Bales, and Anita
Alvarez."[6] Robbins, in particular, devised dances that made use of the modern group. Bird, who began as a Graham dancer and also worked with
Limón and in Broadway musicals with de Mille and Helen Tamiris, further
recalls that "beginning in the mid-1940s, quite a number of Martha Graham
dancers could be found at the School of American Ballet on Madison
Avenue."[7] These included Anna Sokolow, who took ballet class barefoot.
Bird herself worked at the School of American Ballet teaching plastique
and ballet.

Journalists today may still marvel when modern choreographers like
Mark Morris or David Parsons make dances for major ballet companies; or
when the renowned ballet virtuoso Mikhail Baryshnikov founds White
Oak, a modern dance company; or when Baryshnikov takes as his dancing
partner Kate Johnson, a multifaceted performer who has appeared in both
the modern dance company of Paul Taylor and the Eliot Feld Ballet. And
by the 1990s, professional training schools like Juilliard and SUNY-
Purchase—and even the once staunch strongholds of modern dance like
Bennington College, Mills College, and the University of Wisconsin—
expect dance majors to study both ballet and modern dance technique.
Today's dancers need to be ambidextrous to be marketable to dance companies like Ballet Hispánico, the Merce Cunningham Dance Company, and
Bill T. Jones/Arnie Zane Dance Company, in which skills in both idioms,
or the ability to combine the two, are required. To some, the fusion reaches
back a bit further, to the entry of José Limón's *Moor's Pavane* into the repertory of several ballet companies in the early 1970s, or to the appearance
of Rudolf Nureyev and Margot Fonteyn as guest stars with Graham's
company in 1975. These were shifting points when, it was said, modern
dance lost its distinctive, combative edge—when it capitulated to the arch-
enemy, ballet.

But these fusions between ballet and modern dance are nothing new.
Graham dancer Mary Hinkson appeared in Balanchine's *Figure in the Carpet*
in 1960. In the Graham/Balanchine collaboration *Episodes*, produced by
NYCB in 1959, Sallie Wilson (who was then dancing for NYCB) appeared,
along with members of the Graham company and the choreographer herself, in Graham's half of the work, while Paul Taylor had a solo in
Balanchine's half, which was otherwise danced by members of NYCB. John

Butler, a former Graham dancer, choreographed *The Unicorn, the Gorgon, and the Manticore* for NYCB in 1957. Merce Cunningham's *The Seasons*, with music by John Cage and scenery by Isamu Noguchi, was commissioned for Ballet Society in 1947, not long after Cunningham had left Graham's company, and it remained in the New York City Ballet repertory for several years.

In fact, just look at the photographs of Balanchine's *Serenade* in 1934. The pictures of the first cast of his very first ballet choreographed in the United States could have been taken at the Bennington School of the Dance, the summer home for the major modern dance companies: despite the dancers' pointe shoes and short tunics, their chunky bodies, wide stances, bent knees, lunges, outstretched arms, and exposed strength and effort all seem to compose a frozen image of modern dance as much as, if not more than, classical ballet.[8] (As it happens, the Bennington School of the [Modern] Dance held its first session in 1934, six months after the School of American Ballet opened its doors, and its founder, Martha Hill, spoke at length then with Lincoln Kirstein about both enterprises.)

Facing page: PAUL TAYLOR in *Episodes,* 1959. *Martha Swope/LIFE Magazine © TIME Inc.*

The first performance of *Serenade* at Woodlands, the Warburg estate in Westchester, 1934. *Dance Collection, The New York Public Library for the Performing Arts, Astor, Lenox, and Tilden Foundations.*

Also, as dance critic and historian Marcia B. Siegel points out, *Serenade* is an "assertion about the theoretical equality of all dancers, about the right each one of them has to belong—to fit in and to stand out."[9] This was the message too of Doris Humphrey's equally abstract *New Dance* (1935)—which had its official premiere the same year as the American Ballet premiere of *Serenade* in New York—and of a plethora of other works by modern dance choreographers at the time.

Ballet choreographers in both Europe and America have since the turn of the century repeatedly made use of modern dance techniques, styles, and themes to revitalize their art. But in the United States, where ballet had a checkered history and only mixed prestige, perhaps recurring contests for artistic domination and reversals of status also account, in part, for the convergences and divergences between these rival art-dance idioms. If in Europe academic dance could turn confidently to modern dance, pilfer it, and move on, in the United States, ballet was not so surefooted. So, any narrative of the conflict between these two forms must take into account the chronology of their struggle for hegemonic power and preeminence.

Ballet was the only known high-art concert dance form in late nineteenth-century America, and it was simultaneously part of low-art, even tawdry, forms of dance entertainment, in vaudeville and burlesque. Modern dance, then, arose as a self-consciously adversarial form on two fronts, declaring *itself* the only serious form of art dance and denouncing European ballet and its American derivatives as decadent, frivolous, and unnatural. By the time Balanchine arrived in New York in 1933, modern dance was established as *the* uniquely American form of serious dance. And American artists and intellectuals had trained their sights on their own landscape, history, and rhythms, rather than trying to emulate Europe. However, Kirstein and Balanchine, like the modern dancers, also saw European ballet—as embodied in the Ballet Russe—as outmoded. Even though their visions were not identical, both felt that American ballet had to abandon European "decadence" and find uniquely native subjects and techniques—a project modern dance had long since embarked on.

So Balanchine and Kirstein hoped to create yet another new form, neither modern dance nor ballet as they knew it. Yet rather than wage open war against their rivals, as the early modern dancers had against European ballet, these proponents of the new American ballet engaged a more subtle strategy, colonizing the sister arts in various ways: borrowing techniques, styles, moves, structures, themes, ideas, and values, as well as composers and designers, from modern dance and synthesizing it with classical ballet, as well as jazz and social dancing. Ruthanna Boris wrote of the first performance of Kirstein's new troupe, Ballet Caravan, at Bennington College in 1936, that "when Bennington applauded us we felt more than ever that we were headed in the right direction, for there our audience was composed of young dancers who, though their technique was different, had been doing for a long time what we were beginning to do."[10] In launching a new American ballet, Kirstein and his collaborators realized they had something to learn from the successes of modern dancers like Humphrey and Graham.

During the 1910s and 1920s, in both Western Europe and Russia, ballet dancers had experimented with modernism in various forms, extending and in some cases completely distorting classical technique and choreography beyond recognition. Michel Fokine, Anna Pavlova, and Alexander Gorsky, among others, while heeding Isadora Duncan's call for a more natural dancing body, remained within the classical academy. Vaslav Nijinsky's *Rite of Spring*, made for Serge Diaghilev's Ballets Russes in 1913, was a radical departure from the *danse d'école*, closer in spirit to the experiments of Emile Jaques-Dalcroze, Rudolf Laban, and (somewhat later) Mary Wigman.

The years during World War I and immediately following, especially after the Bolshevik Revolution, saw a blossoming of experimental dance studios in Russia. In order to make dance Soviet, and in an era of intense avant-garde activity, ballet masters incorporated constructivist figures, machine dance movements, and music-hall chorus lines into their works—and even into pre-Revolutionary relics like *The Nutcracker* and *Swan Lake*. As Yuri Slonimsky later disparagingly put it, "In the 1920's Soviet Ballet went through all the phases of barefoot naturalism, strident constructivism, unnatural plastic expressionism and erotic orientalism."[11] It was in this milieu that Balanchine himself began to choreograph, and his

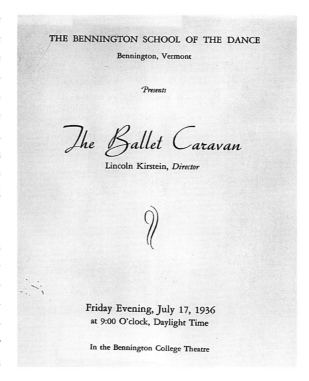

THE BENNINGTON SCHOOL OF THE DANCE

Bennington, Vermont

Presents

The Ballet Caravan

Lincoln Kirstein, *Director*

Friday Evening, July 17, 1936
at 9:00 O'clock, Daylight Time

In the Bennington College Theatre

Program for the debut performance of Ballet Caravan at the Bennington School of the Dance, 1936. On the bill were LEW CHRISTENSEN'S *Encounter*, EUGENE LORING'S *Harlequin for President*, and seven divertissements. *San Francisco Performing Arts Library and Museum.*

early efforts in his group the Young Ballet show influences from a range of sources—folk dance, music hall, *apache* dancing, acrobatics, plastique, German Expressionism, and jazz.[12] Like the American modern dance choreographers, Balanchine aspired to create a revolutionary dance idiom.

Thus, Balanchine brought first to Diaghilev's company, where he worked from late 1924 to 1929, and then to his various American enterprises an emerging choreographic sensibility formed in a European crucible of mixed dance forms. Kirstein writes that unlike the conservative custodians of the ballet tradition he met in Europe in 1933, Balanchine thought ballet "must be reconstructed for service in our twentieth century, speeded up," made to achieve "the snap and brilliance propelled by syncopation since Stravinsky and jazz."[13] Despite its classical theme, Balanchine's *Apollo* (1928), revived for the American Ballet in 1937 and New York City Ballet in 1951, and revised several times thereafter, included torso contractions and striking asymmetries, as well as other movements seemingly borrowed from both modern dance and jazz.

Prodigal Son (1929), which Balanchine revived for NYCB in 1950, reveals the emotional saturation, constructivist effects, erotic acrobatic partnering, and fascination with the grotesque typical of the 1920s. De Mille's description of the hero's drinking companions in the original production recalls the expressionism of German choreographers such as Mary Wigman:

Bald as eggs, dressed identically, moving identically, crowded together as closely as possible, the dancers hop over one another's back, circle around alternately squatting and rising, rear themselves into architectural formations, crawl down each other to the earth again, scramble about sideways in ridiculous positions like crabs. . . . They are abortions, gargoyles, abnormal, undeveloped creatures.

And of the Prodigal's crushing, humiliated return home, she writes:

In an excess of shame and grief he pulls himself up until his body hangs pilloried, shrunken with loathing, knees drawn taut. In this manner he comes to the earth. In this manner he crawls away. He thrashes in the dust, draws himself into a knot, kicks free, turns feverishly over and around and back again.[14]

Balanchine made other ballets in an expressionist mode, most notably *Opus 34* (1954), to music by Arnold Schoenberg and with costumes by Esteban Francés that made the dancers' bodies look like skeletons. John Martin described it as "morbid, solemn . . . altogether in [Laban's] idiom, torso, grotesqueries, and all." Francisco Moncíon, who danced one of the male leads, recalled that "it was absolutely eerie, obscenely eerie, having the connotation of foulness and death." And playing into the rhetoric of the ballet-modern

dance competition, B. H. Haggin observed that the first section (First Time) was "a demonstration of how much more effectively Balanchine uses [elements of modern dance] than the modern dancers themselves."[15]

With Balanchine's second U.S. ballet, *Alma Mater* (1935), a satire of college life, the Americana project Kirstein had dreamed of even before meeting Balanchine bore its first fruit. As early as 1933, Kirstein wrote to his friend A. Everett Austin, Jr., the director of the Wadsworth Atheneum in Hartford, about the plans for an American ballet he had discussed with Balanchine in Europe. The repertory Kirstein proposed to Balanchine, "out of American life," included: *Pocahontas*; *Doomsday*, with scenery by John Benson inspired by New England gravestones; *Uncle Tom's Cabin*, with a libretto by e.e. cummings and music by Stephen Foster; *Moby Dick*; and *Custer's Last Stand*.[16] While most of these ballets were never realized (nor were later projects like *Memorial Day*, about the Civil War, and *The Birds of Audubon*), Ballet Caravan, the company Kirstein founded in 1936, did produce *Pocahontas* (1936), which had choreography by Lew Christensen, music by Elliott Carter, and a libretto by Kirstein himself, as well as several other ballets on American themes set to new American music, including *Yankee Clipper* (1937), *Folk Dance* (1937), *Filling Station* (1938), *Billy the Kid* (1938), and *City Portrait* (1939).

Kirstein seems to have ushered in the era of Americana dance not only through his work with Ballet Caravan but also through writings such as *Blast at Ballet: A Corrective for the American Audience* (1938), in which he called for a specifically American style of ballet dancing, "bred . . . from basket-ball courts, track and swimming meets and junior-proms."[17] Pointing out that American ballet companies, like those of Catherine Littlefield and Ruth Page, were also working with native themes, he called for "an alliance of American ballets" that could compete with imported Russian troupes and build a national performing circuit and a national audience.

But Kirstein's fascination with American themes, styles, and textures was not unique. It was part of a large-scale movement in ballet and modern dance—and the American arts in general in the 1930s. During the Depression, an urgent search for a national identity, as well as for both past American traditions and possible future directions, led artists of varying political persuasions to base their work on studies of American life at every social and economic stratum. There were new turns toward realism and toward politically engaged art, efforts to uncover a critical American history as well as to celebrate nostalgically a mythic American past. The American experience was captured by Edward Hopper's desolate landscapes as well as by Thomas Hart Benton's reactionary populism; by Dorothea Lange's photographs; by writers of the Harlem Renaissance like Langston Hughes and Zora Neale Hurston; by muralists like

George Biddle; and by the thousands of other artists—musicians, theater people, dancers, writers, and visual artists—hired by the WPA.

In dance, Tamiris had begun her suite of *Negro Spirituals* and choreographed *Prize Fight Studies* in 1928; Doris Humphrey had created *The Shakers* in 1930; Sokolow choreographed *City Rhythms, Part 2* in 1931; Martha Graham made *American Provincials* in 1934 and *Panorama* in 1935. By the mid-1930s, themes of American identity—both critical and celebratory—pervaded ballet as well as modern dance, especially as both idioms, along with show dancing, were produced on Federal Theater Project stages.

In founding Ballet Caravan and in calling for an organization of American ballet companies, Kirstein followed an institutional model more like the small American modern dance company than the traditional ballet troupe. (Perhaps the democratic, collective administrative methods he aspired to even surpassed the modern dance companies, which were often run as dictatorially as any Ballet Russe troupe.) "Ballet Caravan was conceived as a miniature," Kirstein later wrote. "I had no ambition to make it more than a pilot experiment. . . . Primarily it attempted to produce a new repertory by native choreographers, musicians, and designers working with national themes. Prospective audiences would come from colleges across the country, and we would play in civic auditoriums as we could find them."[18] Kirstein was no stranger to left-wing politics, which in part accounted for his politically informed vision of organization and administration. But also, perhaps following the principle that "the enemy of my enemy is my friend," in attempting to create an alternative to the émigré Russian companies that he had come to despise, despite his classical taste he looked for allies in the modern dance world.

Kirstein's ready-made college audiences had recently been built by touring modern dance companies and the network of college dance teachers who came to the summer sessions of the Bennington School of the Dance. Further, in *Blast at Ballet*, Kirstein proposes that American ballet companies consider participating in a circuit for "dance attractions" that would include modern dancers and that might take as its model the modern dance series at Washington Irving High School run by Joseph Mann or that at the YMHA run by William Kolodney.[19]

Kirstein engaged Frances Hawkins as his manager for Ballet Caravan. Hawkins managed a number of modern dancers, including Martha Graham, and it was she who arranged for the company to give its first performances at Bennington, the stronghold of modern dance. As Kirstein later wrote, "Ballet Caravan first appeared in an auditorium usually given over to the dauntless experiments of progressive dancing, supposedly in violent opposition to the academic classic ballet. . . . In an important sense, Modern Dance may be said to have launched Ballet Caravan."[20]

Thus, Kirstein allied himself institutionally to modern dance. His aesthetic could also—like the moderns—be seen as antiballet, or at least anti-European. Recounting the genesis of *Filling Station*, he wrote that he had considered adapting Mark Twain's *Mysterious Stranger*, but that "its medieval, romantic locale was reminiscent of *Giselle*—a locus which at the moment was anathema."[21]

And yet Kirstein's aesthetic, as contemporary and vernacular as modern dance if not more so, was still rooted in classicism. He still wanted to produce ballets, not defect to the arena of modern dance. Similarly, his friend Paul Cadmus, who designed the costumes and scenery for *Filling Station*, made paintings that could be seen simultaneously as shocking slices of tawdry contemporary life *and* classical or Renaissance nudes. (Cadmus also created a mural of *Pocahontas Saving the Life of Captain John Smith* in 1938, two years after Ballet Caravan first produced Lew Christensen's ballet on the same theme.) Kirstein later wrote of Cadmus's early painting *Shore Leave*:

A solidity of firm flesh and muscle swells the flush health within the tightness of navy blues and whites. Infectious good humor and hearty slapstick playfulness, sport without caricature, fix a transient carnal innocence. Uniforms italicize biceps, deltoids, and pectorals, recalling the convention of Renaissance armor plate laid close over nudity, as cut in classic marble for the Medici.[22]

He might have been speaking of Jerome Robbins's Americana ballet *Fancy Free* (1944), which entered the NYCB repertory in 1980. Robbins first made *Fancy Free* for Ballet Theatre because he was vexed by the continuing Russian influence on American ballet companies, a frustration similar to what had led Kirstein to found Ballet Caravan in the late 1930s.

Fancy Free is an example not only of the Americana theme shared by ballet and modern dance, but also of the ballet-modern dance convergence of technique and style during this period. The ballet shows the same homoerotic iconography of desire as Cadmus's paintings of sailors, despite their heterosexual narratives about shore-leave innocents and fast women. (Indeed, Cadmus's *Sailors and Floosies* [1938], which shows three sailors with three women—a redhead, a blonde, and a brunette—could almost be a forerunner to *Fancy Free*.) Although it has a plot and is indebted to both classical and popular dance traditions, *Fancy Free* also recalls the abstract modern dances of Ted Shawn and his Men Dancers, a troupe devoted to enhancing the status of the male dancer by displaying his athleticism and bare-chested virility in scenes of contest and cooperative labor.[23] Reviewing *Fancy Free* in 1944, Edwin Denby called it "a direct, manly piece."[24] The sailors often stand at the bar with their backs to the audiences, flexing their muscles and revealing the buttocks under their tight pants; they synchronize identical moves in a line or spread out, like a deck of cards, in canon; they dance with big, open chests and outspread arms; they devour space in wide leaps; and, arguing over women, they fight lustily—recalling paintings of nude Greek athletes.[25] (In fact, the opening movement of Balanchine's *Agon* [1957], in which four men in T-shirts and tights line up with their backs to the audience and then move either in tight synchrony or in canon, also calls to mind Shawn's Men Dancers.)

Either through Frances Hawkins or de Mille, Kirstein was introduced to Martha Graham. Though he had disdained modern dance, the two became close friends. They found they had a common enemy in European-style ballet and a common interest in American themes and an American athleticism and use of space. In *Blast at Ballet*, Kirstein writes:

I have been deeply impressed by a use of a lateral breadth in her leaps and in her extended profile which is far more satisfactory for some athletic American dancers than a complete adherence to the perpendicular stylistic rigidity of the Russo-Italian [ballet] pedagogy. In Martha Graham's finished work as in her strict professional classes, I can find nothing inimical to the developed classic dance as expounded, for example, by George Balanchine's *Apollon*.[26]

Perhaps it was under Kirstein's influence that Graham began to experiment—in *American Document* (1938) and in *Letter to the World* (1940)—with the spoken word. Of *American Document*, with its minstrel show format and its themes of Native American spirituality and the emancipation of the slaves, topics dear to Kirstein's own heart, he wrote, "The subject matter . . . is our time, our place, our dangers, and our chances of survival. It is the most important extended dance creation by a living American, and if there has been another in any other time more important, there is no record of it."[27]

Graham first saw Erick Hawkins dance, with Ballet Caravan, in 1936. And it was through Kirstein that Graham got to know Hawkins and invited him to join her company; he became her dance partner and her lover. De Mille writes that once Kirstein met Graham, "He became addicted. He hung around her studio. And with him was Erick Hawkins."[28] As Graham's friend, de Mille hoped that Kirstein might provide funding for Graham's own financially unstable company, but Kirstein proved to be something other—and more important—than a financial backer: a mentor.

Lincoln Kirstein was rich and had access to great wealth and great sources of wealth. One could accordingly expect that as his enthusiasm waxed for Martha he would certainly help her. It seemed that at last she had found the patron whom she so desperately needed.

Three years after she met him, I asked her, "Has he given you much?"

"Not a penny," she said. "However, he's around the whole time." He was around, counseling and criticizing, writing, praising, and courting, but he gave not a cent and he opened no doors. He did give Erick: he released him from his continuing contract with Ballet Caravan.[29]

But if Hawkins defected from Balanchine and Kirstein to join Graham, less than a decade later Merce Cunningham moved in the opposite direction. Even before he left Graham's company in 1945, Cunningham had begun to present his own modern dance choreography. After leaving Graham, he also began teaching at the School of American Ballet (where he had studied while dancing with Graham), and he choreographed *The Seasons* for Ballet Society in 1947. Robert Sabin's description of the piece—"experimental and challenging . . . a blending of modern dance and ballet"—is not only an apt characterization of the choreography and technique Cunningham eventually developed for his company, but also pinpoints the very spirit of Ballet Society, which in 1947 alone presented modern dancer Iris Mabry in concert and a program of Balinese court and popular dances.

Balanchine may also have been influenced by Cunningham's use in *The Seasons* of simple leotards for costumes and a spare stage stripped of scenery—stylistic innovations at the time that later became hallmarks of an important strand of Balanchine's oeuvre. And perhaps it was the chance techniques favored by Cunningham (who in 1966 gave NYCB a version of *Summerspace*, a piece to music by Morton Feldman he had made for his own company in 1958) that influenced the look of Balanchine's *Agon* (1957) and *Stravinsky Violin Concerto* (1972). *Stravinsky Violin Concerto* opens with stillness—something unusual for ballet, but not surprising in Cunningham's chance-generated dances. The disconnectedness of the dance phrases in both *Agon* and *Stravinsky Violin Concerto* and the seeming autonomy and impersonal interactions of the dancers, even when in a group, as well as the independence of individual body parts, all recall the look of Cunningham's dances. So too does the focus in both ballets on rhythm rather than melody, with staccato, often minute movements following or providing syncopated contrasts to a steady pulse. In many ways Cunningham, who had hungrily absorbed ballet at the beginning of his career as a modern dancer, and Balanchine, who had opened himself to modern dance as a young ballet choreographer, seemed to be approaching each other and meeting on a common ground of dance abstraction.

Not only styles and techniques crossed over between the two idioms—so did personnel. Kirstein and Graham had shared a composer (with other choreographers) in Aaron Copland, who wrote the music not only for Eugene Loring's *Billy the Kid* (Ballet Caravan, 1938), and for Graham's *Appalachian Spring* (1944), as well as for Page's *Hear Ye! Hear Ye!* (1934) and de Mille's *Rodeo* (Ballet Russe de Monte Carlo, 1942). Another composer shared by the two was Robert McBride, who did the music for *Show Piece* (1937), choreographed by Erick Hawkins for Ballet Caravan, and *Punch and the Judy* (1941), a work choreographed by Graham. For both *The Seasons* and *Orpheus* (1948), Balanchine and Kirstein commissioned the scenery and costumes from Isamu Noguchi, who had collaborated regularly with

Graham since the mid-1930s and whose distinctively expressive, symbolic sculptures had come to mark Graham's work.

A precursor to the 1948 *Orpheus*, Balanchine's 1936 production of Gluck's *Orpheus and Eurydice* at the Metropolitan Opera was created in a style somewhere between aesthetic dancing and expressionism, with costumes and sets by Pavel Tchelitchew made of draped cloth over chicken wire. The dancers were barefoot—a famous emblem of modern dance, but seldom a practice in ballet, whose standard costume continues into the 1990s, no matter how unusual the rest of the clothing, to include pointe shoes for women. The novelist Glenway Wescott wrote, "This *Orpheus* is the only ballet I can think of that Isadora Duncan would have approved whole-heartedly."[30]

KAY MAZZO and PETER MARTINS in *Stravinsky Violin Concerto*, 1976. *Martha Swope/LIFE Magazine © TIME Inc.*

DAPHNE VANE, LEW CHRISTENSEN, and WILLIAM
DOLLAR in *Orpheus and Eurydice*, 1936. Photo by George
Platt Lynes. *The Metropolitan Museum of Art, Gift of Mr. and
Mrs. Russell Lynes, 1983.*

The new *Orpheus* bore striking similarities not to Duncan, but to Graham's *Night Journey* (1947), and not only because of the familiar Noguchi visual style, the ritual quality, and the Greek mythopoetic theme of doomed love. Orpheus's dance of mourning in the opening section is marked by contractions—a trademark of Graham's technique—and a repeated movement of his lyre to his pelvis that emphasizes the prop's phallic symbolism, recalling the genital imagery of Graham's choreography. The Dark Angel brings Orpheus a rope reminiscent of the one that links Oedipus and Jocasta, as well as an eye mask that resembles the brooch with which Oedipus blinds himself in *Night Journey*. Both Orpheus, in his dance of mourning, and Eurydice, in her solo in the Underworld, use hieratic gestures to shield their eyes (although a similar gesture appears in many Balanchine ballets, including *Serenade*). And both Orpheus's duet with the Dark Angel and his pas de deux leading Eurydice out of the Underworld are characterized by a sinuous muscularity of tangled bodies and flexible torsos; like Jocasta in Graham's dance, Eurydice clings to her husband and climbs on his body in a Kama Sutra pose. Then, when Orpheus gazes at her, she falls to the floor, rhyming Orpheus's fall of grief in the opening scene as well as Oedipus and Jocasta's fall in *Night Journey*. A great deal of the movement is earthbound and angular throughout, from the group scene in the Underworld to the destruction of Orpheus by the crouching Bacchantes. And yet whereas *Night Journey* ends bleakly with Jocasta's suicide, *Orpheus* ends with a sunlit apotheosis, a clarifying moment that restores classicism, as Apollo appears and raises Orpheus's lyre to the heavens.[31]

Of the sixteen works commissioned by Ballet Society, at least half seem to have some relationship

MARTHA GRAHAM as Jocasta in *Night Journey. Dance
Collection, The New York Public Library for the Performing Arts,
Astor, Lenox, and Tilden Foundations.*

DIANA ADAMS and NICHOLAS MAGALLANES
in *Orpheus*. Photo by Baron. *Hulton Getty Picture
Collection, London.*

DIANA ADAMS and NICHOLAS MAGALLANES
in *Orpheus*. Photo by Baron. *Hulton Getty Picture
Collection, London*.

to modern dance, including *The Four Temperaments* (1946), *Divertimento* (1947), *The Triumph of Bacchus and Ariadne* (1947), and *Elégie* (1948) by Balanchine; *The Minotaur* (1947) by John Taras; *Zodiac* (1947) by Todd Bolender; and Cunningham's *Seasons*. Some of these entered the repertory of New York City Ballet when it was founded in 1948, and during the early years of the new company, even as it was building a repertory of more classical works like Balanchine's *Symphony in C* (1948), *Scotch Symphony* (1952), and *Divertimento No. 15* (1956), various choreographers continued to experiment with borrowings from modern dance styles and themes. These included *The Cage* (1951) by Robbins, a depiction of women (either Amazons or insects) devouring a man in a blood lust ritual reminiscent of Humphrey's *Life of the Bee* (1929), Balanchine's *Opus 34* and *Ivesiana* (both 1954), and *The Unicorn, the Gorgon, and the Manticore* by Butler (1957).

The hegemonic struggle between ballet and modern dance included courtship and flirtation until ballet achieved its own niche in the United States in the 1960s. Marcia B. Siegel muses about *Ivesiana*, in which she sees a family resemblance to Sokolow's *Lyric Suite* (1953) and other modern dances of "agonized discommunication": "In this ballet one can . . . detect the sardonic Balanchine, in the golden age of Graham, Humphrey, and Limón, saying, You think you want modern dance—I'll give you antiballet."[32]

With a new home in the New York State Theater and bolstered by a large Ford Foundation grant, by the mid-1960s the New York City Ballet had arrived. As Nancy Reynolds puts it, "Balanchine the avant-gardist and his selfless dancers were becoming 'Establishment.' . . . What had been an elitist art was becoming a popular one, perhaps the leader in the 'culture boom' of the Sixties."[33] At the same time, modern dance had reached a plateau as its major figures aged. Doris Humphrey died in 1958, Louis Horst in 1963; Graham could no longer dance the roles she had created for herself. And in an expanding postwar economy, Americans developed a taste for a luxurious, royal art on a par with that of important European companies like Britain's Royal Ballet and the Bolshoi Ballet. They wanted ballet. But they also liked what was new. And New York City Ballet, with its diverse menu of classics and experimental works, absorbing the best of modern dance as well as jazz and social dancing, could provide that.

In retrospect, *Episodes* seems to mark the end of an era of modern-dance anxiety for NYCB. Modern dance and ballet literally competed on the same stage, and Balanchine's abstract neoclassicism, what Denby called his "counter-classic classicism," won.[34] It proved to be far more radical and avant-garde than Graham's story-and-costume ballet. Modern dance was no longer the avant-garde art. It appeared antiquated. And ballet took its position on the cutting edge.

After the 1959–60 season, Graham's section was removed from the ballet; the following year Balanchine's section alone, without the Paul Taylor solo, became the newly constituted *Episodes*. Thus the showdown between the two idioms ended with ballet triumphant and modern dance banished, as experimentalism on the ballet stage continued. Historical modern dance now seemed traditional, if not moribund. In fact, the modern dance of Graham's generation became more and more balletic. In a sense, ballet triumphed through what might be called invasion and annexation—it diluted orthodox modern dance technique, made it look refined and attenuated. And yet simultaneously, the incorporation of ballet technique—the verticality, the crisp port de bras, the quick footwork— was what made Cunningham's work look so new and so brilliant.

So Balanchine, Robbins (after his return to the company in 1969), and other NYCB choreographers turned their attention away from historical modern dance, although not from other movement forms. Robbins, especially, found new stimulation in watching postmodern dance. This had emerged in the early 1960s as a reaction to the stylized emotion and monumentalism of modern dance, but it also criticized the strict, formal canons of

ROBBINS'S *Glass Pieces* (1983), to a score by PHILIP GLASS, recalled the minimalism of postmoderns such as LUCINDA CHILDS. Photo by Paul Kolnik.

beauty and symmetry in classical ballet. Although not united stylistically, postmodern dancers like Simone Forti, Yvonne Rainer, Steve Paxton, and others (many of them associated with the Judson Dance Theater in Greenwich Village) often rejected musicality, plot, character, and meaning. Like Cunningham and Balanchine, these choreographers explored pure dance and the possibilities of the moving human body, but their rejection of virtuosic technique put them at the edge of dance experimentation.[35]

Robbins said at the time that his *Dances at a Gathering* (1969) was a reaction to the work he had seen by the Judson Dance Theater and by other avant-garde choreographers. "What's the matter with love, what's the matter with celebrating positive things?" he asked.[36] And yet this romantic "piano ballet" to the music of Chopin—harking back to Michel Fokine's 1909 ballet *Les Sylphides*, which in turn was an homage to the romantic ballet of the nineteenth century—includes many elements familiar to postmodern dance. Robbins had his dancers walk casually, as if in daily life. At times they "marked" phrases, dancing them tentatively as if rehearsing them with reduced energy. There were intimations of improvisation. The small ensemble of ten dancers, permutating into different smaller group relationships, created a sense of close community. And although there is certainly virtuoso ballet technique in the piece, Robbins himself described some of the movements in postmodern task dance terms: "At the end of Eddie [Villella]'s pas de deux with Pat [McBride] . . . it looks as though he were lifting a sack onto his shoulder."[37] Robbins's fascination with capturing movement as it would look in rehearsal, instructing the dancers at times to relax and shed both drama and virtuosity, and simply to perform the movement *qua* movement, without asking what it meant, parallel precisely Yvonne Rainer's experiments with tasks and baring "levels of performance" during this period.

After Balanchine's death in 1983, a general malaise set in, not only at the New York City Ballet but also at the many ballet companies that had established themselves around the country thanks to the dance boom and federal arts dollars. Ballet seemed to be exhausted, unable to generate ideas of its own or choreographers capable of moving the form into the post-Balanchine era. For a variety of reasons, in the mid-1980s several ballet companies—including the Joffrey Ballet and American Ballet Theatre—hired postmodern choreographers to rejuvenate the repertory.[38] NYCB made a gesture in this direction with *Brahms/Handel* (1984), co-choreographed by Twyla Tharp and Jerome Robbins, though Tharp was by then no stranger to the ballet stage.

Then in 1988, NYCB suddenly, if belatedly, followed suit when Peter Martins, the company's co-artistic director with Robbins, organized the American Music Festival, commissioning works from modern dance choreographers Lar Lubovitch and Paul Taylor, postmodern choreographer Laura Dean, and ballet choreographers William Forsythe, Eliot Feld, and Martins himself, whose work was at least partly indebted to varieties of modern dance. For the festival, Martins proposed a collaboration between himself and Taylor on the model of the Graham/Balanchine *Episodes*. Martins created *Barber Violin Concerto*, to music by Samuel Barber, which not only mixed modern dance and ballet but also paired two Taylor dancers with his own NYCB dancers. The Taylor piece, *Danbury Mix*, conceived entirely in the modern dance idiom and set to music by Charles Ives, included both dancers from Taylor's company and NYCB dancer Peter Frame.

At that time, Martins acknowledged frankly that NYCB was searching for new directions, that it needed "a change of menu." He insisted that "classical ballet will always be the basis for our wanting to exist, but it's important not to exclude everything else and become stifled."[39] Paradoxically, in the annals of American dance, it seems that ballet has been the open-minded, flexible form, surviving by virtue of its ability to absorb and adapt alien techniques, while modern dance has more often defined and protected its perimeters with rigid purism.

For the first half of the twentieth century, it seemed the quintessential form of American dance was the new democratic, innovative genre, invented on this continent, of modern dance. Yet since the post–World War II era, ballet—born in European courts, and long despised as elitist, conservative, and tradition-bound—has come to dominate dance culture in the United States, attracting popular audiences and becoming a staple of national arts broadcasting. The ballet companies and schools founded in the 1930s survive and flourish, while their modern dance counterparts of the same period (except when affiliated with universities) blossomed for a generation and then declined, superseded by postmodern dance. One might ask why, if there was regular intercourse between

Facing page: HELÉNE ALEXOPOULOS (*left*), MARIA CALEGARI, and JERRI KUMERY in *Antique Epigraphs*. In this 1984 ballet, Robbins used the same Debussy music he had used in *Ballade* (1952). Photo by Paul Kolnik.

ANNA SOKOLOW conducting a choreography class at the School of American Ballet, 1953. Photo by Peter Basch. *Dance Magazine, June 1953, p. 37.*

the two dance forms in the 1930s, 1940s, and 1950s, ballet was stimulated and renewed by the exchange, while modern dance became enervated.[40]

If Kirstein is right, the problem lies in modern dance's stress on the individual: idiosyncratic and therefore evanescent techniques, emanating from charismatic individuals, have no staying power. But, he argues, the impersonal traditions of the ballet academy, based on laws of anatomy and geometry rather than on personality, are resilient and capable of regeneration.

However, in the American context there is quite another explanation for this paradox. The answer may lie in the specific historical conditions of the sibling rivalry between the two idioms—their struggle for hegemonic power. Modern dance was already in decline when it finally began to import ballet technique and ballet dancers. And thus modern dance was taken over, usurped, and weakened by ballet, as if by an invasive virus. But ballet encountered modern dance while on the upswing, and rather than defeating the alien form in a Darwinian struggle for survival, adapted to and absorbed it, taking it in its stride.

The Making of Agon

Agon WAS EXACTLY THE RIGHT WORK at exactly the right time. It burst
onto the New York ballet scene during the late autumn of 1957—the same
autumn, in fact, that the Soviet Union hurled a tiny artificial satellite into
orbit around the earth, marking the dawn of the Space Age. It seemed
inevitable that Stravinsky and Balanchine's "futuristic" ballet, as *Agon* was
sometimes called, would evoke astronautical comparisons. *Agon* was "like
travel in outer space," Edwin Denby wrote, pushing the envelope of the
dance universe with its "jetlike extensions," "soundless whirl," and "intent
stillness." Just as the Russian space shot redefined the edge of gravity-bound
existence, Stravinsky and Balanchine's newest collaboration challenged the
conception of musical/balletic time and space, producing, as A. V. Coton
wrote, "a celestial marriage of music and movement." Precision was the
byword. Balanchine likened the ballet to an IBM electronic computer: "It is
a machine," he wrote in the opening night program, "but a machine that
thinks . . . a measured construction in space, demonstrated by moving bodies." The work's computerlike temporal exactness was emblematic; its
techno-precision, both musically and choreographically, matched the spirit
of a new era. *Agon* was, as Denby noted, a bold new work poised on "the
acute edge of risk."[1]

The success of the premiere (the composer's associate Robert Craft called
the ballet "a smash hit") caught Stravinsky entirely off guard. Only a few days

before its first publicly staged New York performance, Stravinsky wrote to a friend: "Are you going to the premiere of *Agon* tomorrow? I can imagine the reaction of the listeners paying $50 a seat to hear my new score." So skeptical was the composer that he skipped town, retreating to his California home. By the mid-1950s Stravinsky had good reason to be anxious about first nights. When *Agon* was first performed as an orchestral work the previous summer in Los Angeles, critics greeted it politely, but coldly. The composer's recent scores had found little favor in the United States. Old loyalists felt betrayed by Stravinsky's conversion to Schoenberg's serialism, and *Agon* stepped way over the line. While many couldn't keep pace with the seventy-five-year-old composer, Balanchine always instinctively sensed dance movement in any Stravinsky score. His realization of *Agon* confirmed that there were still new Stravinskyan worlds to explore, at least when someone with Balanchine's acuity could imagine them. His young and exciting New York City Ballet offered Stravinsky's music a very public forum, just as Diaghilev's Ballets Russes had done almost a half century earlier. With the staging of *Agon*, it became evident that the composer's much-maligned serial works were every bit as vibrant and powerful as the old Diaghilev ballets upon which Stravinsky's reputation was still, even in 1957, largely based.

For all of its "modernism," *Agon* is firmly rooted in the past—a past marked by an assortment of literary, musical, numerological, and dance-based models that guided Stravinsky even before he began composing. The making of *Agon* was a protracted journey, lasting almost a decade. Ever since *Apollo* (1928), Lincoln Kirstein had envisaged a Stravinsky/Balanchine trilogy based upon the classic Greek myths. Following the 1937 Stravinsky Festival, presented by the American Ballet at the Metropolitan Opera House, Kirstein and Balanchine had jointly "begged" the composer for "a sequel" to *Apollo*. And while that ballet had been almost exclusively Stravinsky's idea from the start, he considered *Orpheus*, its 1948 "sequel," a "Balanchine-Kirstein inspiration." Immediately after the April 28 premiere, Kirstein wrote to Stravinsky, recalling his persistent dream: "To me *Orpheus* is the second act of a great lyric-drama. Which leads me on the day after the second act, to ask you to write a third."

Several erroneous assumptions have infiltrated the writings about *Agon*'s convoluted history.[2] The first that should be dispelled is that Stravinsky himself shared Kirstein's enthusiasm for such a grand triptych. One should not make too much of the composer's August 1953 letter suggesting that he was "quite willing to compose a ballet . . . to complete the *Apollo*-idea." Not one to burn bridges before they were built, the composer gave a characteristically prudent response. But the notion of writing structurally linked works never appealed to him. Each composition, he often proclaimed, presented a specific problem in search of a specific solution. Conversely, Balanchine and Kirstein had eagerly envisioned an epic trilogy. In their minds, each of the three so-called Greek ballets was part of a logical, inevitable evolution. No such progression entered Stravinsky's thinking. When the composer did once speak about a combined performance of all three ballets on a single program, he suggested that *Apollo* appear first, *Agon* second, and *Orpheus* last in order.

Someone should have advised Kirstein that the quickest way to dissuade Stravinsky from writing a "third act" was to dictate too specific a scenario. As heroically supportive and astute as Kirstein was, Stravinsky didn't trust him any more than he had Diaghilev. But Kirstein was a veritable idea-mill, churning out one scenario after another in the hope of interesting the composer. From 1948 to 1951, while Stravinsky was preoccupied with his most ambitious composition to date, *The Rake's Progress*, Kirstein—with help from W. H. Auden and even Balanchine—came up with a menu of sensible ideas: Euripides' *Bacchae*, *Apollo Architectons*, *Nausicaa*, *Amphion*. Stravinsky rejected them all. Some possibilities were discussed with Balanchine, and apparently in considerable detail. A draft sketch for a ballet entitled *Terpsichore*, included in a letter sent by Kirstein to the composer in late 1951, outlined the proposed work's seven sections. And while an edited version of the letter is reprinted among Stravinsky's published correspondence, the original shows that Kirstein went so far as to match specific roles with specific dancers—an indication of how serious the proposal was, at least in Kirstein's mind. Though nothing came of the idea, the original letter reveals not only that Jerome Robbins was to have portrayed Mercury but also that the ballet was to end with "a big jazz finale."[3]

The only suggestion catching Stravinsky's attention was offered by the poet T. S. Eliot. Although his contribution to *Agon* is often slighted, it was only when Eliot suggested that the two collaborate on a ballet to complete Kirstein's trilogy that Stravinsky's interest was stirred. Writing to the composer on August 23, 1950, Kirstein relayed Eliot's idea that his controversial *Sweeney Agonistes: Fragments of an Aristophanic Melodrama* might make a workable scenario.[4] Stravinsky studied Eliot's two "agon" poems, first published separately in 1926 and 1927. Often criticized as profane, grotesque, enigmatic, experimental, and a vacuous statement about "the jazz age," they were just the kind of offbeat creative forays that intrigued the composer. The title of Stravinsky's ballet is almost certainly indebted to the Eliot poems, just as Eliot's use of the Greek concept to explore the psychological corridors of Sweeney's complex mind goes to the very heart of *Agon*'s hard-edged, abstract message. *Sweeney Agonistes* dwells on duality, blackness and whiteness, the tensions between men and women, contrast, sensuality, on both contesting and celebrating difference. It was only after reading Eliot's "agon" fragments that Stravinsky had a vision of the ballet he would compose.

This vision only partly coincided with the idea of an Olympian contest. It also embraced the larger "Greek" issues that Sweeney had grappled with in Eliot's poems. For Stravinsky an agon represented the idea of struggle, of a contrast between Good and Evil, of oratory and debate as effective rhetorical devices employed by Euripides (as in Orestes' agon with Tyndareus). Collectively, these provided the working basis for Eliot's poetry. Sweeney must combat his internal demons; he must face the discordant claims of humanness, animalism, and spirituality. Eliot's agons were consumed with self-reflexivity, and Stravinsky would have understood this as well as he understood any of antiquity's classical metaphors. The rehearsal costume adopted by Stravinsky and Balanchine for *Agon* was surely intended to showcase the athleticism of the dance. But as Glenn Watkins suggests, *Agon* is far more than a contest: "This reduction of costume is also a symbol that not only projects an abstraction and confirms the absence of a narrative but serves as a ritual body mask that announces the presence of multiple identities." Just so, in a 1933 production of Eliot's *Sweeney* fragments at Vassar College, Terrence Diggory reports that Eliot wanted "the stiff movement of actors—'like marionettes,' in Yeats' phrase—and the wearing of masks."[5] A year later the poems were staged by the Group Theatre, and again the players wore masks.

The importance of contrast is underscored by the ballet's clearly defined gender relationships and frictions—the very same realities starkly portrayed in the treatment of sexuality and hopeless finality of *Sweeney Agonistes*: "Birth, and copulation, and death. That's all the facts when you come to brass tacks," says Eliot's protagonist. The music for *Agon* was also profoundly influenced by the temporal rhythms of Eliot's words—even if, as was typical of Stravinsky's literary models, the influence was oblique. As an ardent student of linguistic

ARTHUR MITCHELL and ALLEGRA KENT in the pas de deux of *Agon*, 1963. *Martha Swope/LIFE Magazine © TIME Inc.*

morphology, the polyglot Stravinsky was exceedingly sensitive to the flow of language, syllabication, accent, meter, and inflection. His interest in French versification is particularly notable. How can one hope to understand the rhythmic fabric of *Apollo*, for example, without recognizing the composer's reliance upon the alexandrines of the Renaissance poet and biographer Nicolas Boileau? Nor was the composer's curiosity about English prosody—including Eliot's poetry, of course—any less fervent, especially since while reading *Sweeney Agonistes*, Stravinsky was also immersed in Auden's text for *The Rake's Progress*, and thus attentive to the rhythms of the opera's libretto. Eliot's poetry was replete with linguistic rhythms, especially jazz rhythms. Can it be mere coincidence that in describing *Agon*, Stravinsky spoke of jazz rhythms, of "traces of boogie-woogie," specifically referring to the "Bransle de Poitou" and "Bransle Simple"? Or that Eliot's own Aristotelian analysis of drama was as a "ritual consisting of a set of repeated movements [which] is essentially a dance."[6] Poetry, music, dancing—these were the fundamental ingredients of ritual; and ritual was the focus of Stravinsky's attraction to dance and theater.

Within a month of the September 1951 Venetian premiere of *The Rake's Progress* (or a year after Stravinsky had read *Sweeney*), Kirstein resumed his prodding. Three years had passed since Kirstein first raised the idea of a ballet, yet the composer still did not set to work. The truth is, Stravinsky had reached a compositional wall. As Craft reveals, in March 1952, Stravinsky confessed that "he was afraid he could no longer compose and did not know what to do. For a moment he broke down and actually wept." The *Rake* had not brought the hoped-for critical acclaim.[7] The opera held little appeal for a younger generation sympathetic to the serial tenets of the recently deceased Arnold Schoenberg. Stravinsky's brand of neoclassicism had drawn its last breath, and he knew it. It was a critical juncture that might well have further impeded, or perhaps even prevented, the completion of the ballet. It was now four years since Kirstein first approached Stravinsky, and still not a note. Fortunately, with the ministrations of Robert Craft, Stravinsky regrouped, embracing the compositional techniques of serialism that would serve him well for the remainder of his life.

It was at this juncture that Kirstein and Balanchine suggested a new idea for their ballet, "a ballet to end all ballets," as Kirstein wrote on August 31, 1952, "a competition before the gods . . . [through] a series of historic dances." Along with the letter came "a book which may possibly interest you along these lines." It was a turning point. F. de Lauze's *Apologie de la danse* (1637) provided the composer with the model on which *Agon* would largely be built. De Lauze's *Apologie* was one of many "how to dance" manuals popular during the reign of Louis XIV. But it went a step further: it was also a book of protocol, a philosophical treatise extolling the cardinal virtues of classicism. Kirstein sent the composer a 1952 British reprint of the book, not a copy of the original publication.[8] Greatly supplemented by its editor, Joan Wildeblood, the introduction begins: "In an age when the manner of the Court was becoming increasingly artificial, the observance of the correct mode of behaviour became a matter of supreme importance, especially for those members of society who desired to appear to have advantage in courtly circles." The de Lauze manual was written even earlier than Boileau's *L'Art poétique* (1674), the treatise that had sparked Stravinsky's conception of *Apollo*. The alexandrines of Boileau's magnum opus (which espoused the constancy of classical principles) were a counterpart to Eliot's words and rhythms. It was this odd alchemy of Renaissance and modernism that opened the way to Stravinsky as he now prepared to compose his new ballet.

Cover page of F. DE
LAUZE'S *Apologie de la
danse (Geneva: Minkoff
Reprint, 1977)*.

Kirstein and Balanchine's vision of a grandiose ballet, unlimited in scope,
was unacceptable to a composer who liked precise boundaries. He replied to
Kirstein on September 9: "Thank you . . . for the book: I am studying it 'poco
a poco.' On the other hand, the idea you and George have of doing a 'ballet to
end all ballets' may prove to be a limitless affair."[9] De Lauze's *Apologie* provided
the boundaries Stravinsky needed to begin to work. The composer's interest
in Renaissance music had deepened by the 1950s. Craft had not only introduced Stravinsky to the serial techniques of Schoenberg's most famous pupil,
Anton Webern, but had also nudged the composer toward several Renaissance
composers whose relationship to Webern was close. Stravinsky became

"Lady Snapping Her Fingers in Dancing," from Stravinsky's copy of *Apologie de la danse. Paul Sacher Stiftung, Basel.*

absorbed in the music of Ockeghem and Isaak (the latter being the subject of Webern's doctoral dissertation), even studying musicological works about their individual compositional styles. Moreover, Stravinsky was already familiar with the music of de Lauze's contemporary, Claudio Monteverdi, that musical giant who spans the great divide between the pretonal and tonal music of the late Renaissance and early Baroque. For all of these reasons, the de Lauze manual proved a timely stimulus.

The indispensability of the *Apologie* is perhaps best confirmed by Stravinsky's claim that the manual influenced him only indirectly—a statement typical of his denial of so many other models (the most famous canard being that *The Rite of Spring* did not rely upon folk sources, when in fact the entire 1913 ballet springs from one Russian folk song after another). An examination of the *Apologie* sent to him by Kirstein, now in the collection of the Paul Sacher Stiftung in Basel, reveals how deep the composer's reliance upon the dance patterns outlined by de Lauze really was. The many illustrations, for instance, clearly played a role in Stravinsky's fashioning both the sound and the look of *Agon*. With two trumpeters playing from a balcony, "A Nobleman Leading a Bransle" is the visual inspiration not only for the ballet's fanfare opening but also for the Second Pas de Trois (Bransle Simple), which calls for two trumpets scampering in a musical canon of close pursuit. Balanchine's choreography has two male dancers mirroring each other at the same close temporal interval as the music—one of many mirrors in *Agon*, in fact, and analogous to a standard compositional technique in the music of the Renaissance. Other engravings caught Stravinsky's eye as well. What Arlene Croce calls the "bright finger snap" in the Double Pas de Quatre almost certainly owes its origin to the manual's engraving "Lady Snapping Her Fingers in Dancing."

Stravinsky, who always annotated books that he studied, frequently under-lined portions of the de Lauze treatise or added marginalia highlighting partic-ular passages. These telltale signs reveal a composer familiarizing himself with the choreographic conventions of the Renaissance at least a year before he and Balanchine first met in August 1954 to discuss the ballet. The notion that Stravinsky tailored the music to Balanchine's preconceived scenario and chore-ography is thus not true. If anything, it was the other way around. In *Agon*, as in virtually every ballet that he wrote, the composer was intimately involved from the beginning, often envisioning quite specific choreographic patterns, which he notated on his compositional sketches. Balanchine, to be sure, brought Stravinsky's suggestions to life as the two worked together, finalizing the details of *Agon*. But to suggest that the composer wrote music to fit some predeter-mined choreographic scheme is to misrepresent the way the two collaborated. Stravinsky was a serious student of dance, and his annotations of the de Lauze volume only confirm that he did his homework.

Stravinsky was as struck by Wildeblood's editorial commentary as by the explanation of the dance patterns themselves. He marked several passages in red, indicating his particular interest in the bransle. Significantly, Wildeblood spoke of a ritualistic connection that Stravinsky also noted: "The world-wide use of this form of the dance is well known . . . it may be of interest to record that this salient feature of pagan festivals was preserved in the clandestine rit-uals of the dying religion in Western Europe for many centuries." The com-poser also underlined a few sentences Wildeblood quotes from Margaret Murray's *The Witch-cult in Western Europe*: "The ring dances were usually round some object, sometimes a stone, sometimes the Devil. The round-dance was . . . essentially a witch dance." He marked several other pertinent passages:

(a) The Bransle—The circle, or round dance . . . recognized to be one of the oldest forms of the group dance. (b) Bransle, with a string of dancers holding hands. (c) For Arbeau describes the clapping of hands, shaking of fingers, and so forth in certain Bransles. (d) Bransle, Brawls or Rounds. (e) A tree . . . which they erected, bedecked with ribbons and garlands. (f) Throughout the seventeenth century there is evidence that the ball was always commenced by dancing a Bransle.

The Bransle—The circle, or round-dance, in which the dancers form either a complete or partial circle, is generally recognized to be one of the oldest forms of the group dance. It is natural that this should be so, for it is a pattern into which a man or people will easily form if they are either dancing round some object, as in worship, or, if being joined one to another by holding hands, linking arms, or placing their arms

LES CAVALIERS. 41

DV TROISIESME BRANSLE.

E troifiefme eft le Branfle de Poiƈtou, auqnel
le commun ne compte que dix pas. mais pour
le faire comprendre auec moins de peine, il en
faut compter douze.

Ce Branfle fe commence par vne reuerence qui fe
doit faire femblable à celle du premier, mais parce que
l'entree de celuy-cy fe faiƈt de differentes fortes, i'ay
choifi celle qui fuit, comme eftant à mon opinion la
plus graue, fans s'arrefter donc apres la reuerence (comme font plufieurs, qui manque de bonne oreille font
contraints d'attendre pour choifir le temps propre à
prendre leur cadance.) Il faut partir par vn temps ou
deux, en tournant deuant la femme, felon que la Mufi-
que obligera, à fin de finir cefte entree par vn pas en-
trecoupé.

Mais à fin de bien pourfuiure le refte du Branfle, cefte entree fe doit finir les pieds efloignez de demy pied,
les pointes fort ouuertes, principalement celle du droit,
& en cas que l'Efcolier foit defia auancé, faudra luy faire couler tout ce branfle fur le mouuement des pieds,
que s'il ne fait que commencer, il luy faut au premier
pas faire plier vn peu les genoüils & affembler le talon
droiƈt au gauche, en fe releuant fur la pointe des pieds,
puis faire porter le pied gauche fur la pointe à cofté &
le droiƈt deuant. Au quatriefme, defgager doucement
le pied gauche de derriere, & le glifier à cofteà demy

F

DE LAUZE's explanation of the "Third" or "Bransle
de Poitou."

across each other's shoulders, or backs, their dance continues to progress, either forwards, backwards, or sideways, without leaving the same dancing ground.

As Robert Craft remarks, Stravinsky's particular
interest in the bransle began with the 1940
Symphony in C, the first major work he completed
after settling in America. The third movement,
"Allegretto," is based upon the same fundamental
rhythmic pattern Stravinsky employed for *Agon*'s
"Bransle Gay." Later in the *Apologie*, Wildeblood
summarizes de Lauze's explanation of the dance,
and Stravinsky again marked the entire passage:

In 1623, de Lauze's *Suite* consists of five *Bransles*, which he
names the *Bransle Simple*, *Bransle Gay*, *Bransle de Poitou*,
Bransle Double de Poitou, the "Fifth" *Bransle*, and lastly, the
Gavot, which made the sixth dance in the *Suite*.

Finally, we have Mersenne's *Suite*. Though the date of
his book is 1636, he had obtained the King's Privilege in
1629, six years later than the date of de Lauze's book. As
the names and the order of the *Bransles* he gives are identical with those of de Lauze . . . one may assume that they
were speaking of the same dances. He writes: "There are
six kinds (of *Bransles*) which are danced now-a-days at
the opening of a Ball, one after the other, by as many persons as wish; for the entire company, joining hands, perform with one accord a continual *Bransle*, sometimes forwards, sometimes backwards; it is done with divers movements to which are adapted various kinds of steps,
according to the different airs which are used. They dance
round very sedately at the beginning of the Ball, all with
the same time and movements of the body. The first of
which is named the *Bransle Simple* . . . the second is called
the *Bransle Gay* . . . the third is named *Bransle-à-Mener*, or
de Poitou . . . the fourth *Bransle Double de Poitou* . . . the fifth
is called *Bransle de Montirande*, and the sixth is *La Gavot*."

The order of the *Bransles* in the *Suite* is important, for
one may thereby ascertain whether the *Suite* retained a
definite form in *tempo* and *time*, throughout the years.

Arbeau explains that the dances in his day were divided into four kinds, as in ancient Greece. There were the *Grave*, the *Gay*, and a combination of the two, *Grave-and-Gay*. . . . He then places the *Bransles* in these various categories, and his explanation is that the order of the *Bransles* in the *Suite* was regulated by the persons taking part. The slower *Bransles Double* and *Simple* were danced sedately by the "old people," the quicker Bransle Gay by those of the next degree of dignity, the young marrieds, and the *Bransle de Bourgoyne*, seemingly a very quick dance, by the "youngest of all."

The mention of Marin Mersenne provides another key to uncovering *Agon*'s models. Stravinsky marked on the title page of his copy of the *Apologie*, "with some musik [sic] by Marin Mersenne (1636)." A renowned French theorist and composer whose interest in mathematics and music frequently brought him into contact with Descartes, Pascal, and other contemporary theologians and philosophers, Mersenne was just the kind of paragon Stravinsky admired. Mersenne's thirteen-hundred-page *Harmonie universelle* (extracts of which appear liberally in the Wildeblood edition) is considered a major contemporary treatise on seventeenth-century music and instruments. Moreover, several pages are dedicated to a discussion of coordinating dance and music. Mersenne insisted that "the poets, musicians, and composers of dances and ballets of his own times would benefit by studying the ancient Greek rhythms in order to apply them to songs and dances which they composed." Stravinsky's identification with Mersenne is critical, for it leads to the deeper Greek concept underlying *Agon* that is not immediately obvious.

Stravinsky also marked this quintessentially Greek admonition of Marsenne's: Once a melody is chosen, "one must join it to its proper movements, which the Greeks called Rhythm"—a statement that recalls Eliot's *Sweeney*. Mersenne advises composers to write bransles because of their rhythmic opportunities, "since they were not restricted by the words as when composing music for songs." Throughout his copy of the *Apologie*, Stravinsky noted these passages, especially those addressing the bransles used in Mersenne's "Suite." Even more specifically, Stravinsky understood Wildeblood's explanation that: "[Mersenne] writes at some length on his subject, and includes a 'Table of the movements or measured feet' of 'Twelve Movements Simples.' . . . These rhythmic feet are based on the long and short syllables of ancient Greek rhythms." The invocation of prosodic versification rings yet another familiar Stravinskyan bell—the rhythmic feet of the alexandrine in Calliope's variation in *Apollo*. Borrowed from Boileau's *L'Art poétique*, it was, in the composer's own words, "the real subject" of the entire ballet. This pronouncement is borne out by an examination of *Apollo*'s compositional sketches, in which scansion notations appear on numerous manuscript pages.

Virtually every pattern that Stravinsky and Balanchine employ in the Second Pas de Trois is explained in Mersenne's outline for a *Suite of Bransles*. Several tables were included, graphically demonstrating the many seventeenth-century patterns that found their way into the composer's initial thinking and the choreographer's eventual realization, for example, "Take the Left foot forward and outward to the side, so that it describes a semi-circle in moving, with the toe turned well out, and step on to the whole foot." Just how closely Stravinsky heeded both de Lauze's and Mersenne's advice, especially in the trio of bransles comprising this part of the ballet, is confirmed by examining a few of the fundamental

FIGURE 1: MERSENNE'S example of the "Bransle Gay" with Stravinsky's scansion of the music in poetic meter.

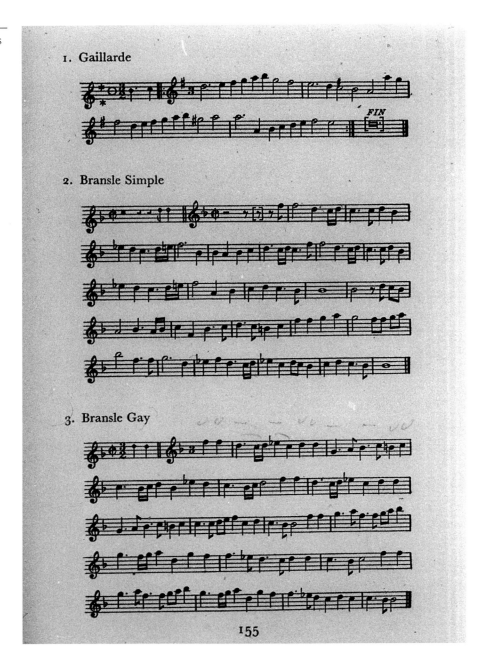

melodic and rhythmic aspects of Mersenne's musical examples. Stravinsky bracketed several melodic segments included in his copy of Wildeblood's edition. These divisions, marked by Stravinsky's scansion, served as the rhythmic fabric of the ballet. The notation entered by the composer in Mersenne's melody no. 3 "Bransle Gay," ∪∪__ __ (see fig. 1) is directly transferred to *Agon's* own Bransle Gay. There it appears as the signature rhythm accompanying the

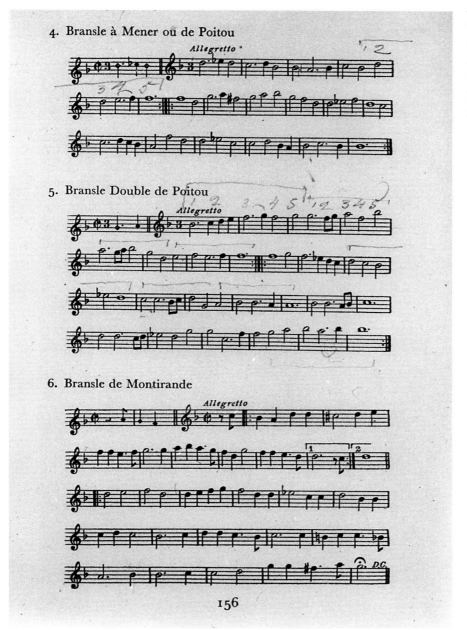

single female dancer flanked by the two males who mimic the orchestral castanets part.

Other bracketed divisions are found in Mersenne's "Bransle à Mener ou de Poitou" and the "Bransle Double de Poitou" (see nos. 4 and 5 in fig. 2). The use of these same rhythmic and dance patterns in *Agon* reveals an unmistakable counterpart. The *Apologie* holds that in the "Bransle de Poitou"—entitled

"Bransle Double (de Poitou)" in *Agon*—"the rhythm is counted in five beats whilst the measure is triple." The Mersenne example, as marked by Stravinsky, displays the same five-beat grouping used in *Agon*. Even the melodic and harmonic pitch material that Stravinsky employs in the 1957 ballet is often traceable to the melodic contour of the examples reproduced in the de Lauze manual—in the same way that Stravinsky often transformed melodic lines (such as folk songs in his earlier works) by retaining the essence of the model while modifying it to fit his needs. In examining Mersenne's tune (no. 3 in fig. 1), it becomes apparent that the opening pitches of his "Bransle Gay" are replicated exactly in *Agon*, comprising the harmonic and melodic pitch material of the entire opening passage. Moreover, Stravinsky marked in red and boxed the de Lauze passage that applied: "The second (bransle) is named Bransle Gay, which is composed of four steps and in order to get the cadence better begins with the last (of these) by bending knees a little so as to join both heels in rising on the toes." The composer actually highlights the expression "rising on the toes," and just as one would expect, Balanchine's choreography follows the de Lauze/Stravinsky direction. Later in the same paragraph Stravinsky marks "one must set aside the left foot, and make the other follow it . . . let it go gently to the side, in sliding on the heel," a gesture once again imported into *Agon*.

FIGURE 3: STRAVINSKY'S sketch of the *Coda* dated (by him) 23 December 1954. *Paul Sacher Stiftung, Basel.*

The overall spirit of the bransles depicted in *Agon* is also directly attributable to Stravinsky's reliance upon de Lauze. For example, the aforementioned "Bransle Simple," as used by Stravinsky and Balanchine, employs two men in a fast catch-as-catch-can canon. According to the manual, "Young men who have an excess of agility make these divisions at their pleasure." Moreover, de Lauze explains those divisions as a dance having eight definable steps. Musically, the Mersenne example Stravinsky studied allows six measures of double time for these same eight steps in setting the "Bransle." Stravinsky copies this pattern almost exactly in laying out the opening passage of the same dance.

Even the three dances of *Agon*'s First Pas de Trois have their origin in both de Lauze and Mersenne. The latter remarked that "a Sarabande is danced to the sound of the guitar and castanets—its steps are composed of tirades or glissades." Just so, Stravinsky includes both instruments in *Agon*'s version of the courtly dance. His attempt to bring choreographic authenticity to *Agon*'s Sarabande may be further corroborated by consulting his compositional sketches, wherein he marks on the manuscript: "Sarabande Step (male dancer)—Five Steps forwards and Three Steps backwards." Here again his model was the *Apologie*, where, under an explanation of the dance, he underlined "sometimes forwards, sometimes backwards." The composer genuinely wished to re-create the essence of both the de Lauze and Mersenne models. In this same Sarabande, for instance, Stravinsky composed four different opening passages, each with different instrumentation and all progressing toward the overall temporal duration of the one minute and fifteen seconds he and Balanchine originally sketched for the dance.[10]

In *Agon* the male solo of the Sarabande is followed by the Gailliard for two female dancers. Again, the Mersenne musical example furnishes the blueprint (see fig. 1). The rhythmic figure of the Mersenne illustration and the *Agon* Gailliard are noticeably similar. While there is no evidence to suggest that Stravinsky had studied Arbeau's 1589 *Orchésographie* (that the composer denied knowing the treatise at that point, however, makes one suspicious), Arbeau's description of the dance as containing six steps and six notes played in triple finds its analogue in Balanchine's choreography and Stravinsky's music. Here Stravinsky turned to additional sources in studying the dance form. In his early sketches (dated November 1954), the composer actually notates what appear to be several preexisting samples of gailliards on the manuscript page itself. These seem to have served as a handy guide as he drafted his preliminary ideas. In fact, Stravinsky was just then studying the music of the sixteenth-century lutenist Luis Milan, and as Craft confirms, the composer actually used a tune from a Milan "Fantasy" as a reference for *Agon*'s Gailliard. Stravinsky also perused the well-known gailliards of John Dowland. Such models account for Stravinsky's use of a mandolin in the Gailliard. Although Stravinsky actually once referred to the lute as his favorite instrument, the mandolin's more piercing sound could cut through *Agon*'s instrumentation more distinctly. Finally, the de Lauze manual states, "From the Italians come the Gaillarde; or Romanesque," and Stravinsky writes at the top of his compositional sketches: "*Gaillarde*, (Garliarde) Saltarello, Romanesca," suggesting that he had been exploring such dances. So thorough was his scrutiny that he consulted Littré's *Dictionnaire de la langue française* published in 1874 (Stravinsky owned the entire five-volume set). The composer copied Littré's definition directly from a well-worn page 1816, writing it on a small index card and stapling it to his compositional sketches as yet another "crib" to guide him.

Left and above: BALANCHINE and STRAVINSKY during rehearsals of *Agon*, 1957. *Martha Swope/LIFE Magazine ©
TIME Inc.*

Much has been made of the supposed congruence between the twelve-tone vocabulary of the music and *Agon's* twelve dancers. While there is certainly an overarching duodecimal significance to the ballet, this has little to do with the twelve-tone method of composition Stravinsky employed. Indeed, the structural divisions of the ballet and the number of dancers were both decided before Stravinsky began writing in the dodecaphonic style. The first section of *Agon* exhibiting a fully established twelve-tone row appears in the closing passage of the "Coda," written at the very end of 1954 (fig. 3)—a particularly critical juncture in Stravinsky's serial conversion, reached well over a year after Stravinsky and Balanchine had charted the choreographic structure of the work. The ballet's opening fanfare and the recurring interludes are not built upon twelve-tone rows, and those passages that are serial are only freely so. It is true that certain numerals did carry a "charismatic" weight for Stravinsky, but numerical "sums" did not interest him as much as numbers' divisibility into symmetrical subsets. As the composer told an interviewer in September 1954 (and thus years before the premiere), the subject of the ballet was "figures and the relation of figures."[11] In *Agon*, the number twelve arithmetically lends itself to obvious symmetrical groupings—3 x 4, 4 x 3, 8 + 4, 4 + 8—all of which are realized in the music's formal structure and choreographic pairings of duos, trios, quartets, and double quartets. The one choreographic division that is not employed is conspicuous: two groups of six. Such a hexachordal segmentation of pitch was the one most commonly used by twelve-tone composers—even in the hexachordal structure of *Agon's* tone rows—but the partitioning was completely avoided by Stravinsky and Balanchine in the dance, suggesting that there was no grand plan to match twelve notes with twelve dancers in any systematic way.

The magic of *Agon's* "twelveness" springs from poetic versification, and specifically from Stravinsky's transliteration of poetic meter, not pitch—just as in his hemistich structure of *Apollo's* alexandrines ("Suspende l'hémistiche et marque le repos" is the Boileau directive that Stravinsky faithfully followed in the 1928 ballet). Nor was the efficacy of versification as a means of attaining structural coherence rekindled only by Stravinsky's reading of Eliot. Mersenne speaks of splitting twelve movements into duple or triple time (temps), and sometimes "two bars of ternaire (triple) time have six movements." It is these divisions, harkening back to the Renaissance, more than any association with serialism that account for the symmetry of the ballet's architecture. The Bransle Simple (two male dancers), the Bransle Gay (one female), and the Bransle Double (two male and one female) are all divisions to which de Lauze refers. Even the tempo and metric markings of Stravinsky's music—moving from duple to triple, with each bransle successively faster—are borrowed from de Lauze, just as such divisions are reflected in *Agon*'s bransles. Wildeblood's explanation of de Lauze's principles includes diagrams and step-by-step instructions—all of which Stravinsky studied, and many of which are explained in movements of twelve specific steps comprising a circle or pattern. For example, in the manual's demonstration of the "Bransle de Poitou," we learn that the dance "had only ten steps but to make it understood with less difficulty we will count twelve." Stravinsky was always particularly fascinated by the parameters of rhythmic patterns, and several sketches and index cards disclose his drafting of various rhythmic schema prior to working out a melodic contour. Many of these sketches appear at the top of a draft and apparently were used as a precompositional guide, before the actual writing process began.

Ultimately, *Agon* is not about the composer's adoption of the twelve-tone system; rather, it is about the temporal flow of rhythm, "architectonics," to use Stravinsky's own term. It is about how the beauty of architecture multiplies in splendor the more it is limited by the discipline of classical templates—templates that the composer became familiar with long before he sat down to write the ballet's first note. In tracing *Agon*'s history, the importance of the composer's precompositional preparation should not be underestimated. Especially for a ballet whose gestation was so long, the early stages of incubation were particularly crucial. In which direction would Stravinsky have moved without Lincoln Kirstein's intercession? Without the writings of Eliot, the music of Mersenne, and the de Lauze dance manual as guides, would the composer have found the catalyst he needed to jump-start his thinking or to edge it down the path it eventually took? As always, Stravinsky, the indefatigable classicist, found inspiration by turning to the past, to models that would provide the structural foundation he needed to assemble his "futuristic" creation. *Agon* is justly hailed as a masterpiece of abstraction, of stark, powerful contrasts producing a cohesive, wondrous musical/balletic unity. That the power of this "Space Age" ballet owes its genesis to sources as old as the Renaissance seems fitting. For in Stravinsky's estimate, the pathway of the future could never be separated from the achievements of the past.

Watching Music

"YOU CAN'T IMAGINE how great the New York City Ballet was, forty years ago. Too bad you weren't around." My own memories have little to do with this, the usual revenge of aging balletomanes on youth. I'd never seen a ballet before 1961, when I left Chicago to study the cello and conducting in New York, and it was a revelation when I did—the ballet taught me about music. Over the course of the last four decades, I've puzzled over the relation of these two arts, a story shaped for me, as for other musicians, by George Balanchine's particular genius; a story also shaped by New York City.

In principle, musicians and choreographers face the same problem. Musical scores are set texts; the positions, steps, and movements of ballet are elaborately defined: the problem is how to bring such careful instructions to life onstage. George Balanchine formed a bridge between the two arts. Himself a capable pianist, Balanchine had worked closely with Stravinsky, Prokofiev, Hindemith, and other composers; he had once famously declared that he sought to make music visible in his ballets.

The trouble in my generation was that few classically trained musicians took this statement seriously—a failure that reveals something about the state of music forty years ago. In part we were simply ignorant; "ballet music" con-jured up only the thump-boom-boom of Minkus and similar composers who wrote the Muzak of the nineteenth century. So super-snobbish were students at Juilliard, Curtis, and Mannes that even Tchaikovsky's music seemed unworthy; we were embarrassed by its directness. My generation of musicians also loathed self-dramatizing wildness onstage—the agonizing pianist or the balletic conductor, epitomized in New York then by Leonard Bernstein. Our ideal was the physically serene performer: Arthur Rubinstein, Gregor Piatigorsky, Pierre Monteux.

I was therefore surprised when a conducting teacher chided me one night at the Metropolitan Opera: "Why are you wasting your time *here*? Go to the New York City Ballet; that's where you will learn to conduct." She was so insistent that I decided to give it a try, dragging the pianist Murray Perahia with me down to the City Center on Fifty-fifth Street, where the New York City Ballet performed in those days.

First on the program was a dance set to Tchaikovsky, which confirmed our prejudices and derailed us from looking. But then came *The Four Temperaments*, the dance Balanchine made to music by Hindemith, and all at once we got it.

This 1940 piece of Hindemith's is not satisfying to hear in concert because it is so spare. Balanchine's ballet doesn't so much represent the action of the music as analyze and develop it, like a jazz musician mining the possibilities of a tune. The choreographer takes Hindemith's spareness as an opportunity rather than a limit, so that the movements onstage explore what the severely economic sounds might imply—a hand raised at an unresolved dissonance, then moving downward to complete the missing harmonic progression. The works of Balanchine that have since come to move me most use music of a kindred sort: Stravinsky's *Apollon Musagète* is also lean and astringent; his Violin Concerto is as much about silence as sound. The choreography builds on musical absence.

That evening, all I knew was that we were suddenly watching *The Four Temperaments* in order to hear it. I began going to the ballet night after night, in order to understand the music I was elsewhere performing. It's not that I tried to dance when I conducted, but in ways I still can't fathom my gestures became more free and expressive to others. And I began to hear Bernstein better. One thing that struck me as I moved between the two worlds of classical music and ballet was how different, for audiences, Bernstein's Carnegie Hall felt from Balanchine's City Center.

Musical life in New York during the 1960s was still living out the consequences of the Second World War. Fascism and Nazism had sent to America, and particularly to New York, many great musicians, as well as a large, knowledgeable audience of European exiles. For this public music was an important link—

perhaps the most important one in New York—with a life that nearly had been destroyed; the exiles were reverent about concerts in a way that reminded me of churchgoers back in the Midwest.

It would be wrong, though, to imagine New York musical life in 1961 as simply turned toward that past. Bourgeois culture, in the age before mechanical recording of music, had emphasized making music in the family; that emphasis continued in the exiles' family lives after the war, as it did in the families of Jewish, Italian, and German immigrants who had earlier come to New York. This made for a sense of immediate connection and presence between listener and performer that is hard to convey today; forty years ago, audiences were filled with young people, and many of them had played as amateurs the same music we performed onstage.

This connection partly accounts for how much music was performed all over the city. A musician would make his or her way in New York because there was an active concert life in the boroughs as well as in Manhattan; people went to what have sometimes been called "little concerts" because they wanted the pleasure of hearing live music, even if they'd never heard of the "little" musicians playing it.

The scene at the City Center was quite different. To be sure, Balanchine had come to America bringing a culture, as well as dance teachers and dancers, from Europe. However, classical ballet had far more shallow roots historically in New York than classical music; before Balanchine's arrival in 1934, ballet appeared only sporadically on the local stage, and Balanchine would only found a permanent company in New York in 1948. Equally, few of the people who watched Balanchine's dances had themselves danced; nor had ballet spread out through the city in quite the same way. The City Center was its only real home, and over this Balanchine reigned single and supreme. In one way there was nothing surprising about this; Balanchine was as great an artist as Picasso or Mozart, and a public formed around him.

Yet what struck me about the atmosphere at the old City Center was that, if reverent, it was very informal. People dropped into the theater whenever they could, and there always seemed to be plenty of tickets available; performances seldom started on time; ballets were suddenly added or subtracted. A foreigner weaving through the lobbies of the faux-Moorish interior of the City Center might have imagined, from the use of first names and dish about private life, that half the audience was on an intimate footing with the dancers. And the company's performances were among the few places in the city where gay men and women appeared easily and unselfconsciously.

The architecture of City Center served this social informality well. A hall based on the German theater model, it had a big balcony that protruded over much of the orchestra. The closeness of the upper tier to the stage helps create a sense of intimacy in the theater that can be reinforced by curtaining off the back of the balcony when the house is not full.

So, to compare the worlds of classical music and ballet forty years ago, you have to imagine two very different scenes for high art—Carnegie Hall on Fifty-seventh Street and City Center on Fifty-fifth Street. Carnegie Hall, for many of its public, was a monument to the survival of European culture despite the disasters of war; for many others, it was the place in which the art they practiced themselves was performed better—at least in theory. Above all, Carnegie Hall was a musical *center*, fed by concert halls and concerts throughout the city.

In contrast, City Center housed an art evoking memories of elsewhere only for its principal choreographer and some of his fellow artists. Few who watched the ballet could dance what was performed onstage. And despite its name, City Center was not a center in the same urban sense as its neighbor, but rather a singular institution presided over by a single genius. Yet the City Center was easy and free in spirit, anything but a monumental cultural "institution."

Historians of New York culture like Thomas Bender and Irving Howe have observed how isolated cultural activities were from one another forty years ago—ghettos of culture were as strong in the city as racial or class ghettos. The separations between dancers and musicians in my generation also existed between both these performing arts and the "New York Intellectuals," which meant then people still in the orbit of *Partisan Review*. Susan Sontag was the only writer I knew who moved knowledgeably in other worlds. But even within the dance world, as I soon found, Balanchine worked in a certain isolation.

One paradoxical reason for this was that, if New York lacked a long history of ballet, it did not lack for other kinds of dance. Modern dance had deep roots in the city. By 1960, Martha Graham had become a well-established presence in New York, and "mother" to several generations of choreographers. This other dance world had networks throughout the city; the youngest and most adventuresome found a home in Greenwich Village at the Judson Church as well as in lofts and temporary studios. Though I can't reckon the split in any statistical way, the faces of the audience at City Center were seldom those one saw at Judson.

When I began playing and conducting for modern dance groups, I quickly learned how much they resented the New York City Ballet. Some modern dancers rejected it because it was ballet, a European rather than an American idiom. Others, who acknowledged Balanchine's stature, felt that by the early 1960s he had reached an artistic dead end, his best work behind him. And almost all the dancers working outside his orbit resented the arrangement with City Center, a public institution that used—so they believed—public money to support Balanchine's solitary genius rather than the modern dance native to the country and the city.

There was a certain cruelty in this resentment, for it had taken a long time for Balanchine to stabilize the conditions in which he worked. In 1924, as a young Russian exile in Paris, he had joined

Diaghilev's Ballets Russes. After the impresario's death in 1929, the company collapsed. Balanchine drifted: he worked in Copenhagen, Paris, and London, where Les Ballets 1933, a company founded to showcase his choreography, also collapsed. Invited by Lincoln Kirstein, Balanchine sailed to America in 1933—a second exile. There was money for a year, and with it, Balanchine and Kirstein started both a company and a school.

Even so the choreographer's career remained unsettled; the Great Depression, and after it the Second World War, taught him that the streets of America were hardly paved with gold. In the 1930s and early 1940s, Balanchine worked on Broadway and made ballets for Hollywood movies. Only in 1948, with the help of the civic leader Morton Baum, did Balanchine and Kirstein gain regular access to a theater. Balanchine had waited fifteen years in America for a home; he was forty-four years old.

Most of the modern dancers I knew were too American to understand Balanchine's double exile, too young to sympathize with his long wait for a home. To some extent, Kirstein's presence helped mollify the resentment other dancers and choreographers felt about the New York City Ballet. A poet, writer on photography, and social flâneur, the Boston-born impresario inhabited many worlds, rather than working in solitude and submission within Balanchine's orbit. My impression was that Kirstein, though fiercely protective of everything concerning the New York City Ballet and its choreographer, didn't have much of a social relationship with Balanchine; he was certainly friendly with many people who were not well disposed toward the company, and who, for the sake of his friendship, kept their discontents to themselves.

Balanchine's isolation, at least from other musically based arts, was slated to end even by the time I began going to the ballet. Since the mid-1950s the city fathers had been working to create Lincoln Center. This great square for the performing arts is modeled, architecturally, on Michelangelo's Campidoglio in Rome, grouping different government buildings around a common space. The Roman planners had hoped to make government more coherent; in New York, the planning mavens hoped for artistic "synergy." Clustered together, they argued, the performing arts would interact more strongly by sharing sets, costumes, musical personnel, and maybe even artistic ideas.

The New York City Ballet was included in the project almost from its inception. City Center was, in truth, hardly an ideal place for dance. When the New York City Ballet first used it, the sharp tilt of the orchestra-level seats meant viewers in the first rows could not see the dancers' feet; backstage everything was cramped, and the lighting system was a fireman's nightmare. Lincoln Kirstein was therefore anxious to build a home where the dancers were more comfortable and safer, the stage was larger, and the public out front could see better.

These plans aroused mixed emotions. It was easy forty years ago for a young artist to live in the very heart of the city; musicians like myself preferred the Upper West Side because its solid bourgeois apartments, though cheap and cockroach-infested, were blessedly soundproof. My neighbors and I resented the fact that the city fathers thought our community, its streets filled in summer with the mingled sounds of salsa and Schumann, its traffic islands in all seasons crowded with elderly ladies recalling the prewar glories of Frankfurt, needed renewing.

But as a musician who had stumbled by chance on another art, I also found the larger rationale for Lincoln Center compelling; it seemed reasonable that the accident that had so enriched my life might occur to many others in the new space. To me, the best thing about Lincoln Center was the inclusion of the Juilliard School. Then, as now, Juilliard required two things of its students: they should be exceptionally gifted and exceptionally driven. Juilliard students stewed in these requirements with few other urban seasonings; the school, then located up near Columbia University, was perhaps the most isolated artistic ghetto in the city. Now Juilliard was to move, and its students' isolated sufferings would perhaps be relieved by synergy; at least, encountering ballet would be physically easier.

That was perhaps a parochial interest. Historians of the New York City Ballet might take a larger view: Did the company's immediate presence in fact affect the music performed around the square—the operas, orchestral concerts, or chamber music? And did the ballet gain by the association? When the New York City Ballet moved to Lincoln Center, many critics pointed out that Balanchine didn't need an expensive new building to "synergize." He had only to lift the telephone and summon any composer—or for that matter, any lighting designer, set designer, or instrumentalist—he needed. After the move, the company in essence remained what it was; Balanchine made more great ballets, like *Jewels* and *Davidsbündlertänze*; great dancers retired, great dancers like Suzanne Farrell appeared; pretty much the same public came to hang out, dish, and revere. It's true that as an organization NYCB seemed a tighter ship; performances started more nearly on time, and getting tickets became more efficient. But better bureaucracy and safer, bigger quarters seemed to have little effect on the artistic enterprise itself.

Sadly, the presence of this amazing dance company has done little to raise the standards of choreography at the opera next door, as anyone who has sat through any Met *Aida* in the last thirty-five years can attest. As to the specific connections between musicians and dancers, the opening up of the Juilliard School to other arts has occurred in ways that didn't follow the script of 1965. Juilliard expanded and diversified within itself. But the connections of its students to the city are now "downtown" connections; I see composition students often at the Joyce Theater, seldom at the New York State Theater. It may be that, in time, the gleaming new home of the School of American Ballet behind Juilliard will finally knit musicians and dancers together. But the institutional spread of the company's work has occurred outside New York, thanks to former Balanchine dancers who have created companies in Washington, Pennsylvania, Florida, and elsewhere.

For all these reasons I think it's fair to say that Lincoln Center has not on the whole made much difference to the relations between classical music and ballet in the city. Perhaps institutional design isn't the answer to strengthening artistic connections. Yet this conclusion, I've come to think, leaves something out: Balanchine's own practice as an artist.

Despite his work on Broadway and for films, or the ballet *Stars and Stripes*, a loving sendup of apple-pie America, there is something in the very nature of Balanchine's art that sets him apart from his adopted country. I think he would have subscribed to Stravinsky's credo of 1936: "In classical dancing, I see the triumph of studied conception over vagueness, of the rule over the arbitrary, of order over the haphazard."[1] This love of form Stravinsky also calls ballet's "aristocratic austerity."[2] If one thing marks American high culture, however, it is the value we put on impulse, on the spontaneous outburst on the sudden confession whose truth breaks through conventions. We are by temper not aristocrats of Balanchine's or Stravinsky's sort.

Artistic labels are crude, but certainly the "neoclassical art" of Balanchine or Stravinsky requires an engagement with questions of form bred in the bone, in particular a loving engagement with the studied simplicities of eighteenth-century art. It is the very taste for aristocratic austerity, for studied simplicity, that prompts the neoclassical artist to play with form. For instance, Arlene Croce writes about Terpsichore's solo in *Apollo* that "we see leaps that do not advance, leaps that go *down*, back-front reversals that seem to maintain the mysterious constancy of a shape even as it changes. We see, in other words, an examination and also an expression . . . of the complex logic of classicism."[3] The neoclassical temperament does not seek to preserve sights or sounds exactly intact, as though in a museum. Rather, it wants to discover the inner logic of a form by experimenting with its rules—particularly when the rules are as seemingly strict as in ballet or eighteenth-century musical composition.

This temperament kept Balanchine a foreigner in America, I think, as much as it made Stravinsky's neoclassicism difficult for American musicians to digest. I had a taste of this separation in 1979, when Balanchine unveiled his last reworking of *Apollo*. Like other people in the first-night audience, I watched in stunned surprise. In his old age the choreographer had radically altered his own creation; the beginning and the end were cut; Stravinsky's music was cut; at one stroke, nearly a third of the ballet was missing.

Balanchine had declared in a 1948 issue of *Dance Index*: "In 'Apollo' and in all the music that follows, it is impossible to imagine substituting for any single fragment the fragment of any other Stravinsky score. Each piece is unique in itself; nothing is replaceable."[4] Yet he had also declared in the same breath, " 'Apollo' I look back on as the turning point of my life. . . . It seemed to tell me that I could dare not to use everything, that I, too, could eliminate."[5] It is precisely this contradiction that animates the self-critical attitude of neoclassicism—and we, Balanchine's audience, had trouble following him. How could a man not keep faith with something near perfect he had made? In *Ballet Review*, Robert Garis called the production a "depredation."[6]

For all these reasons—social, urban, and artistic—it has seemed to me that Balanchine remained apart even as he made his way in New York. In particular, the connections between dance and music in his work could not be received in the same spirit he offered them. I don't mean that either he or we failed one another; perhaps connections between arts occur obliquely, or only by happy chance, or through puzzlement, rather than in the direct, businesslike fashion imagined by the planners of synergies. And perhaps also the aloof relation to his adopted home ensured Balanchine's own freedom. But as an American musician watching music, thanks to him, I've never ceased to feel I'm crossing a real boundary of difference.

A serious study remains to be written about connections between performers of dance and music in New York City. Since the Second World War, the lives of dancers have become more secure, thanks to the institutionalization of dance. Classical musicians have, paradoxically, suffered from the institutions designed to protect them; the recording industry has been driven out of New York City, for instance, due to union constraints. And we know all too little about the parallels or divergent shapes of artistic careers in the city. Dancing is of course a shorter-lived activity than playing music, but today there are more opportunities for those embarking on that short career than there are for young violinists or conductors in New York.

One connection between these two realms of performance, with which I'd like to conclude these reflections, concerns the sense of the generation to which middle-aged performers belong. The New York I entered can be dated two ways, "the 1960s" or "The Sixties." When we talk about "The Sixties," we usually mean a watershed in American history—the civil rights movement, the Vietnam War and its protests, the counterculture. This aspect of the decade did not much intrude into the high arts of ballet and classical music, at least in New York; the chronology of culture was different for them. In ballet, a long generation spanned the birth of the New York City Ballet in 1948 until Balanchine's death in 1983; in classical music, there was a roughly similar time span after the Second World War; by the 1980s young people, who no longer played music at home or thought of the great European tradition as their own, had deserted the concert halls.

Now that this long generation has come to an end, those who lived through it are often prone to regret. This may be natural, though chiding the young for missing out on the great times isn't much solace. Balanchine refused such temptations. Shortly before he died, he declared, "I don't want my ballets preserved as museum pieces for people to go and laugh at what used to be. *Absolutely not.* I'm staging ballets for today's bodies. Ballet is NOW."[7] Somewhere, surely, is a choreographer who will shock us again into watching music, though it may look like nothing we've seen before.

Substitute and Consolation

The Ballet Photographs of

George Platt Lynes

ONE OF GEORGE PLATT LYNES's most extraordinary ballet photographs is of Francisco Monción and Nicholas Magallanes reenacting a scene from George Balanchine's *Orpheus.* "Reenacting" is probably not the right word, since they are not actually dancing, but carefully posed for the camera. And unlike when they performed the work in public, they are both nude, stripped by Lynes of the costumes designed for them by Isamu Noguchi. The scene is from a moment in the ballet when the Dark Angel leads the masked and blinded Orpheus through the underworld. The Angel moves behind him, slipping the lyre over the singer's head. He is about to run his hands across the strings as a gesture for Orpheus to play and thus win Pluto over to restoring Eurydice to life. The effect is of the two bodies joining in an erotic embrace. Ostensibly, the lyre seems placed out of modesty to cover the singer's genitals, but the extreme phallic form of the instrument's arms has the effect of exaggerating what is hidden. And so the Angel's handling of Orpheus's instrument takes on the quality of foreplay, even as his position behind the bard suggests penetration. In a sense the Angel is seducing Orpheus, so that his music will seduce the god of the underworld. With his arms in a high circling fifth, Orpheus gazes upward as if responding ecstatically to the Angel's embrace. The bodies of the dancers merge in a formal configuration that itself is intensely phallic.

Although Monción and Magallanes are obviously posed in the studio—in the background we can make out the mottled stains of a photographer's backdrop—they are bathed in a light that is intensely theatrical; indeed, everything about Lynes's ballet photography is meticulously staged. For the most part, Lynes had little interest in creating naturalistic effects in which light seems to emanate from a single source. In his pictures electric light pours in from multiple angles, including from behind. We are not asked to imagine these two figures inhabiting any world but that of the studio. The artifice of his lighting resolves potential conflicts: Lynes can be both specific and general. The strong contrast of shadows and highlights creates a clear sense of line and gesture, so crucial to Balanchine's choreography, even as the intense sculptural effect delineates the musculature of the bodies. We are intensely aware of the ways in which the dancers are both separate and complicatedly entwined. Lynes's carefully manipulated light works like a surrogate for touch. It moves over the smooth surfaces of the muscular bodies, the curves of the waists, the folds of the stomach muscles and rib cages. A shadow across Magallanes's stomach has the effect of emphasizing the indentation of his navel, which marvelously echoes the hole of the lyre.

It is no coincidence that Lynes was particularly drawn to Balanchine's *Orpheus*. Not only did he photograph the ballet extensively, clothed and nude, but he also documented Balanchine's earlier encounter with the theme, the 1936 *Orpheus and Eurydice*, which had sets and lighting by Pavel Tchelitchew and used the music of Gluck. The Orpheus story allowed for intimate dancing between two males that was otherwise rare in ballet. Photographing what amounted to a pas de deux between the Dark Angel and Orpheus was a way for Lynes to reconcile his private work of photographing beautiful men with his public activities as a portraitist and photographer of ballet.

Lynes worked closely with Balanchine to pose the dancers, even asking him at times to click the shutter when the image seemed right. But how can a still and silent image suggest an art form that is essentially about movement in relationship to music? Film would seem better for this task of remembrance. Lynes felt that most attempts to film dance were failures, either because "the lens seems obliged to sit farther away than any balletomane ever sat" or because "the cameraman weaves in and out among the dancers" so that "the unity of the dance-design is lost."[1] Balanchine shared Lynes's distrust of the motion picture camera, but for a different reason. He was worried that film would freeze his choreography, reduce it to a single, unvarying performance of a work, while fostering a standardized and stagnant repertory. He did not exempt his own ballets when he said that "even the best of them deserve to die and let in new

MARIA TALLCHIEF in
Prodigal Son, 1950.
Dance Collection, The New
York Public Library for the
Performing Arts, Astor,
Lenox, and Tilden
Foundations.

vision." "I have energy," he added, "to make new works, not to recall old ones with original accuracy." One of the great appeals of Lynes's photographs for Balanchine was that they made little attempt to capture actual performance steps. Instead they suggested what might be called the ambience of a particular dance, its "echo" or perfume. "They contain something of the secret and seldom realized intention of choreography," he wrote. "They are pure miniatures, while dance-films are always improvised or impoverished." He paid Lynes the ultimate compliment: his "pictures will contain, as far as I am concerned, all that will be remembered of my own repertory in a hundred years."[2]

And so the *Orpheus* series not only conveys something of Balanchine's original choreography but also suggests Lynes's longing for the dancers who were Balanchine's tools and inspiration. The Orpheus story itself could serve as an allegory for the problem dance posed for the camera. Lynes wrote of the enormous difficulties involved in trying to make permanent this most impermanent of art forms: "The design of the choreographer has to be passed from one company to another, handed down from generation to generation. Each dancer re-creates his role, often with a lesser, in any case with a different ability. Choreographers and dancers and audiences forget; and generally speaking, a revival harks backs inaccurately to its first night, its heyday." But, he adds, "an essential factor in our response to dancing is the wish that it might go on forever."[3] Like Orpheus, Lynes sees his task as cheating death. His photographs are intended to bestow immortality, to make the dance go on forever.

From the moment of its invention, the camera has been celebrated as an instrument that has the power to arrest time. Yet paradoxically, this very ability to freeze a likeness ends up reasserting the mortality of the original. More than any other photographer, Lynes captured the beauty and grace of Maria Tallchief. Yet in contemplating an arresting image of her as the Siren in *Prodigal Son* I become painfully aware that she is irretrievably gone. Or returning to the picture of Monción and Magallanes in *Orpheus*, I realize that they no longer exist as young, beautiful bodies and, even worse, that I will never see them dance. Roland Barthes, whose *Camera Lucida* is an extended reverie on precisely the way death is always inscribed on a photograph, writes: "The photograph does not call up the past (nothing Proustian in a photograph). The effect it produces upon me is not to restore what has been abolished (by time, by distance) but to attest that what I see has indeed existed."[4] Like Orpheus, we need to be warned of the perils of using Lynes's photographs to look back. To the degree that his ballet pictures are documents, it is not because they reconstitute what took place at an actual performance, but because, in a Barthian sense, they are evidence that such beautiful dancers existed, performing for Lynes's camera. Barthes writes: "The Photographer's 'second sight' does not consist in 'seeing' but in being there. And above all, imitating Orpheus, he must not turn back to look at what he is leading—what he is giving me!"[5]

Lynes himself had no illusions about his photographs replacing Balan-chine's dances. He wrote with modesty that his ballet photographs were only an "adjunct" to memory or, for those who had never seen the original performances, "a sort of substitute and consolation."[6] Such terms put the emphasis on the fetishistic character of his ballet photographs rather than their archival role. They are replacements for love objects, images for devotion and mourning. In truth, Lynes never had much interest in the documentary photography that was so popular among his American contemporaries. His roots were in the European avant-garde. In his teens he imagined becoming an avant-garde writer and publisher and had sought advice and encouragement from Gertrude Stein. Originally, photography was a sideline to his literary career, but he found in his portraits of Stein and Jean Cocteau, as well as more intimate pictures of his friends and lovers, René Crevel, Glenway Wescott, and Monroe Wheeler, an expressive voice that was missing in his literary efforts. Lynes was particularly drawn to the photography of the American expatriate Man Ray, whom he met in Paris. Indeed, Man Ray's success in reconciling avant-garde experimentation with a thriving commercial career in portraiture, fashion photography, and even, occasionally, ballet photography provided a model for Lynes's career. Like Man Ray, he experimented with montage in which negatives were superimposed and manipulated. Although he did not advocate retouching or soft focus techniques, he was no subscriber to the aesthetic of the "straight photograph," in which the image was cropped in the camera. But it was his use of studio lights, glamorizing his subject so that whatever he photographed—portraits, nudes, dancers—resembled a staged performance, that put his work most at odds with the documentary style of photographers like Walker Evans, Edward Weston, and Paul Strand.

If Lynes's photographs were not intended to record dance movement in an archival sense, they did serve a functional purpose. Many were used in souvenir programs or as press material, helping to publicize ballets and the companies and artists that produced them. The lavishness of the Kirstein-Balanchine souvenir programs, which were produced for every major season and most important events starting in the mid-1930s, belied the economic precariousness of the enterprise at large. But that was precisely the point: the image of the company was successful, elegant, and glamorous, a worthy heir to the high artistic tradition of Diaghilev's Ballets Russes, which had made the souvenir program a collector's item earlier in the century. In his dance portraits Lynes applied the same techniques he used in his fashion work for *Harper's Bazaar*. He imbued his dance subjects with the appeal of models or, better yet, movie stars. Lynes's habit of lighting his subject from behind, a technique associated with Hollywood star shots, emphasized the silhouette of his subject, no less crucial to a choreographer than to a fashion editor. At the same time, his use of sharp contrast eliminated skin imperfections: his photographs are always flattering to his sitters. There is a richness to his tonal contrasts and sense of pattern; this, combined with the evocative poses of his sitters, conveys a sense of luxury and excess. The final effect was to imbue Balanchine's dancers with the aura of America's leading celebrities. For those who lived through the extraordinary ballet boom of the 1970s, when ballet superstars regularly turned up in gossip columns and even on television, this may not seem like much of an accomplishment. But in the 1930s, 1940s, and 1950s, when Lynes worked with Balanchine, ballet did not have anything like this appeal. His pictures were thus an essential part of Kirstein's campaign to create an audience for ballet among New York's sophisticated elite. They did so not simply through their glamour but by presenting the dance in a manner that seems eternal and classic.

The 1951 souvenir program, which followed New York City Ballet's first European tour, is particularly beautiful. The cover features an extremely cropped image of male dancers grasping a mask from

Orpheus. Inside, along with several portraits of the principal dancers, are pictures of Magallanes, Monción, Tallchief, and Tanaquil LeClercq in poses from *Orpheus* arranged cinematically in strips to suggest movement. Even though the company had yet to celebrate its third birthday, a sense of history was created by including a photograph of the American Ballet's 1936 *Orpheus and Eurydice*. Of course, mythological subjects, no matter how nonconformist their presentation, reinforce a sense of tradition. But also important is Lynes's sculptural technique, his way of lighting the dancers from all angles, intensifying voids and solids in their forms, so that they seem fully embodied and concrete. In this context, his fondness for photographing dancers at rest or in carefully contrived poses, while potentially static, conveys the message that ballet is not a medium of flux but an instrument of tradition. Balanchine wrote that Lynes's "secret was his sense of plasticity," which enabled him to suggest the "quintessential permanence of characteristic silhouette and massive form" in the choreographer's ballets.[7]

ORPHEUS, New York City Ballet Souvenir Program, Seventh New York Season, June 1951.
Ballet Society Archives.

Despite Balanchine's (later) words of praise, many of Lynes's best ballet pictures were not deemed suitable for public dissemination and so did not make it into print until long after he died. Lynes complained of NYCB's "prudishness" to the sexologist Alfred Kinsey, who actively collected some of the photographs that had been turned down.[8] Of course, Lynes's nude *Orpheus* pictures were not published in his lifetime; after all, they were not made to be used in advertisements and programs. But also excluded were many of his pictures of male dancers, probably because they seemed too homoerotic and too seductive. From the very beginning of his career as a dance photographer, Lynes seemed more interested in photographing male than female dancers. And he

LEW CHRISTENSEN as
Mac in *Filling Station*,
1938. *San Francisco
Performing Arts Library
and Museum.*

tended to photograph men differently, so as to emphasize their physicality. For example, in his photograph of Lew Christensen in the American Ballet's 1937 revival of *Apollo*, the dancer's tunic is carefully draped to expose his muscular arms and legs. Dark shadows make it difficult to see if he is wearing anything below his waist. Lynes seemed particularly taken with the transparent costume designed by Paul Cadmus for Mac, the gas station attendant in *Filling Station*— a see-through uniform that clung to Christensen's body, accentuating his right nipple and his crotch. In the 1940s and 1950s Balanchine often dressed his dancers in tights, shirts, and form-fitting leotards that resembled practice clothes. Lynes went further, longing for the men to wear nothing at all. And in the privacy of his studio he was able to get a number of male dancers to shed their clothes completely. In contrast, the female dancers in Lynes's photographs are nearly always elaborately costumed and made up. In a 1950 portrait of Beatrice Tompkins, the NYCB dancer seems almost embalmed in clothes. Not only is her body hidden under a cape and ball gown, but her face is concealed by a veil. Thick stage makeup accentuates her eyebrows and lips, adding yet another layer to her body's disguise. Her outfit is so excessive and artificial that she resembles a man in drag. If being a woman in Lynes's photographs is usually a matter of putting clothes on, being a man is usually about taking them off.

In addition to shooting them in elaborate costumes and makeup, Lynes tended to distance his ballerina subjects in space. Diana Adams, in a tutu (from *La Valse*) that reaches her ankles, is seen from afar, pressed against a wall, a figure isolated in an expanse of empty space. Instead of engaging the viewer with her eyes, she looks up and out of the photograph: in general, the women in Lynes's ballet pictures tend to look away from the camera. The men are far more likely to confront the viewer. John Kriza, as Billy the Kid, nude from the waist up, flexes his muscles and stares at the lens. Lynes's women are more distant idols, their glances suggesting ethereal concerns or self-absorption; his men seem aware of the viewer's presence and thus are more seductive.

The homoeroticism of Lynes's photographs is present even when all the principals are fully clothed. In another picture from *La Valse*, Tanaquil LeClercq reaches for the bouquet her death-bringing partner holds aloft, a dramatic moment disturbed by the presence of a handsome male figure looming in the background with a mirror in his hand, a surrogate for the camera and Lynes's desiring gaze. In general, Lynes's photographs of men and women dancing in close physical proximity have a chaste quality. The *Jones Beach* pictures have the potential to be sexy since the couples wear nothing but bathing suits. But whether because of the obvious artificiality of the setting—the cloud backdrop and thin layer of sand on the floor look borrowed from a physique magazine—or the strain of athletic movements that do not translate into still photographs, the dancers are not convincing as an erotic couple.

How do Lynes's photographs of male dancers relate to his more explicit photographs of male nudes? James Crump charts the photographer's growing dissatisfaction with having to do commercial work for fashion magazines.[9] At the end of his life

TANAQUIL LECLERCQ with FRANCISCO MONCIÓN and EDWARD BIGELOW in *La Valse*, 1951.

Facing page (*top*): JOHN KRIZA as Billy the Kid, 1949.

(*bottom*): TANAQUIL LECLERCQ and NICHOLAS MAGALLANES in *Jones Beach*, 1950. All three photos from *Dance Collection, The New York Public Library for the Performing Arts, Astor, Lenox, and Tilden Foundations.*

he actually destroyed most of the negatives for his fashion photographs, as if he were ashamed of the very stylishness and elegance that make them so appealing today. If not for the necessity of earning a living, he would have focused all his attention on photographing nude men. From 1930 to his death in 1955, Lynes produced an extraordinary series of male nudes that because of the homophobia and censorship of the period were known only to his circle of artists and friends.

What was new and dangerous about Lynes's erotic photographs was not just their nudity per se, but their sense of intimacy between men. Where it might be possible to attribute individual pictures of a lone male figure to a refined appreciation of the human form, it is impossible to ignore the homosexual content of his pictures of young men completely naked and physically entwined. His series of photographs of the painters Paul Cadmus and Jared French are, as far as I know, the first extensive photographic portraits of male lovers by a professional American photographer. Their semi-nude state is not only a necessary component to this picture's beauty, but an unmistakable sign of the physical nature of their attachment. Yet despite the eroticism of his photograph, Lynes insists on his high art ambitions by placing Cadmus and French in an abstract setting so that the subtle curves of the male physique contrast with the geometric lines of a box.

Lynes also photographed men who appear to be outside his artistic circle and class. We can guess that the man covered with tattoos was a sailor and hustler (or "trade," to use the gay subculture's nomenclature for male prostitutes drawn from the working class), whose sexual prowess is reinforced by the bizarre backdrop embossed with explicitly phallic patterns. The image is certainly related to pornographic photographs that were circulated clandestinely in the gay underworld around the time of

World War II. However, the contrast of the hypermasculine body with the elegant neoclassic chaise, combined with the dramatic and mysterious lighting, underscores Lynes's artistic intentions.

Indeed, Lynes insists on both the erotic and the aesthetic. In another photograph, the tattooed sitter is juxtaposed with a classical bust, hanging improbably from the ceiling. We are given both an earthly and a celestial version of male beauty. In Lynes's world the two were inextricably linked. He merged them in a series of montages based on Greek myths. According to Glenway Wescott, Lynes's project of photographing beautiful boys in the guise of Actaeon or Pan was a way to "put a stop to all the questioning and quibbling and moralizing" that would otherwise greet the depictions of male nudes.[10] However, the photographer's use of classical themes was not just a means to present sexy male bodies to a prudish audience. He longed for a classical golden age in which the male body and homosexual love were celebrated Unfortunately, the discontinuity between the camera's realism and the

Facing page (top): PAUL CADMUS and JARED FRENCH, late 1930s. *The Kinsey Institute for Research in Sex, Gender, and Reproduction, Indiana University.*

(bottom): MALE NUDE WITH TATTOOS, 1934. *The Kinsey Institute for Research in Sex, Gender, and Reproduction, Indiana University.*

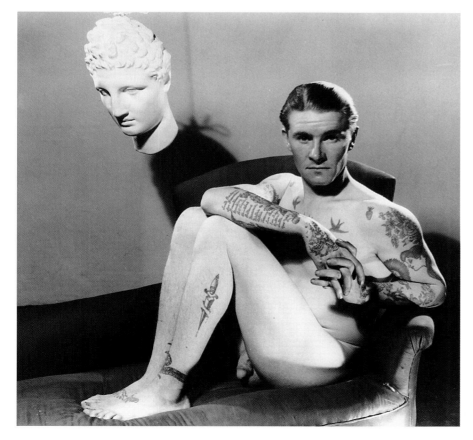

MALE NUDE WITH STATUARY, 1934. *The Kinsey Institute for Research in Sex, Gender, and Reproduction, Indiana University.*

MALE NUDE, 1951. *The Kinsey Institute for Research in Sex, Gender, and Reproduction, Indiana University.*

mythological setting produces a somewhat campy effect. The models never really seem to be anything but modern Americans. But such discontinuity reinforces the enormous gulf between Lynes's fantasy of a free space of gay desire and the repressive reality of American culture.

If Wescott was right in thinking that classical myths were a convenient mask for the homoerotic content of Lynes's work, how much more so was his ballet photography? In this context, the photographer's description of his ballet pictures as a "substitute and a consolation" takes on a distinctly different meaning from the original sense as providing a surrogate for the experience of the dance. Surely, photographing male ballet dancers in mythological contexts—like his pictures of Balanchine's *Orpheus* and *Apollo*—was a way for Lynes to explore some of the themes of his private nudes. Indeed, there is no absolute dividing line between Lynes's so-called erotic photography and his ballet photographs. Often the studio settings are identical. One of his most radical erotic photographs shows a figure crouched on the floor in a ball so that his rectum and testicles are in the center of the picture. Such an explicit focus on the genitals of his subject may seem very far from the decorum of the ballet pictures—until we realize that the background may be the same phony sky he used for the *Jones Beach* series. And given the obvious limberness of the faceless subject, it is probable that the model is a dancer. The nude *Orpheus* series, when removed from the context of Balanchine's ballet, reads like the narrative of a love affair between two men, underscoring that in the original myth, Orpheus ends up renouncing the love of women.

It is not just that Lynes struggled to get something from his private nude photographs into his ballet pictures; his ballet work powerfully influenced his male nudes. Perhaps Lynes's most extraordinary series of photographs depicts an erotic encounter among three men in a highly stylized bedroom setting.[11] This triangle may be Lynes's attempt to represent his complex relationship with Monroe Wheeler and Glenway Wescott. In any case, the sequence reads like a passionate ballet or pantomime—and seems just as choreographed.

It was because the demarcation between Lynes's ballet photographs and his private homoerotic pictures was not clear that many of his best dance pictures were not seen until after his death. Arguably, the danger of many of the photographs of male dancers was the way they suggested the crucial role of homosexuality in the formation of modern ballet. Dance historians and critics of visual culture have only just begun to explore the homosexual presence in ballet. Certainly, in the case of the New York City Ballet, homosexual men were part of its core audience from the beginning. The company and its predecessors employed many gay and bisexual male artists—designers like Tchelitchew, Cadmus, and Cecil Beaton; composers like Aaron Copland, Virgil Thomson, and Leonard Bernstein; as well as any number of dancers and choreographers. Ballet Caravan's productions of *Filling Station*, *Yankee Clipper*, *Billy the Kid*, and *Show Piece* all had a strong homoerotic component. Kirstein himself was initially drawn to ballet through the aura of Diaghilev's Ballets Russes and its androgynous virtuoso Vaslav Nijinsky. Kirstein never actually saw Nijinksy dance; he fell in love with him, he wrote in *Nijinsky Dancing*, "through his reflection in . . . photographs,"[12] which may well explain why he hired Lynes in the first place: he wanted the potential audience for ballet to experience the same thrill.

Paradoxically, the fact that the ballet was a safe harbor for homosexuals and a locus of desire for a gay audience had a closeting effect. The stereotype that only effeminate and "deviant" men would be interested in dance encouraged the repression of overt homosexual content in order to broaden the audience for ballet and, in time, to attract mainstream institutional support.[13] There is a marked difference between the sometimes homoerotic content of many American Ballet and Ballet Caravan productions of the 1930s and the repertory of the New York City Ballet in the late 1940s and 1950s. Although classical tradition and Balanchine's own heterosexuality were key factors in this shift, there may well have been the worry—all too real at a time when McCarthyism drove more gay men than leftists from government jobs—that displaying the male body was too risky. Even earlier works like *Filling Station* and *Yankee Clipper*, for all the opportunities they offered for men to dance together, veiled their homoeroticism in traditional romantic narratives and a populist glorification of America. Having dancers take the roles of sailors and gas station attendants was also a way of negating the idea that dancing was necessarily effeminate.

Lynes mediated between ballet as a space of homosexual desire—a place where it is possible for men to embrace or become the passive objects of a viewer's gaze—and ballet as a mask, or really *masque*, for that desire, glorifying traditional modes of romantic love. It is tempting to see Lynes's photography as somehow revealing the essential homosexuality of the ballet. I find something wonderfully honest about his picture of Frederick Ashton with three of the African-American dancers of *Four Saints and Three Acts*. Ashton rests his hands lovingly on the necks and arms of two of the nude men, suggesting his desire for their beautiful bodies. Ashton's display of affection is perhaps not so surprising in the 1930s when many downtown whites—gay as well as straight—found love uptown in Harlem. More unexpected is the fact that the third reclining figure returns Ashton's gaze even as he fondles the leg of a fellow dancer. This

FREDERICK ASHTON with three of the dancers of *Four Saints in Three Acts*, 1934. *The Kinsey Institute for Research in Sex, Gender, and Reproduction, Indiana University.*

picture suggests that homosexual desire is not just a matter of an older man voyeuristically gazing at beautiful boys, but of reciprocal affection between young men. Yet Lynes's daring revelation about male-male intimacy in ballet is not the *truth* of ballet in the 1930s, any more than Balanchine's obsession with teenage ballerinas was the truth later. To the degree that gender can add to our understanding of ballet, it has to do more than bring homosexuality out of the closet: It has to explore ballet's invitation to its audience to inhabit multiple bodies and genders. When Lynes wrote of the problem of filming ballet, he said that "a ballet is not indeed conceived to be seen from any particular seat," precisely because it is experienced from multiple viewpoints by multiple viewers, all of whom have different expectations of and responses to what they see.[14] The

BALANCHINE rehearsing
NICHOLAS MAGALLANES
and TANAQUIL LECLERCQ
in *The Triumph of Bacchus
and Ariadne,* 1948.
*Dance Collection, The New
York Public Library for the
Performing Arts, Astor, Lenox,
and Tilden Foundations.*

BALANCHINE with NICHOLAS MAGALLANES and MARIE-JEANNE, 1941. *Private collection.*

empathetic connection of a viewer with a particular dancer is not limited to the gender identity of either. For example, as a gay man, I might well become fixated on the arabesque of a male dancer, while also imagining what he looks like naked, but I might just as well become fixated on a female dancer's arabesque. I might want to sleep with a male dancer, or I might want to be that dancer, supporting a ballerina in a gravity-defying lift.

The ability of dance to cross gender boundaries is suggested by Lynes's remarkable photographs of Balanchine himself. In one picture the choreographer is shown refining a moment in the 1948 Ballet Society production of *The Triumph of Bacchus and Ariadne*. In order to demonstrate a movement to Tanaquil LeClercq (as Ariadne), he actually takes her place with Nicholas Magallanes (as Bacchus). She watches as Balanchine takes Magallanes's hand and gently leans against his shoulder. The photograph succinctly suggests Balanchine's ability to identify completely with both male and female roles. This idea is reinforced by a 1941 picture of Balanchine, in a well-cut suit and tie, embracing the naked stars of his American Ballet Caravan— Magallanes and Marie-Jeanne. In this portrait, Lynes seems to be saying that Balanchine's tools and the very matter of his art are the male and female body, and that these two sexes are fused in the choreographer. The fact that Balanchine wears a business suit and the dancers are naked could allude to the idea that choreography is a businesslike art of order, the work of the mind over the body. However, the effect is to throw into question both clothing and nudity. Both modes are costumes: indeed, the dancer's muscular body is the result of a daily discipline that is as much a product of artifice as the most fashionable suit.

That ballet is a matter of grueling work is, I think, behind the joke of another 1941 Lynes portrait

of Balanchine, this one showing him with a drill in one hand and a hammer in the other, which has been replaced by a bizarre-looking prosthetic arm. But these hardhat tools are in sharp contrast to the elegantly folded handkerchief, carelessly tossed-back silk tie, and tweed jacket worn over the shoulders like a cape. Lynes and Balanchine are playing with the stereotypes of ballet as antithetical to masculinity and everyday American work. Yet when this picture was later reproduced in an NYCB souvenir program, the tools and the prosthetic arm were cropped so that the joke of the picture was obliterated. What remained—the tweed, silk tie, and pocket-handkerchief—was the outfit of a gentleman dandy, the proper uniform for a serious choreographer. Such radical cropping on the part of the designer suggests a feeling of unease about the original portrait. My guess is that what was disturbing was not the prospect that Balanchine would seem effeminate—such an association came with the territory of ballet—but the possibility that the choreographer might be both masculine and feminine at once. Gender identity can seem most dangerous when it refuses to keep its place, when it cannot be easily described or identified—

SELF-PORTRAIT, mid–
1940s. *Private collection.*

that is, when it is most *queer*. In many Lynes photographs the male dancer is a
similar puzzle. He is an athlete capable of lifting a woman over his head, yet he
wears tights (or nothing at all) and makes exaggerated theatrical gestures. He is
both the passive object of male and female fantasies and an active performer
filled with aggressive energy. Whether he happens to be gay or straight, he is
paired with extraordinarily beautiful women. And he almost always gets the girl,
even if he himself may be a little girlish.

There is one more way in which Lynes's ballet photographs are a kind of
substitute and consolation. In 1945 Lynes posed himself in front of the cam–
era dressed in a leotard and tights. Raising his arms, he places one across the

eyes and the other behind his head. The space in the photograph is unusually shallow for Lynes's figure compositions. It is as if he cannot quite imagine himself dancing in a large open space, even as his pose suggests something less than the grace and physical awareness of a trained dancer. Indeed, his black and white costume is vaguely reminiscent of a joker's outfit, as if he were mocking his own aspirations. Other Lynes self-portraits are far more dignified and consciously artistic; in one, for example, he poses with a large format camera and lights, squinting at the viewer like the shutter of a lens. But the self-portrait of himself as a ballet dancer is all the more poignant for his very inability to conjure up the beauty and confidence of the male dancers that were his usual subjects. His talent was elsewhere. Balanchine said that Lynes was such a good photographer of the dance because he "loved dancers around his studio and his home. They were not alone his subjects but his intimates—like his beautiful pictures: his early Picasso, the Klees, the magnificent Tchelitchew *Golden Leaf,* and his fine modern American drawings."[15] Balanchine's remark strangely fuses the photographer's dancer friends with works of art. Of course, this is exactly what Lynes accomplishes in his ballet photographs. Longing to be a dancer and loving dancers, he turns them into still pictures. Their dance cannot go on forever, but as photographs they remain eternally seductive and beautiful. Despite Lynes's declared aim, such pictures are no real substitute and consolation for seeing Diana Adams, Lew Christensen, or Maria Tallchief dance—how could they be? They only have the power to suggest what we have missed. There is no looking back.

Listening to Balanchine

THE FOLLOWING COMMENTS by George Balanchine are taken from interviews conducted by Nancy Reynolds in December 1974 and January 1975 as
part of the research for her award-winning book *Repertory in Review*. Although
some of Balanchine's remarks were included in the book, others are published
here for the first time. At the time of the interviews, Balanchine was preparing
the Ravel Festival, presented by the New York City Ballet from May 14 to 31,
1975.

On music:

NR: How do you hear about a lot of the music you use? Some of the scores
you find have never been recorded, so one has to know about them. I
understand how you know about Stravinsky, of course, but how did you
find—say, Louis Moreau Gottschalk (*Tarantella*, 1964) or Charles Ives
(*Ivesiana*, 1954)?

GB: That takes years. About Gottschalk: I remember when I was a young boy
in Russia we had a ballet called *[Die] Puppenfee*. There was a dance of two
dolls in blackface, wearing American trousers and big boots with the toes
cut out. They were doing tap, and the music was Gottschalk. When I came
here, I decided to look for this music, and then I found there is lots more.
First of all, I'm interested in everything that I played four hands with my

EDWARD VILLELLA in *Tarantella. Martha Swope/LIFE Magazine © TIME Inc.*

mother. Then what I played with teachers at school [and] with my friends—two pianos. I went to the library to find what had been written by someone like Mendelssohn. And I took everything.

When I came here, I think it was Morton Gould who told me to listen to Ives.[1] First, I was thinking of having him make an arrangement of Stephen Foster, someone everybody knows. I was friendly with Gould, and sometimes he played things. And there were some friends of Lincoln's who were composers, and they knew about . . . a lot of things that were not published yet.

The modern composers I met. I worked with [Darius] Milhaud and [Georges] Auric. [Erik] Satie was still alive, and I staged his piece (*Jack in the Box*, 1926).[2] I also worked with Ravel. He came to the Opera [at Monte Carlo]—[which] at the time was nothing amazing—and played. I did not understand French, but I understood the music. I staged. . . *L'Enfant et les Sortilèges* in 1925, the first time ever on stage. Then, when I came here, I said, "Lincoln, why don't we stage *L'Enfant et les Sortilèges*?" And he translated it as *The Spellbound Child*. We staged it in [1946]. Now, because it will be [Ravel's] hundredth anniversary, we have decided to do whatever Ravel is possible.[3] But apart from this [one] opera, we don't want any singing. It's not our business to present singing. But anything written to play we would like to do.

As for the rest, you buy music. You go to the library. I knew *all* the Russian music—all the Glinka, all the Tchaikovsky. I knew everything. Except—there was a Russian emigré shop here, and I discovered Tchaikovsky wrote [incidental music] for Ostrovsky's play *The Snow Maiden* (1873). It was a beautiful piece, and I had never seen it before. I loved the score, and I gave it to Stravinsky to play; he also didn't know it. He knew that there was such a thing, but he [had] never s[een] it. So, I gave it to him. Now I can't find it anymore, and he's died. . . .

On *Apollo* (1928):

GB: First of all, it was done like Rousseau, in the style of Douanier Rousseau. [André] Bauchant was a peasant in France somewhere. Diaghilev passed by and saw the farm. Outside were little pieces, little paintings, and Diaghilev liked them. He bought from him. So, that's how we started. It was a *primitive* Apollo. Small Apollo, a boy with long hair. The paintings were like that. All the little mountains and hills were painted primitively. The first curtain was a big vase of flowers—standing. So that's why I made the ballet a little bit like Rousseau. Youknow, the man lying down, or walking with his head tilted slightly, all wooden.

Diaghilev himself [did the first] costumes. He made lousy costumes, and the [girls'] hairpiece was like an egg with no hair; [the head looked] shaved, like an Easter egg. The tutus were all grayish and dirty looking. One girl had it cut long in back and [short] in front. The other one had it cut [short] in back and long in front. And the third one [was] cut [short] in front and back. Idiotic, awful, the idea. And very badly made. [Serge] Lifar's [costume] was red and gold. Gold hair. And then Chanel came and said, "Those [tutus] are awful. Come on, send me the girls." [So] they all three went. . . . And she just took pieces of white cloth, put it this way and that, and [added] three handkerchiefs [neckties]. It was kind of modern, short for the girls. [Chanel's costumes replaced the originals in 1929.]

Later, I didn't want to have scenery because then you have to have Greek costumes. You think Apollo is Greek. [With] a toga and long hair. The scenery is passé, no good any more. It only was good the way it was done at the time of Diaghilev—primitively.

NR: Could you comment on the intent or meaning behind some of the movements—Apollo and Terpsichore touching fingertips; Apollo lenching his fists and splaying his fingers, Apollo and the Muses shuffling forward, Apollo laying his head on the Muses' palms?

SUZANNE FARRELL and
JACQUES D'AMBOISE in
Apollo, 1969. *Martha Swope/
LIFE Magazine © TIME Inc.*

GB: [The fingertip gesture] is stolen from Michelangelo. Why not? It's a pretty picture. [The fists]—that's nothing; it doesn't mean anything. [Shuffling]: I never can say what it is, because I don't know myself. I just did it that way.

I don't put meanings to any of my gestures. In modern dance, every gesture *means*—it has a literary meaning. Also, Balinese dances have a literary meaning—this is a flower, this is love, this is "I." A dance of mine is just a dance. There's no meaning in it except dance. You will never find any literary meaning in my dance.

I'm against words. I don't understand words; [they're] a menace. I can only hear and see music. But I don't understand words at all. [Apollo's head on the palms] doesn't mean anything. Nothing at all. It's sweet music, and he's a young boy—that's all. It's just a gesture. He also walks on his knees. After the first performance there was a big reception, and a Russian critic, a very important critic in 1928, was there. He said, "Young man, tell me, where did you see Apollo walking on his knees?" And I said to him, "Mr. So-and-So, you know what I want to ask you: 'Where did you see Apollo?' " It doesn't mean anything. And Apollo doesn't "walk on his knees"—he's dancing.

On *Prodigal Son* (1929):

GB: Prokofiev came and wrote [the music]. When it was done, he presented it to [Diaghilev]. And Diaghilev asked me to [stage] it. Then [Georges] Rouault came. I [had] never s[een] him before. Strange man. He balanced chairs on his nose . . . during our rehearsals. He was a little bit—not crazy, but kind of a man of God. He couldn't do anything—costumes, scenery—nothing. So Diaghilev locked the door [of his room], took the key, and said to him, "You're not going to get out of here until you do something." He kept him there, supplied with food. And finally Diaghilev opened [the door], and there was a pile of drawings. Little things, like that window, stained—blue little things, red, black. But there were no costumes, nothing. So Diaghilev said, "What's that for?" And Rouault says, "Do what you like with it." So he asked Vera Stravinskaya [Stravinsky] to come—she was very clever—and [Boris] Kochno, and they collected the pieces for the boys.[4] I don't believe [Rouault] ever saw the ballet. As soon as he finished, he left.

I invented the [flower crowns] for the men, also the bald head. They are celebrating, because they stole things. So I decided to make them sinister. I shaved them, and then I put on these things like Christ wore. Flowers. There's no sex in it, you know; they're insects—awful, terrible, disgusting.

EDWARD VILLELLA in the final scene of *Prodigal Son*, 1967. *Martha Swope/LIFE Magazine © TIME Inc.*

VIOLETTE VERDY in costume for *Divertimento No. 15,* 1960. *Martha Swope/LIFE Magazine © TIME Inc.*

Violette Verdy danced with the New York City Ballet from 1958 until 1977. Balanchine created Tschaikovsky Pas de Deux *for her in 1960, as well as roles in* Episodes *(1959),* Liebeslieder Walzer *(1960),* A Midsummer Night's Dream *(1962),* Jewels *(1967),* La Source *(1968), and* Sonatine *(1975), among others. These excerpts are from an interview conducted by Charles France in March 1974 as background for* Repertory in Review.

Technique is not an end for Balanchine. . . . It doesn't satisfy him. He's always calling for the spirit to come through. [He does this] in many ways. . . . It can be an impassioned plea that is extraordinarily touching as a confession of belief, or a sort of humble prayer, or it can be slightly insulting . . . . In spite of everything he says about not distorting the material, what he's looking for is to be surprised, to have the lid taken off. The great mystery of what makes us do what we do—he's after that, always.

Class is often the time when he comes up—seemingly out of nowhere—with the greatest distillations of his experience and philosophy. One: "Just do it. What does it matter if you're going to die the next minute? You want to have done something full out before you die." And: "Look at a flower in the woods. Nobody is going to see that flower; nobody is going to take that flower; nobody is going to do anything about that flower, and yet there it is being a flower, for nobody, for no reason other than being what it is supposed to be." When he talks about those things, there is the whole mystery, right there, you see.

Dancers are afraid to displease him, to invest themselves at their own risk and peril in front of him. I think it's because they have heard, often quite wrongly, that one type pleases him more than another. They do not accept what they are, which is something they cannot change—and which he already knows better than they, as they find out when he choreographs for them. Thus, they do not invest themselves totally in what they are doing and miss the totality of their own effort and achievement. For me the most fantastic thing about working for Balanchine was finally to realize who I was, what I was, how I could please him, also how I displeased him. It took courage, and was not without despair, discouragement, and depression. I didn't leave to seek the non-truth somewhere else; I stayed even if that truth seemed a little hard to bear, because this is the only game that is interesting and this is one of the only companies where dancers have a chance to play it—to find out who and what they are.

On his early years in America, creating for the first Balanchine-Kirstein company, the American Ballet:

NR: You did *Dreams* in Europe (1933) and then in America (1935). Why was the music changed?

GB: Because we couldn't find Milhaud, so [George] Antheil wrote something. Not very good, I wouldn't even mention it. We owned the costumes, we took [them] with us from France, very pretty costumes [by André Derain].[5]

NR: You created *Alma Mater* (1935), but how did you know about American football?

GB: [Edward M. M.] Warburg told me about football.[6] It was Yale [vs.] Princeton; he told me there are cheers, yelling, that they take the poles away and that people wear coats with that fur—raccoon. And Princeton doesn't like Yale, so I made a Yale boy marry a Princeton girl. Kay Swift wrote it like a waltz. She was friends with [George] Gershwin and an excellent songwriter on her own. You can't do that ballet any more. It was only good at the time. Of course [John] Martin probably said it was a disaster.

NR: What kind of composer is [Benjamin] Godard (*Reminiscence*, 1935)?

GB: Oh, Godard was a very well-known composer, French—like Chabrier, like Gounod, that type. Danceable. I knew him because when I was in Russia, studying piano, we all played Godard. In France, nobody played Godard. I found lots of things he wrote; it's cute, very nice, melodic. We had to give [the ballet] a title. No matter what, they demand a title—all the time. I didn't start [with] the idea to do reminiscences of something—not at all. I just took Godard's music and made a ballet—you know, like I usually do—variation, coda, pas de deux, and finale. And so, what to call it? You can't say "Godard." So you say, "It looks like a style of old time on pointes—not modern. Let's call it 'Reminiscence.' "

[The first *Orpheus* (1936)] was very beautiful. Singers were in the pit. Pavlik's [Pavel Tchelitchew] things were beautiful. But it [had] very bad [press]. Can you imagine two hours of singing? The whole thing I did in pantomime. I had a lot of energy. Now I wouldn't *start* [such a thing]. You have to be young. It was classical dancing without pointes. We didn't use the [end], the big ballet. We finished with Death. Eurydice died at the end.

[In 1934] we didn't have any place to dance. We had a school to teach people, [but] the people who came to the school were in and out. There was only one girl, Marie-Jeanne; she came when she was about ten. And

Barbara Weisberger, she came at about nine. [But] they all disappeared because we didn't have anything. We did several performances at a little theater here—the Adelphi. After that, we didn't have anything. Then I went to the Metropolitan, and I brought people with me. We stayed for three years, then [the company] dissolved. We had absolutely nothing. There was nowhere to go. And we didn't have anything to do. [We were] finished. I worked on Broadway making a living.

On Hindemith (*The Four Temperaments*, 1946; *Metamorphoses*, 1952; *Kammermusik No. 2*, 1978):

GB: I worked on Broadway, and I had a little money, about $500. And I said, "What am I going to do? Maybe write music." I wanted to have something for myself at home. I used to have concerts at home every month or two weeks. And I had musicians. And I did unknown music. They would come and play quartets—this and that. And I had lots of food prepared and I invited people, friends, [to these] "musicales." I did [it all] myself, alone. Nobody was around. Nice apartment, two pianos, friends. So I asked Hindemith. At that time he was at Yale. I called him up and asked if he can do something for me. He says, "Oh yes, I just now have some time. A few weeks. What do you want?" I say, "Write something for a piano with a little strings that I can play at home." "Fine." I said, "I have five hundred dollars." And he said, "Fine." Then when he finished, I went to see him. It was in summer. He was sitting in a nice big garden, [with] trees [and] a small table. He had some tea. His wife came in. And he told me it was finished. He himself named the variations. He invented themes, made variations, and called them "the four temperaments." "The four temperaments" is a gothic thing; instead of writing in Italian or German—"allegro," "presto," "schnell" (fast)—he wrote a temperament—not that somebody's good or bad, but a temperament as applied to music.

[For the costumes], Lincoln brought this man [Kurt Seligmann]. He was a Swiss surrealist. He covered everything, so you couldn't see anything. It was lousy, so I decided to throw away the costumes.

Hindemith also offered me another piece. I said, "Thank you," and took it. [It was] the "Metamorphoses" [*Symphonic Metamorphoses on Themes of Carl Maria von Weber*, 1943]. He told me that Miassine [Léonide Massine] had asked him to orchestrate Weber—you know, like Hershy Kay. He was going to ask Hindemith, because Hindemith orchestrated very well. But

Hindemith didn't orchestrate. He made a new composition, like Stravinsky with *Le Baiser de la Fée*. And when he showed it to Miassine, Miassine didn't like it: "No, I don't want your music. I want an orchestration." "Then, you ask in Hollywood someone else. There's lots of people who orchestrate very fast for you." And Miassine did ask someone else. And [Hindemith] said: "Now it's free. Do you want to take it?" And I said, "Yes, I do." There's another piece he gave me that we never did—an excellent piece—because we didn't have enough musicians in the orchestra. We couldn't afford three trombones, two tubas, four horns, things like that. It was called *Tanz Symphonia* [1937]. It's never been done. And nobody will ever do it. I asked [the composer Nicolas] Nabokov at that time to make it for piano, which he did.[7] Remember [John] Colman [composer and accompanist at School of American Ballet]?[8] He was a pupil of Hindemith. I gave him Nabokov's transcription and never received it back. He probably lost it.

On *Firebird* (1949):

GB: "Firebird" is the wrong word. It's not about "fire," but . . . there is no word in English to compare to the Russian word. So, it's all wrong. You can never make it convincing that a dancer, a ballerina, *is* fire—not [Maria] Tallchief [or] [Natalia] Makarova in a red tutu dancing pirouettes. Right from the beginning [the ballet] didn't work. And it never will. The story is too complicated. I have books in Russian [with] about twenty versions or so of "Firebird." It's a Russian legend about a bird, a bird that is made of gold. And when you look at it, [it's] like the sun; you can't look at it because it's so glittery. And the reason the bird becomes gold is because she was eating apples in the territory of a king who had a special apple tree that was pure gold. And she became gold, and you couldn't look at her.

You can't make a ballet out of it. There is nothing but beautiful music. . . . It's much better to listen to the music than to see [the ballet].

What happened is that Ballet Theatre asked Chagall [to design it]. So they presented it once or twice [in 1945, with choreography by Adolph Bolm] and then abandoned it because it was not a success. So [Morton] Baum said to Hurok, "Give it to us. We will pay you what we can."[9] We gave him five thousand—[or was it] three?—for the whole production, which was just the scenery. The costumes were rags, certainly not by Chagall. We used them the way we could, because it's the title again, "Firebird." [The stage] was in complete darkness because the costumes were so bad. So, it became just the pas de deux for Tallchief and [Francisco] Monción. We made just this red costume. Tallchief danced very well. Strong. But the finale had only five people on stage. When we went to Paris [in 1952], Chagall didn't even see the ballet. But his daughter saw it, and she said, "This is awful." And Chagall said, "I don't want you to use my name any more." So, we stopped using his name.

Until, in 1970, because of the big theater here, we decided to make everything new. So I went to Antibes, where Chagall lives, and I asked him to give me everything—there was a pile of things, colored drawings of everything. The insurance cost maybe two hundred thousand dollars, and he sent [everything]. Karinska made the costumes exactly—absolutely—the way he designed them. And we sent him back the things.[10]

But then I decided that "Firebird" meant nothing any more. In the first curtain, there's a woman who hangs upside down. I said, "That probably would be good. That's the way it should be." [The costume was changed from a tutu to an elaborate gown and headdress in June 1972; after several further modifications of the costume, the original red tutu was restored.] Because everything else is monsters. It's a strange world. Most important is the music accompanying Chagall. As for the rest—you're not supposed to do anything. You're supposed to let the costumes flow.

GELSEY KIRKLAND as the *Firebird* in the 1970 revival. *Martha Swope/ LIFE Magazine* © *TIME Inc.*

On *Nutcracker* (1954):

GB: Everybody always asks why do I want to do *Nutcracker*—even in Russia they ask me. It's not that I *want* to. It's my business to make repertoire. My approach to the theater—to ballet—is to entertain the public. I always say it's like a restaurant. You have to cook; you have to please lots of people. One person wants soup, one wants oysters. Before, I couldn't do it, because we didn't have a theater, didn't have musicians, didn't have money. Then, finally, we had a little bigger company. *Nutcracker Suite* in America is a free title, a million-dollar title—free. So Baum asked me to do it. I said, "If I do anything, it will be full-length and very expensive." Most important was the tree.

I knew all about *Nutcracker* because I was in it, and because in Russia Christmas is a German invention. Our Christmas is German. Everything that's on the tree—pfefferkuchen, lebkuchen, everything like that is there. We had German postcards with snow, little deer—very pretty. Also, the little cards you open every day. Things like that. Also, it's religious. Christ is born, so grown-ups never gave each other any presents out of respect for religion. But children are told beautiful stories about it, and they have to have presents. And you dress up. And you eat from the tree. Our tree was full of food—chocolate, oranges, apples. You just pick from the tree and eat. It's a tree of plenty. It represents food, plenty, life. We used to sing German songs all night—like "Tannenbaum." There was no Russian translation.

So Baum gave me $40,000. We studied how the tree could grow both up and also out, like an umbrella. The tree cost $25,000, and as soon as he had to sign the check, Baum was angry. He told Betty [Cage, the company's general manager], "Stop that fool. George, can't you just do it without the tree?" I said, "[The ballet] *is* the tree." It cost $80,000 instead of $40,000. We

BALANCHINE conducting a *Nutcracker* rehearsal with the drop of Act II in the background. Photo by Costas.

A young EDWARD VILLELLA in the Hoop Dance. *New York World-Telegram and Sun Collection, Prints and Photographs Division, Library of Congress.*

had lots of beautiful costumes. I used all the music, and I used the story by Hoffmann—not the whole thing, but the prologue of the Hoffmann story.

I named Dewdrop myself. [In Russia] we had a waltz called the "Golden Waltz"—lots of girls dressed in gold tutus. It's written in the score "Waltz of the Flowers"—"Valse des Fleurs"—but it was renamed by Ivanov, I think, when they staged [*Nutcracker*], because we already had *[Le] Corsaire*, a ballet with a flower waltz in a big garden, so they probably didn't want to repeat the same thing. [My] Hoop Dance is [the] original—absolutely authentic. In the Imperial Kappelle the boys who sang in the choir were also the mice.

Drosselmeyer is not evil. When you read the book, you'll find out who Drosselmeyer is. [He's] Coppélius. A strange man who makes toys. They call him "uncle" because he brings toys every Christmas, and they always expect these mechanical things. And he invented the nutcracker. He gave it to [the little girl]. Then, when it got sick, she had the dream. Actually, it's not a dream—it's the reality Mother didn't believe. The story was written by Hoffmann against society. He said that society, the grown-ups, really have no imagination, and they try to suppress the imagination of children. In Germany they were very strict—no nonsense. They didn't understand that nonreality is the real thing. Goethe was against Hoffmann; that's why [the story] was never published in Germany. It was published in Russia and in France, but in Germany it was banned.

On *Agon* (1957):

GB: I said to Stravinsky, "I would like to have something." And he said, "All right; I have time." And because his music is so . . . *hard* on the ear, he doesn't like to write very long, and it's not too good to write *too* long. That kind of impact—they [the audience] wouldn't even follow. So, I said "about twenty minutes—maximum twenty-two." And we talked. All the introductions to everything are the same music. Because it's difficult to get the first time. So, we repeat it, because you have to hear it several times. Then we decided that the variations would be not more than a minute. The girl's variation was a minute and twenty-five [seconds]—something like that.

Not everything is atonal, or serial—not the whole of *Agon*. Serial music—it's a series that you pick. It's twelve-tone instead of harmonic—a Schoenberg invention. Stravinsky would never say "Symphony in B-flat *minor*." He was always against saying things like that, because with tonality you have to stay. Atonal means that there is no tonality; there is no B-flat. Each note becomes a note in itself; it is not a half-tone or a tone. (It's rather complicated.) But Stravinsky liked this, because even [early on], he said there is no tonality (he never said "atonal"). Or sometimes, certain early things, he called "Symphony in C"—not C-minor or C-major, but C. Later on he abandoned [serialism] completely, like everybody else.

You can always [tell] Stravinsky. With almost all [serial] composers except Webern and Schoenberg, you never know who wrote the music. It's a mechanically made-up thing. You couldn't say "Concerto for Strings by Mr. Johnson," because it could have been made up by somebody else: you'd never know. It's the same thing with electronic music. You don't know who wrote it. But Stravinsky, no matter what, you always know Stravinsky. He cannot escape.

NR: Diana Adams [the ballerina in the original pas de deux] said she felt you wanted to do the pas de deux first. I wondered if you thought this would give you the key to the rest.

GB: I don't know. I cannot tell you. I decided probably I would like to see the pas de deux first. I do things like that. I do the finale first. Then I know where I'm going, where's the end. You have to know where you're going. If you start on the road, and you don't know where you're going, you never arrive anywhere. So I usually like to finish first, and then I know where my possibilities will be.

NR: How do you feel about *Agon* now? Is it more or less the way it was originally?

GB: I don't know. I'm not going to analyze any more of it.

On *Coppélia* (1974):

NR: Why did you wait so long to do *Coppélia*?[11]

GB: Why should I do, even? I'm not interested in *Coppélia*. So I didn't do it. I was doing something else that was much, much more important, because it was not Ballet Russe. I didn't do *The Sleeping Beauty*. I didn't do a full-length *Swan Lake*. I didn't do *Giselle*. *Nutcracker*—it was beautiful music and a title, so it brings people. *Coppélia* is like *Giselle*. Why don't I do *Giselle*? Why don't I do *Swan Lake* full-length? Because they're impossible, absolutely impossible. It's difficult to explain. Even Robert [Irving, music director] told me, after *Coppélia* was done, "Ahh—next, *Sleeping Beauty*."

Coppélia was done by Ballet Russe all the time. *Schéhérazade*, one act of *Nutcracker*, one act of *Sleeping Beauty*. Fifteen minutes each. It's only *now* you could do [the complete version]. I think it's because of all this Baryshnikov and Makarova stuff that *Coppélia* became more known. You see, the ballet's not written for male dancers. There are no variations, no pas de deux.[12] You have to put things together. In the last act, nobody did it that way. You have to think, "should we do it, or shouldn't we do it?" We did it, finally, because of Saratoga. It's special for them. And [it's also special] for children.

A Portfolio of Photographs of Jerome Robbins

With THE ORIGINAL CAST of *Fancy Free*, 1944.
Photo by George Hurrell.
Dance Collection, The New York Public Library for the Performing
Arts, Astor, Lenox, and Tilden Foundations.

With MARIA TALLCHIEF in *Prodigal Son*, 1950. Photo by
George Platt Lynes. *Dance Collection, The New York Public
Library for the Performing Arts, Astor, Lenox, and Tilden
Foundations.*

With MARIA TALLCHIEF and NICHOLAS MAGALLANES
in *The Guests*, 1949. Photo by George Platt Lynes. *Dance
Collection, The New York Public Library for the Performing Arts,
Astor, Lenox, and Tilden Foundations.*

Rehearsing *Prodigal Son* with MARIA TALLCHIEF under
Balanchine's direction at the School of American Ballet,
1950. Photo by Walter E. Owen. *Dance Collection, The New
York Public Library for the Performing Arts, Astor, Lenox, and
Tilden Foundations.*

Facing page: In the title role of *Prodigal Son*, 1950. Photo by
George Platt Lynes. *Dance Collection, The New York Public
Library for the Performing Arts, Astor, Lenox, and Tilden
Foundations.*

With MARIA TALLCHIEF in *Jones Beach*, 1950. Photo
by George Platt Lynes. *Dance Collection, The New York
Public Library for the Performing Arts, Astor, Lenox, and
Tilden Foundations.*

Facing page: In *The Age of Anxiety*, 1950. Photo by Gerda
Peterich. *Dance Collection, The New York Public Library for the
Performing Arts, Astor, Lenox, and Tilden Foundations.*

BACKSTAGE AT COVENT GARDEN, 1952. Photo by
Roger Wood. *Dance Collection, The New York Public Library
for the Performing Arts, Astor, Lenox, and Tilden Foundations.*

With TANAQUIL LECLERCQ in *Bourrée Fantasque*, 1949.
Photo by George Platt Lynes.
The Metropolitan Museum of Art, Gift of Lincoln Kirstein, 1986.

In *The Age of Anxiety*, 1950. Photo by Melton–Pippin. *Dance
Collection, The New York Public Library for the Performing Arts,
Astor, Lenox, and Tilden Foundations.*

Facing page: With ROBERT FIZDALE at Sneedans Landing.
Photo by Tanaquil LeClercq. *Courtesy Tanaquil LeClercq.*

Rehearsing *West Side Story*, 1957. *Martha Swope/LIFE
Magazine* © *TIME Inc.*

Rehearsing *Dances at a Gathering* with ALLEGRA KENT and
CAROL SUMNER, 1969. *Martha Swope/LIFE Magazine* ©
TIME Inc.

With Bolshoi Ballet artistic director YURY
GRIGOROVICH, at a reception for the New York City
Ballet, Moscow, 1972. *Special Collections Division, University
of Arkansas Libraries, Fayetteville.*

With BALANCHINE rehearsing *Pulcinella* for the
Stravinsky Festival, 1972. *Martha Swope/LIFE Magazine*
© *TIME Inc.*

Above: Partnering MERRILL ASHLEY in *Firebird* as JOSEPH
DUELL and the ensemble look on, 1985. *Martha Swope/
LIFE Magazine © TIME Inc.*

Facing page: With PATRICIA McBRIDE in the studio. *Dance
Collection, The New York Public Library for the Performing Arts,
Astor, Lenox, and Tilden Foundations.*

Page 188: As the Ringmaster in *Circus Polka,* 1972. *Dance
Collection, The New York Public Library for the Performing Arts,
Astor, Lenox, and Tilden Foundations.*

Works Choreographed and Staged by Jerome Robbins

If no company name is given, the work was produced by the New York City Ballet. Cities are given only when premieres took place outside New York City.

BALLETS

FANCY FREE[1]

Music: Leonard Bernstein
Scenery: Oliver Smith
Costumes: Kermit Love
Premiere: April 18, 1944, Metropolitan Opera House (Ballet Theatre)
Dancers: Jerome Robbins, Harold Lang, John Kriza (Sailors); Muriel Bentley, Janet Reed, Shirley Eckl (Passersby); Rex Cooper (Bartender)
Note: This entered the New York City Ballet repertory on January 31, 1980.

INTERPLAY

Ballet in Four Movements.
Music: Morton Gould (*American Concertette*)
Scenery: Oliver Smith
Costumes: Irene Sharaff
Premiere: October 17, 1945, Metropolitan Opera House (Ballet Theatre)
Principal dancers: Janet Reed, John Kriza, Harold Lang
Note: An earlier version, minus the pas de deux, premiered on June 1, 1945 at the Ziegfeld Theatre, New York, as part of Billy Rose's *Concert Varieties*. The work entered the New York City Ballet repertory on December 23, 1952.

FACSIMILE

Music: Leonard Bernstein
Scenery: Oliver Smith
Costumes: Irene Sharaff
Premiere: October 24, 1946, Broadway Theatre (Ballet Theatre)
Dancers: Nora Kaye (A Woman), Jerome Robbins (A Man), John Kriza (Another Man)

PAS DE TROIS

Music: Hector Berlioz (from *The Damnation of Faust*)

Costumes: John Pratt

Premiere: March 26, 1947, Metropolitan Opera House (Original Ballet Russe)

Dancers: Anton Dolin, André Eglevsky, Rosella Hightower

SUMMER DAY

Music: Sergei Prokofiev (*Music for Children*)

Premiere: May 12, 1947, City Center of Music and Drama (American–Soviet Musical Society)

Dancers: Annabelle Lyon, Jerome Robbins

THE GUESTS

Music: Marc Blitzstein

Premiere: January 20, 1949, City Center of Music and Drama

Principal dancers: Maria Tallchief, Nicholas Magallanes, Francisco Monción

AGE OF ANXIETY

Music: Leonard Bernstein (Symphony No. 2 for Piano and Orchestra, "Age of Anxiety")

Scenery: Oliver Smith

Costumes: Irene Sharaff

Premiere: February 26, 1950, City Center of Music and Drama

Principal dancers: Tanaquil LeClercq, Todd Bolender, Francisco Monción, Jerome Robbins

JONES BEACH

(with George Balanchine)

Music: Jurriaan Andriessen (Berkshire Symphonies)

Costumes: Jantzen

Premiere: March 9, 1950, City Center of Music and Drama

Principal dancers: Melissa Hayden, Yvonne Mounsey, Beatrice Tompkins, Herbert Bliss, Frank Hobi, Tanaquil LeClercq, Nicholas Magallanes, William Dollar, Maria Tallchief, Jerome Robbins

THE CAGE

Music: Igor Stravinsky (String Concerto in D)

Costumes: Ruth Sobotka

Premiere: June 14, 1951, City Center of Music and Drama

Dancers: Nora Kaye (The Novice); Yvonne Mounsey (The Queen); Nicholas Magallanes, Michael Maule (The Intruders)

THE PIED PIPER

Music: Aaron Copland (Concerto for Clarinet and String Orchestra, with Harp and Piano)

Premiere: December 4, 1951, City Center of Music and Drama

Principal dancers: Diana Adams, Nicholas Magallanes, Jillana, Roy Tobias, Janet Reed, Todd Bolender, Melissa Hayden, Herbert Bliss, Tanaquil LeClercq, Jerome Robbins

BALLADE

Music: Claude Debussy (*Six Epigraphes Antiques*, *Syrinx*)

Scenery and costumes: Boris Aronson

Premiere: February 14, 1952, City Center of Music and Drama

Dancers: Nora Kaye, Tanquil LeClercq, Janet Reed, Robert Barnett, Brooks Jackson, Louis Johnson (guest), John Mandia

AFTERNOON OF A FAUN

Music: Claude Debussy
(*Prélude à l'Après-midi d'un Faune*)

Scenery: Jean Rosenthal

Costumes: Irene Sharaff

Premiere: May 14, 1953, City Center of
Music and Drama

Dancers: Tanaquil LeClercq, Francisco
Monción

FANFARE

Music: Benjamin Britten (*The Young
Person's Guide to the Orchestra*)

Scenery and costumes: Irene Sharaff

Premiere: June 2, 1953, City Center of
Music and Drama

Principal dancers: Yvonne Mounsey
(Harp); Todd Bolender (Percussion);
Jillana (Oboe); Carolyn George, Roy
Tobias (Clarinets); Irene Larsson,
Jacques d'Amboise (Violas); Brooks
Jackson (Double Bass), Frank Hobi,
Michael Maule (Trumpets); Edward
Bigelow (Tuba)[2]

QUARTET

Music: Sergei Prokofiev (String Quartet
No. 2)

Scenery: Jean Rosenthal

Costumes: Barbara Karinska

Premiere: February 18, 1954, City
Center of Music and Drama

Principal dancers: Patricia Wilde,
Herbert Bliss (First Movement);
Jillana, Jacques d'Amboise (Second
Movement); Yvonne Mounsey, Todd
Bolender (Third Movement)

THE CONCERT (OR THE
PERILS OF EVERYBODY)

A Charade in One Act.
Music: Frédéric Chopin

Scenery: Jean Rosenthal

Costumes: Irene Sharaff

Premiere: March 6, 1956, City Center of
Music and Drama

Principal dancers: Tanaquil LeClercq,
Todd Bolender, Yvonne Mounsey,
Robert Barnett, Wilma Curley, John
Mandia, Shaun O'Brien, Patricia
Savoia, Richard Thomas

Note: The 1971 revival had new scenery
by Saul Steinberg.

NEW YORK EXPORT:
OPUS JAZZ

Music: Robert Prince (*Jazz Concert*)

Scenery: Ben Shahn

Costumes: Ben Shahn and Florence
Klotz

Premiere: June 8, 1958, Festival of Two
Worlds, Spoleto (Jerome Robbins'
Ballets: U.S.A.)

Dancers: Patricia Dunn, Jay Norman,
Tom Abbott, Bob Bakanic, John
Mandia, James White, Wilma Curley,
John Jones, Sondra Lee, Gwen Lewis,
Erin Martin, Barbara Milberg, Beryl
Towbin, Joan Van Orden, James
Moore

Note: The first U.S. performance took
place at the Alvin Theatre, New York
City, on September 4, 1958.

3 X 3

Music: Georges Auric (*Wind Trio*)

Scenery: Jean Rosenthal

Costumes: Irene Sharaff

Premiere: September 4, 1958, Alvin
Theatre (Jerome Robbins'
Ballets: U.S.A.)

Dancers: Joan Van Orden, Tom Abbott,
Erin Martin, Gene Gavin, Beryl
Towbin, James Moore

Musicans: William Criss (oboe), Loren
   Glickman (bassoon), Emery
   Davis (clarinet)

MOVES

Music: danced in silence
Premiere: July 3, 1959, Teatro Nuovo,
   Spoleto (Jerome Robbins' Ballets:
   U.S.A.)
Dancers: Erin Martin, Michael Maule,
   Lawrence Gradus, John Jones, James
   Moore, Bill Reilly, Doug Spingler,
   Jamie Bauer, Gwen Lewis,
   Jane Mason, Barbara Milberg,
   Christine Mayer
Note: The first U.S. performance took
   place at the ANTA Theatre, New
   York City, on October 8, 1961. The
   ballet entered the New York City
   Ballet repertory on May 2, 1984.

EVENTS

Music: Robert Prince
Scenery: Ben Shahn
Costumes: Ray Diffen
Premiere: July 12, 1961, Teatro Nuovo,
   Spoleto (Jerome Robbins' Ballets:
   U.S.A.)
Dancers: John Jones, Howard Jeffrey,
   Christine Mayer, Bill Reilly, Jamie
   Bauer, Muriel Bentley, Geryl Donald,
   Fern MacLarnon, Kay Mazzo,
   Charlene Mehl, Helene Petroff,
   Francia Russell, Lawrence Gradus,
   Doug Spingler, Robert Thompson
Note: The first U.S. performance took
   place at the ANTA Theatre, New
   York City, on October 17, 1961.

LES NOCES

Music: Igor Stravinsky
Scenery: Oliver Smith

Costumes: Patricia Zepprodt
Premiere: March 30, 1965, New York
   State Theater (Ballet Theatre)
Principal dancers: Erin Martin (Bride);
   Veronika Mlakar, Joseph Carow (Her
   Parents); William Glassman (Groom);
   Sallie Wilson, Bruce Marks (His
   Parents); Rosanna Seravalli, Ted Kivitt
   (Matchmakers)
Note: This entered the New York City
   Ballet repertory on May 20, 1998.

DANCES AT A GATHERING

Music: Frédéric Chopin
Costumes: Joe Eula
Premiere: May 22, 1969, New York State
   Theater (gala benefit preview May 8,
   1969)
Dancers: Allegra Kent, Sara Leland, Kay
   Mazzo, Patricia McBride, Violette
   Verdy, Anthony Blum, John Clifford,
   Robert Maiorano, John Prinz,
   Edward Villella

IN THE NIGHT

Music: Frédéric Chopin
Costumes: Joe Eula
Premiere: January 29, 1970, New York
   State Theater
Dancers: Kay Mazzo, Anthony Blum,
   Violette Verdy, Peter Martins, Patricia
   McBride, Francisco Monción
Pianist: Gordon Boelzner

FIREBIRD

(with George Balanchine)

Music: Igor Stravinsky
Scenery and costumes: Marc Chagall
Premiere: May 28, 1970, New York
   State Theater
Principal dancers: Gelsey Kirkland (The
   Firebird), Jacques d'Amboise (Prince

Ivan), Gloria Govrin (The Prince's
Bride), Paul Sackett (Kastchei)

THE GOLDBERG VARIATIONS

Music: Johann Sebastian Bach (Aria
with Variations in G, "The Goldberg
Variations")
Costumes: Joe Eula
Premiere: May 27, 1971, New York State
Theater (open working rehearsal July
4, 1970, Performing Arts Center,
Saratoga Springs, New York)
Principal dancers: Renee Estopinal,
Michael Steele (Theme); Gelsey
Kirkland, Sara Leland, John Clifford,
Robert Maiorano, Robert Weiss,
Bruce Wells (Variations, Part I); Karin
von Aroldingen, Peter Martins, Susan
Hendl, Anthony Blum, Patricia
McBride, Helgi Tomasson (Variations,
Part II)

WATERMILL

Music: Teiji Ito
Scenery: Jerome Robbins with David
Reppa
Costumes: Patricia Zipprodt
Premiere: February 3, 1972, New York
State Theater
Principal dancers: Edward Villella, Penny
Dudleston, Colleen Neary, Tracy
Bennett, Victor Castelli, Hermes
Condé, Bart Cook, Jean-Pierre
Frohlich, Deni Lamont, Robert
Maiorano
Musicians: Dan Erkkila, Genji Ito, Teiji
Ito, Kensuke Kawase, Mara Purl,
Terry White

SCHERZO FANTASTIQUE

Music: Igor Stravinsky (op. 3)
Premiere: June 18, 1972, New York State

Theater (Stravinsky Festival)
Dancers: Gelsey Kirkland, Bart Cook,
Stephen Caras, Victor Castelli,
Bryan Pitts

CIRCUS POLKA

Music: Igor Stravinsky
Premiere: June 21, 1972, New York State
Theater (Stravinsky Festival)
Dancers: Jerome Robbins (Ringmaster),
with forty-eight students of the
School of American Ballet

DUMBARTON OAKS

Music: Igor Stravinsky (Concerto in E-
Flat for Chamber Orchestra)
Costumes: Patricia Zipprodt
Premiere: June 23, 1972, New York State
Theater (Stravinsky Festival)
Principal dancers: Allegra Kent,
Anthony Blum

PULCINELLA

(with George Balanchine)

Music: Igor Stravinsky
Scenery and costumes: Eugene Berman
Premiere: June 23, 1972, New York State
Theater (Stravinsky Festival)
Principal dancers: Edward Villella
(Pulcinella); Violette Verdy (Girl);
Michael Arshansky (Pulcinella's
Father); Francisco Monción, Shaun
O'Brien (Devil); George Balanchine,
Jerome Robbins (Beggars)

REQUIEM CANTICLES (II)

Music: Igor Stravinsky
Premiere: June 25, 1972, New York State
Theater (Stravinsky Festival)
Principal dancers: Merrill Ashley, Susan
Hendl, Robert Maiorano,
Bruce Wells

AN EVENING'S WALTZES

Music: Sergei Prokofiev (*Suite of Waltzes*, op. 110)
Scenery and costumes: Rouben Ter-Arutunian
Premiere: May 24, 1973, New York State Theater
Principal dancers: Patricia McBride, Jean-Pierre Bonnefoux, Christine Redpath, John Clifford, Sara Leland, Bart Cook

CELEBRATION: THE ART OF THE PAS DE DEUX (with Victor Gsovsky, Frederick Ashton, Frederick Ashton after Marius Petipa, Enrique Martinez, Erik Bruhn after August Bournonville, Galina Ulanova after Marius Petipa, Alexander Gorsky, and George Balanchine)

Scenery: Rouben Ter-Arutunian
Premiere: June 29, 1973, Teatro Nuovo, Spoleto
Principal dancers: Patricia McBride and Helgi Tomasson; Malika Sabirova and Muzofar Bourkhanov; Antoinette Sibley and Anthony Dowell; Violette Verdy and Jean-Pierre Bonnefoux; Carla Fracci and Paolo Bortoluzzi
Note: Robbins arranged this program, which consists of ten pas de deux (including his *Four Bagatelles* [see below] and *Afternoon of a Faun* [see above]) framed by a specially choreographed prologue (*Entrata* and *Valzer*) and epilogue (*Finale*).

FOUR BAGATELLES

Music: Ludwig van Beethoven
Costumes: Florence Klotz
Premiere: January 10, 1974, New York

State Theater (gala benefit preview as *A Beethoven Pas de Deux*, May 16, 1973, with Violette Verdy, Jean-Pierre Bonnefoux)
Dancers: Gelsey Kirkland, Jean-Pierre Bonnefoux

DYBBUK (*later called* The Dybbuk Variations)

Music: Leonard Bernstein (The Dybbuk Variations)
Scenery: Rouben Ter-Arutunian
Costumes: Patricia Zipprodt
Premiere: May 16, 1974, New York State Theater (gala benefit preview, May 15, 1974)
Principal dancers: Patricia McBride (The Young Woman [Leah]), Helgi Tomasson (The Young Man [Chanon]), Bart Cook, Victor Castelli, Tracy Bennett, Hermes Condé

CONCERTO IN G (*later called* In G Major)

Music: Maurice Ravel (Piano Concerto in G Major)
Scenery and costumes: Rouben Ter-Arutunian
Premiere: May 15, 1975, New York State Theater (Ravel Festival); (gala benefit preview, May 14, 1975)
Principal dancers: Suzanne Farrell, Peter Martins
Pianist: Gordon Boelzner

INTRODUCTION AND ALLEGRO FOR HARP

Music: Maurice Ravel (*Introduction and Allegro* for harp, string quartet, flute, clarinet)
Costumes: Arnold Scaasi
Premiere: May 22, 1975, New York State

Theater (Ravel Festival)
Principal dancers: Patricia McBride,
Helgi Tomasson

MA MÈRE L'OYE

Fairy Tales for Dancers.
Music: Maurice Ravel
Costumes: Stanley Simmons
Premiere: May 22, 1975, New York State
Theater (Ravel Festival)
Principal dancers: Muriel Aasen (Story
Teller, Princess Florine), Delia Peters
(Good Fairy), Tracy Bennett (Bad
Fairy), Deborah Koolish (Beauty),
Richard Hoskinson (Beast), Matthew
Giordano (Hop o' My Thumb),
Colleen Neary (Laideronette), Jay
Jolley (Green Serpent), Daniel Duell
(Prince Charming)

UNE BARQUE SUR L'OCÉAN

Music: Maurice Ravel
Costumes: Parmelee Welles
Premiere: May 29, 1975, New York State
Theater (Ravel Festival)
Dancers: Victor Castelli, Daniel Duell,
Laurence Matthews, Jay Jolley,
Nolan T'Sani

CHANSONS MADÉCASSES

Songs of the Madegasque (Madagascar).
Music: Maurice Ravel
Premiere: May 29, 1975, New York State
Theater (Ravel Festival)
Dancers: Patricia McBride, Helgi
Tomasson, Debra Austin,
Hermes Condé

OTHER DANCES

Music: Frédéric Chopin
Costumes: Santo Loquasto
Premiere: May 9, 1976, Metropolitan
Opera House (Gala Evening for the
Library of Performing Arts at
Lincoln Center)
Dancers: Natalia Makarova, Mikhail
Baryshnikov
Note: This entered the New York City
Ballet repertory on November
26, 1976.

TRICOLORE

(with Peter Martins and Jean-Pierre
Bonnefoux)
Music: Georges Auric
Scenery and costumes: Rouben Ter-
Arutunian
Premiere: May 18, 1978, New York State
Theater (gala benefit preview, May
17, 1978)
Principal dancers: Renee Estopinal, Jay
Jolley, Kyra Nichols, Joseph Duell (La
Garde); Karin von Aroldingen
(Majorettes); Nina Fedorova
("Mademoiselle Marianne" in
Apotheosis)
Note: Robbins choreographed the third
section, "Marche de la Garde
Républicaine."

FENCING DANCES
AND EXERCISES

Music: George Frederic Handel,
Heinrich von Biber
Premiere: June 8, 1978, New York State
Theater
Dancers: Joseph Duell, Daniel Duell,
Laurence Matthews, Peter Naumann,
Peter Frame, Jean-Pierre Frohlich,
Bryan Pitts, Kipling Houston, Bruce
Padgett, Timothy Fox, Paul Boos,
Francis Sackett, Paul Sackett,
Hermes Condé, Gerard Ebitz,
Ulrik Trojaborg, Robert Maiorano

Note: This was the first part of a projected ballet, *The Arts of the Gentleman*. It was presented along with *Solo* and *Verdi Variations* (see below) and a pas de deux by Peter Martins in *A Sketch Book: Works in Progress*.

SOLO

Music: Georg Philipp Telemann (*Fantasy for Unaccompanied Violin*)
Dancer: Daniel Duell
Violinist: Lamar Alsop

VERDI VARIATIONS

Music: Giuseppe Verdi
Principal dancers: Kyra Nichols, Peter Martins

FOUR SEASONS

Music: Giuseppe Verdi (ballet music from *I Vespri Siciliani*, *I Lombardi*, and *Il Trovatore*)
Scenery and costumes: Santo Loquasto
Premiere: January 18, 1979, New York State Theater
Principal dancers: Joseph Duell, Heather Watts, Peter Frame (Winter); Kyra Nichols, Daniel Duell (Spring); Stephanie Saland, Bart Cook (Summer); Patricia McBride, Mikhail Baryshnikov, Jean-Pierre Frohlich (Fall)
Note: The pas de deux from "Spring" was performed as part of *Verdi Variations* (see above).

THREE CHOPIN DANCES

Music: Frédéric Chopin
Costumes: Santo Loquasto
Premiere: February 25, 1979, White House, Washington, D.C.
Dancers: Mikhail Baryshnikov, Patricia McBride
Note: The opening pas de deux was from *Other Dances*, and the solo that followed was from *Dances at a Gathering*. The third dance (solo and pas de deux) was new.

LE BOURGEOIS GENTILHOMME

(with George Balanchine)

Music: Richard Strauss
Scenery and costumes: Rouben Ter-Arutunian
Premiere: April 8, 1979, New York State Theater (New York City Opera)
Principal dancers: Patricia McBride, Jean-Pierre Bonnefoux, Rudolf Nureyev

OPUS 19/THE DREAMER

Music: Sergei Prokofiev (Violin Concerto No. 1 in D)
Costumes: Ben Benson
Premiere: June 14, 1979, New York State Theater
Principal dancers: Patricia McBride, Mikhail Baryshnikov

SUITE OF DANCES

Music: Leonard Bernstein
Costumes: Ben Benson
Premiere: January 17, 1980, New York State Theater
Principal dancers: Helgi Tomasson, Tracy Bennett, Victor Castelli, Hermes Condé, Joseph Duell, Peter Frame, Richard Hoskinson, Kipling Houston, Laurence Matthews, Peter Naumann
Note: This consisted of the men's dances from *The Dybbuk Variations*.

RONDO

Music: Wolfang Amadeus Mozart
(Rondo in A Minor for Piano)
Premiere: November 11, 1980, New
York State Theater
Dancers: Kyra Nichols, Stephanie Saland
Pianist: Gordon Boelzner

PAS DE DEUX (later called
Andantino)

Music: Peter Ilyich Tchaikovsky (from
Piano Concerto No. 1)
Costumes: Ben Benson
Premiere: June 4, 1981, New York City
Ballet (Tchaikovsky Festival)
Dancers: Darci Kistler, Ib Andersen
Pianist: Jerry Zimmerman

VALSE À CINQ TEMPS

(from Tempo di Valse)

Music: Peter Ilyich Tchaikovsky
Premiere: June 9, 1981, New York State
Theater (Tchaikovsky Festival)
Dancers: Christopher d'Amboise, Jean-
Pierre Frohlich
Pianist: Jerry Zimmerman
Note: This was the fourth section of a
work that also included Balanchine's
Garland Dance from *The Sleeping
Beauty* and the Waltz of the Flowers
from *The Nutcracker*.

PIANO PIECES

Music: Peter Ilyich Tchaikovsky (from
Opus 1, 9, 51, 72, *The Seasons*, and
Children's Album)
Costumes: Ben Benson
Premiere: June 12, 1981, New York State
Theater (Tchaikovsky Festival)
Principal dancers: Ib Andersen, Kyra
Nichols, Daniel Duell, Maria

Calegari, Joseph Duell, Bart Cook,
Heather Watts
Pianist: Jerry Zimmerman

ALLEGRO CON GRACIA

(from Symphony No. 6—Pathétique)

Music: Peter Ilyich Tchaikovsky
(Symphony No. 6 in B minor [second
movement])
Costumes: Ben Benson
Premiere: June 14, 1981, New York State
Theater (Tchaikovsky Festival)
Principal dancers: Patricia McBride,
Helgi Tomasson
Note: The fourth movement, *Adagio
Lamentoso*, was choreographed by
Balanchine.

GERSHWIN CONCERTO

Music: George Gershwin (Piano
Concerto in F)
Scenery and costumes: Santo Loquasto
Premiere: February 4, 1982, New York
State Theater
Principal dancers: Maria Calegari,
Christopher d'Amboise, Darci Kistler,
Mel Tomlinson

FOUR CHAMBER WORKS

Music: Igor Stravinsky (*Septet, Ragtime,
Concertino, Three Pieces for Clarinet
Solo, Octet*)
Scenery and costumes: Lawrence Miller
Premiere: June 16, 1982, New York State
Theater (Stravinsky Centennial
Celebration)
Dancers: Maria Calegari, Lourdes
Lopez, Joseph Duell, Peter Frame,
Kipling Houston (*Septet*); Heather
Watts, Bart Cook, Heléne
Alexopoulos, Renee Estopinal, Susan

Freedman, Lisa Jackson (*Ragtime*); Merrill Ashley, Sean Lavery, Mel Tomlinson (*Concertino* and *Three Pieces for Clarinet Solo*); Christopher d'Amboise, Jean-Pierre Frohlich, Christopher Fleming, Douglas Hay (*Octet*)

GLASS PIECES

Music: Philip Glass (*Rubric*, *Façades*, excerpt from *Akhnaten*)
Scenery: Ronald Bates
Costumes: Ben Benson
Premiere: May 12, 1983, New York State Theater
Principal dancers: Heléne Alexopoulos, Peter Frame, Lourdes Lopez, Joseph Duell, Lisa Hess, Victor Castelli, Maria Calegari, Bart Cook

I'M OLD FASHIONED (THE ASTAIRE VARIATIONS)

Music: Morton Gould, based on a theme by Jerome Kern
Scenery: film sequences from *You Were Never Lovelier*, starring Fred Astaire and Rita Hayworth
Costumes: Florence Klotz
Premiere: June 16, 1983, New York State Theater
Principal dancers: Kyra Nichols, Sean Lavery, Heather Watts, Bart Cook, Judith Fugate, Joseph Duell

ANTIQUE EPIGRAPHS

Music: Claude Debussy (*Six Epigraphes Antiques*, *Syrinx*)
Costumes: Florence Klotz
Premiere: February 2, 1984, New York State Theater
Dancers: Kyra Nichols, Stephanie

Saland, Maria Calegari, Simone Schumacher, Heléne Alexopoulos, Jerri Kumery, Victoria Hall, Florence Fitzgerald

BRAHMS/HANDEL

(with Twyla Tharp)
Music: Johannes Brahms (Variations and Fugue on a Theme by Handel)
Costumes: Oscar de la Renta
Premiere: June 7, 1984, New York State Theater
Principal dancers: Merrill Ashley, Ib Andersen, Maria Calegari, Bart Cook

EIGHT LINES

Music: Steve Reich (*Octet*)
Costumes: Florence Klotz
Premiere: February 14, 1985, New York State Theater
Principal dancers: Maria Calegari, Ib Andersen, Kyra Nichols, Sean Lavery

IN MEMORY OF . . .

Music: Alban Berg (Violin Concerto)
Scenery: David Mitchell
Costumes: Dain Marcus
Premiere: June 13, 1985, New York State Theater (gala preview, June 6, 1985)
Principal dancers: Suzanne Farrell, Joseph Duell, Adam Lüders
Solo violin: Cyrus Stevens

QUIET CITY

Music: Aaron Copland (incidental music for Irwin Shaw's play, *The Quiet City*)
Costumes: Barbara Matera
Premiere: May 8, 1986, New York State Theater
Principal dancers: Robert LaFosse, Peter Boal, Damian Woetzel

PICCOLO BALLETTO

Music: Igor Stravinsky (*Dumbarton Oaks Concerto*)
Scenery and costumes: Santo Loquasto
Premiere: June 5, 1986, New York State Theater
Principal dancers: Darci Kistler, Robert LaFosse

IVES, SONGS

Music: Charles Ives
Scenery: David Mitchell
Costumes: Florence Klotz
Premiere: February 4, 1988, New York State Theater
Principal dancers: Heléne Alexopoulos, Stephanie Saland, Alexandre Proia, Jeppe Mydtskov, Laurence Matthews, Stacy Caddell, Katrina Killian, Margaret Tracey, Lauren Hauser, Melinda Roy, Lisa Jackson, Michael Byars, Tom Gold, Robert Lyon, Damian Woetzel, Philip Neal, Jeffrey Edwards, Florence Fitzgerald, Otto Neubert
Singer: Timothy Nolan
Pianist: Gordon Boelzer

A SUITE OF DANCES

Music: Johann Sebastian Bach (Suite for Solo Cello)
Premiere: March 3, 1994, New York State Theater (White Oak Dance Project)
Costumes: Santo Loquasto
Dancer: Mikhail Baryshnikov
Cellist: Wendy Sutter
Note: This entered the New York City Ballet repertory on May 10, 1994.

2 & 3 PART INVENTIONS

Music: Johann Sebastian Bach
Premiere: June 4, 1994, Juilliard Theater (School of American Ballet)
Dancers: Kristina Fernandez, Benjamin Millepied, Eliane Munier, Amaury Lebrun, Riolama Lorenzo, Alex Ketley, Jennifer Chipman, Seth Belliston
Pianist: Nancy McDill
Note: This entered the New York City Ballet repertory on January 19, 1995.

WEST SIDE STORY SUITE

(with Peter Gennaro)

Music: Leonard Bernstein
Scenery: Oliver Smith
Costumes: Irene Sharaff
Premiere: May 18, 1995, New York State Theater
Principal dancers: Robert LaFosse (Tony), Elena Diner (Maria), Jock Soto (Bernardo), Nancy Ticotin (Anita), Nikolaj Hübbe (Riff), Natalie Toro (Rosalia)
Note: This suite was a distillation of the *West Side Story* material in *Jerome Robbins' Broadway* (1989).

BRANDENBURG

Music: Johann Sebastian Bach (Brandeburg Concerto No. 3 and excerpts from Nos. 2, 1, and 6)
Costumes: Holly Hynes
Premiere: January 22, 1997, New York State Theater
Principal dancers: Wendy Whelan, Peter Boal, Lourdes Lopez, Nikolaj Hübbe

In addition to choreographing and/or directing the musicals listed below, Robbins staged Aaron Copland's opera *The Tender Land* (New York City Opera, 1954) and three plays, Bertholt Brecht's *Mother Courage and Her Children* (Martin Beck Theatre, 1963), Arthur Kopit's *Oh Dad, Poor Dad, Mamma's Hung You In the Closet and I'm Feelin' So Sad* (Phoenix Theatre, 1962), and Irene Maria Fornes's *The Office* (1966, closed in previews). Robbins served as production supervisor of *Funny Girl* (Winter Garden, 1964) and "doctored," without credit, *A Funny Thing Happened on the Way to the Forum* (Alvin Theatre, 1962), among other shows.

MUSICALS

ON THE TOWN

Book and lyrics: Betty Comden and Adolph Green, based on an idea by Jerome Robbins

Music: Leonard Bernstein

Scenery: Oliver Smith

Costumes: Alvin Colt

Stage direction: George Abbott

Premiere: December 28, 1944, Adelphi Theatre

Principal players: Adolph Green (Ozzie), Cris Alexander (Chip), John Battles (Gabey), Nancy Walker (Hildy), Betty Comden (Claire), Sono Osato (Ivy), Robert Chisholm (Pitkin), Ray Harrison (The Great Lover)

Dancers: Barbara Gaye, Lavina Nielsen, Atty Vandenberg, Dorothy McNichols, Cyprienne Gabelman, Jean Handy, Virginia Miller, Nelle Fisher, Royce Wallace, Allyn Ann McLerie, Malka Farber, Aza Bard, Ray Harrison, Frank Neal, Carle Ebrele, James Flashe Riley, Ben Piazza, Doublas Matheson, Duncan Noble, Frank Westbrook, John Butler, Richard D'Arcy, Lyle Clark

BILLION DOLLAR BABY

Book and lyrics: Betty Comden, Adolph Green

Music: Morton Gould

Scenery: Oliver Smith

Costumes: Irene Sharaff

Stage direction: George Abbott

Assistant to Jerome Robbins: Anita Alvarez

Premiere: December 21, 1945, Alvin Theatre

Principal players: Emily Ross (Ma Jones), Shirley Van (Esme), Danny Daniels (Champ Watson), Joan McCracken (Maribelle Jones), Mitzi Green (Georgia Motley), Don De Leo (Jerry Bonanza), David Burns (Dapper Welch), William Tabbert (Rocky Barton), Robert Chisholm (Montague), James Mitchell (Rocky [who dances])

Dancers: Jacqueline Dodge, Helen Gallagher, Virginia Gorski, Maria Harriton, Ann Hutchinson, Cecille Mann, Joan Mann, Virginia Poe, Lorraine Todd, Lucas Aco, Allan Waine, Douglas Deane, Fred Hearne, Joe Landis, Arthur Partington, Bill Sumner

HIGH BUTTON SHOES

Book: Stephen Longstreet, adapted from
his novel *The Sisters Liked Them
Handsome*
Music: Jule Styne
Lyrics: Sammy Cahn
Scenery: Oliver Smith
Costumes: Miles White
Stage direction: George Abbott
Premiere: October 9, 1947, New
Century Theatre
Principal players: Phil Silvers (Harrison
Floy), Joey Faye (Mr. Pontdue), Jack
McCauley (Henry Longstreet), Lois
Lee (Fran), Nanette Fabray (Sara
Longstreet), Mark Dawson (Hubert
Ogglethorpe)
Dancers ("Corps de Ballet"): Jean Marie
Caples, Jacqueline Dodge, Evelyn
Giles, Christine Karner, Elena Lane,
Sondra Lee, Kay Lewis, Louisa Lewis,
Audrey Peters, Gloria Smith,
Eleonore Trieber, Vincent Carbone,
Evans Davis, Fred Hearn, Ray
Kirchner, Tommy Morton, Arthur
Partington, William Peirson, Kenneth
Spaulding, William Sumner, Ray
Tobias, Don Weissmuller

LOOK, MA, I'M DANCIN'

Conceived by Jerome Robbins.
Book: Jerome Lawrence, Robert E. Lee
Music and lyrics: Hugh Martin
Scenery: Oliver Smith
Costumes: John Pratt
Stage direction: George Abbott, Jerome
Robbins
Premiere: January 29, 1948, Adelphi
Theatre
Principal players: Don Liberto (Wotan),
Loren Welch (Larry), Alice Pearce

(Dusty Lee), Janet Reed (Ann Bruce),
Virginia Gorski (Snow White),
Harold Lang (Eddie Winkler), Tommy
Rall (Tommy), Robert H. Harris (F.
Plancek), Katharine Sergava (Tanya
Drinskaya), Alexander March
(Vladimir Lubov), Nancy Walker
(Lily Malloy), Raul Celada
(Tanya's Partner)
Dancers ("Members of the Russo-
American Ballet Company"):
Margaret Banks, Mary Broussard, Julie
Curtis, Clare Duffy, June Graham,
Nina Frenkin, Priscilla Hathaway,
Douglas Luther, Bettye McCormack,
Gloria Patrice, James Pollack, Dottie
Pyren, Walter Rinner, Marten
Sameth, Walter Stane, Robert Tucker

MISS LIBERTY

Book: Robert E. Sherwood
Music and lyrics: Irving Berlin
Scenery: Oliver Smith
Costumes: Motley
Stage direction: Moss Hart
Premiere: July 15, 1949, Imperial Theatre
Principal players: Mary McCarty (Maisie
Dell), Charles Dingle (James Gordon
Bennett), Eddie Albert (Horace
Miller), Philip Bourneuf (Joseph
Pulitzer), Herbert Berghof
(Bartholdi), Allyn McLerie (Monique
Dupont), Tommy Rall (The Boy/The
Dandy), Maria Karnilova (The
Girl/Ruby), Ethel Griffies
(The Countess)
Dancers: Virginia Cowell, Coy Dare,
Norma Doggett, Dolores Goodman,
Patricia Hammerlee, Norma Kaiser,
Gloria Patrice, Janice Rule, Tiny
Shimp, Bill Bradley, Fred Hearn, Allen
Knowles, Kazimir Kokic, Erik

Kristen, Joe Milan, Robert Pagent, Eddie Phillips, Bob Tucker

Note: The dance arrangements were by Genevieve Pitot, who also did the arrangements for *Call Me Madam* (with Jesse Meeker) and the ballet music for *Two's Company* (see below).

CALL ME MADAM

Book: Howard Lindsay and Russel Crouse

Music and lyrics: Irving Berlin

Scenery and costumes: Raoul Pène du Bois, with additional dresses by Mainbocher

Stage direction: George Abbott

Premiere: October 12, 1950, Imperial Theatre

Principal players: Ethel Merman (Mrs. Sally Adams), Owen Coll (Supreme Court Justice/Grand Duke Otto), Russell Nype (Kenneth Gibson), Ralph Chambers (Senator Gallagher), Paul Lukas (Cosmo Constantine), Alan Hewitt (Pemberton Maxwell), E. A. Krumschmidt (Hugo Tantinnin), Henry Lascoe (Sebastian Sebastian), Galina Talva (Princess Maria)

Principal dancers: Tommy Rall, Muriel Bentley, Arthur Partington, Norma Kauser; ("The Potato Bugs") Ollie Engebretsen, Richard Fjellman

Dancers: Shellie Farrell, Nina Frenkin, Patricia Hammerlee, Barbara Heath, Norma Kaiser, Virginia LeRoy, Kirsten Valbor, Fred Hearn, Allan Knowls, Kenneth LeRoy, Ralph Linn, Douglas Moppert, Arthur Partington, Bobby Tucker, William Weslow

THE KING AND I

Book and lyrics: Oscar Hammerstein II, based on the novel *Anna and the King of Siam* by Margaret Landon

Music: Richard Rodgers

Scenery: Jo Mielziner

Costumes: Irene Sharaff

Stage direction: John van Druten

Premiere: March 29, 1951, St. James Theatre

Principal players: Gertrude Lawrence (Anna Leonowens), Yul Brynner (The King), Doretta Morrow (Tuptim), Dorothy Sarnoff (Lady Thiang), Larry Douglas (Lun Tha)

Dancers: Jamie Bauer, Lee Becker, Mary Burr, Gemze de Lappe, Shellie Farrell, Marilyn Gennaro, Evelyn Giles, Ina Kurland, Nancy Lynch, Michiko, Helen Murielle, Prue Ward, Dusty Worrall, Yuriko ("The Royal Dancers"); Stephanie Augustine, Marcia James, Ruth Korda, Suzanne Lake, Gloria Marlowe, Carolyn Maye, Helen Merritt, Phyllis Wilcox ("Wives"); Geraldine Hamburg, Maribel Hammer, Norma Larkin, Miriam Lawrence ("Amazons"); Duane Camp, Joseph Caruso, Leonard Graves, Jack Matthews, Ed Preston ("Priests"); Doris Avila, Raul Celada, Beau Cunningham, Tommy Gomez ("Slaves")

TWO'S COMPANY

Book: Charles Sherman, Peter DeVries, Arnold B. Horwitt, Lee Rogow, Nat Hiken, Billy Friedberg, Mort Green, George Foster, Oliver Wakefield

Music: Vernon Duke, Sheldon Harnick

Lyrics: Ogden Nash, Sammy Cahn, Sheldon Harnick

Scenery: Ralph Alswang

Costumes: Miles White

Stage direction: Jules Dassin

Premiere: December 15, 1952,

Alvin Theatre

Cast: Bette Davis, Hiram Sherman, David Burns, Bill Callahan, Nora Kaye, Stanley Prager, Ellen Hanley, George S. Irving, Maria Karnilova, Buzz Miller, Oliver Wakefield, Peter Kelley

Dancers: William Inglis, John Kelly, Ralph Linn, Job Sanders, Stanley Simmons, Florence Baum, Jeanna Beldin, Eleanor Boleyn, Barbara Heath, Dorothy Hill, Julie Marlowe, Helen Murielle; Robert Orton, Francis Edwards, Henry Mallory, Gilert Shipley, Armstead Shobey, Norman Shobey ("Robert Orton's Teen Aces")

THE PAJAMA GAME

Book: George Abbott and Richard Bissell, based on the novel *7 1/2 Cents* by Richard Bissell

Music and lyrics: Richard Adler, Jerry Ross

Scenery and costumes: Lemuel Ayers

Stage direction: George Abbott, Jerome Robbins

Choreography: Bob Fosse

Premiere: May 13, 1954, St. James Theatre

Principal players: Eddie Foy, Jr. (Hines), Stanley Prager (Prez), Ralph Dunn (Hasler), Carol Haney (Gladys), John Raitt (Sid Sorokin), Reta Shaw (Mabel), Buzz Miller (Second Helper), Janis Paige (Babe Williams), Thelma Pelish (Mae), Marion Colby (Brenda), Jack Waldron (Salesman), Peter Gennaro (Worker)

Dancers: Carmen Alvarez, Marilyn Gennaro, Lida Koehring, Shirley MacLaine, Marsha Reynolds, Ann Wallace, Robert Evans, Eric Kristen,

Jim Hutchison, Dale Moreda, Augustin Rodriguez, Ben Vargas

PETER PAN

Book: adapted from the play by James M. Barrie

Music: Mark Charlap and Jule Styne, with incidental music by Trude Rittman and Elmer Bernstein

Lyrics: Carolyn Leigh, with Betty Comden and Adolph Green

Scenery: Peter Larkin

Costumes: Motley

Stage direction: Jerome Robbins

Premiere: October 20, 1954, Winter Garden Theatre

Principal players: Kathy Nolan (Wendy/Jane), Robert Harrington (John), Heller Halliday (Liza), Margalo Gillmore (Mrs. Darling), Cyril Ritchard (Mr. Darling/Captain Hook), Mary Martin (Peter Pan), Joe E. Marks (Smee), Sondra Lee (Tiger Lily)

Dancers: Robert Tucker, Frank Lindsay, Frank Marasco, James Whyte, William Burke, Chester Fisher, John Newton, Arthur Tookoian, Robert Vanselow, Richard Winter ("Pirates"); Robert Banas, Don Lurio, Robert Piper, William Sumner, Richard Wyatt, Linda Dangcil, Lisa Lang, Suzanne Luckey, Joan Tewkesbury ("Indians")

BELLS ARE RINGING

(with Bob Fosse)

Book and lyrics: Betty Comden, Adolph Green

Music: Jule Styne

Scenery and costumes: Raoul Pène du Bois

Stage direction: Jerome Robbins

Premiere: November 29, 1956,
    Shubert Theatre
Principal players: Jean Stapleton (Sue),
    Judy Holliday (Ella Peterson), Peter
    Gennaro (Carl), Sydney Chaplin (Jeff
    Moss), George S. Irving
    (Larry Hastings)
Dancers: Norma Doggett, Phyllis
    Dorne, Patti Karr, Barbara Newman,
    Nancy Perkins, Marsha Rivers, Beryle
    Towbin, Anne Wallace, Doris Avila,
    Frank Derbas, Don Emmons, Eddie
    Heim, Kasimir Kokic, Tom O'Steen,
    Willy Sumner, Ben Vargas,
    Billy Wilson

WEST SIDE STORY

(with Peter Gennaro)

Book: Arthur Laurents
Music: Leonard Bernstein
Lyrics: Stephen Sondheim
Scenery: Oliver Smith
Costumes: Irene Sharaff
Stage direction: Jerome Robbins
Premiere: September 26, 1957, Winter
    Garden Theatre
Cast: (*The Jets*) Mickey Calin (Riff), Larry
    Kert (Tony), Eddie Roll (Action), Tony
    Mordente (A-Rab), David Winters
    (Baby John), Grover Dale (Snowboy),
    Martin Charnin (Big Deal), Hank
    Brunjes (Diesel), Tommy Abbott (Gee-
    Tar), Frank Green (Mouth Piece),
    Lowell Harris (Tiger); (*Their Girls*)
    Wilma Curley (Graziella), Carole
    D'Andrea (Velma), Nanette Rosen
    (Minnie), Marilyn D'Honau (Clarice),
    Julie Oser (Pauline), Lee Becker
    (Anybodys); (*The Sharks*) Ken LeRoy
    (Bernardo), Carol Lawrence (Maria),
    Chita Rivera (Anita), Jamie Sanchez

(Chino), George Marcy (Pepe), Noel
    Schwartz (Indio), Al De Sio (Luis),
    Gene Gavin (Anxious), Ronnie Lee
    (Nibbles), Jay Norman (Juano), Erne
    Castaldo (Toro), Jack Murry (Moose);
    (*Their Girls*) Marilyn Cooper
    (Rosalia), Reri Grist (Consuelo),
    Carmen Gutierrez (Teresita), Elizabeth
    Taylor (Francisca), Lynn Ross (Estella),
    Liane Plane (Marguerita); (*The Adults*)
    Art Smith (Doc), Arch Johnson
    (Schrank), William Bramley (Krupke),
    John Harkins (Gladhand)

GYPSY

Book: Arthur Laurents, based on the
    memoirs of Gypsy Rose Lee
Music: Jule Styne
Lyrics: Stephen Sondheim
Scenery: Jo Mielziner
Costumes: Raoul Pène du Bois
Stage direction: Jerome Robbins
Premiere: May 21, 1959, Broadway
    Theatre
Principal players: Jacqueline Mayro
    (Baby June), Ethel Merman (Rose),
    Jack Klugman (Herbie), Sandra
    Church (Louise), Paul Wallace (Tulsa),
    Maria Karnilova (Tessie Tura), Faith
    Dane (Mazeppa), Chotzi Foley
    (Electra)
Dancers: ("Farm Boys") Marvin
    Arnold, Ricky Coll, Don Emmons,
    Michael Parks, Ian Tucker, Paul
    Wallace, David Winters;
    ("Hollywood Blondes") Marilyn
    Cooper (Agnes), Patsy Bruder
    (Marjorie May), Marilyn D'Honau
    (Dolores), Marle Letowt (Thelma),
    Joan Petlak (Edna), Imelda de Martin
    (Gail); ("Showgirls") Kathryn

Albertson, Gloria Kristy, Denise
McLaglen, Barbara London, Theda
Nelson, Carroll Jo Towers

FIDDLER ON THE ROOF

Book: Joseph Stein, based on stories
    from Sholom Aleichem's *Tevye's
    Daughters*
Music: Jerry Bock
Lyrics: Sheldon Harnick
Scenery: Boris Aronson
Costumes: Patricia Zipprodt
Stage direction: Jerome Robbins
Premiere: September 22, 1964,
    Imperial Theatre
Cast: Zero Mostel (Tevye), Maria
    Karnilova (Golde), Joanna Merlin
    (Tzeitel), Julia Migenes (Hodel) Tanya
    Everett (Chava), Marilyn Rogers
    (Shprintze), Linda Ross (Beilke),
    Beatrice Arthur (Yente), Austin
    Pendleton (Motel), Bert Convy
    (Perchik), Michael Granger (Lazar
    Wolf), Zvee Scooler (Mordcha),
    Gluck-Sandor (Rabbi), Leonard Frey
    (Mendel), Paul Lipson (Avram),
    Maurice Edwards (Nachum), Sue
    Babel (Grandma Tzeitel), Carol
    Sawyer (Fruma-Sarah), Joseph
    Sullivan (Constable), Joe Ponazecki
    (Fyedka), Helen Verbit (Shandel),
    Gino Conforti (The Fiddler); Tom
    Abbott, John C. Attle, Sue Babel,
    Sammy Bayes, Robert Berdeen,
    Lorenzo Bianco, Duane Bodin,
    Robert Currie, Sarah Felcher,
    Tony Gardell, Louis Genevrino,
    Ross Gifford, Dan Jasin, Sandra
    Kazan, Thom Koutsoukos, Sharon
    Lerit, Sylvia Mann, Peff Medelski,
    Irene Paris, Charles Rule,

Carol Sawyer, Roberta Senn,
Mitch Thomas, Helen Verbit
(Villagers)

JEROME ROBBINS' BROADWAY

*Musical revue based on excerpts from shows
choreographed by Jerome Robbins.*
Dialogue, music, and lyrics: James M.
    Barrie, Irving Berlin, Leonard
    Bernstein, Jerry Bock, Sammy Cahn,
    Moose Charlap, Betty Comden, Larry
    Gelbart, Morton Gould, Adolph
    Green, Oscar Hammerstein II,
    Sheldon Harnick, Arthur Laurents,
    Carolyn Leigh, Stephen Longstreet,
    Hugh Martin, Jerome Robbins,
    Richard Rodgers, Burt Shevelove,
    Stephen Sondheim, Joseph Stein,
    Jule Styne
Scenery: Boris Aronson, Jo Mielziner,
    Oliver Smith, Robin Wagner, Tony
    Walton
Costumes: Joseph G. Aulisi, Alvin Colt,
    Raoul Pène du Bois, Irene Sharaff,
    Tony Walton, Miles White, Patricia
    Zipprodt
Assistants to Jerome Robbins: Cynthia
    Onrubia, Victor Castelli, Jerry
    Mitchell
Stage direction: Jerome Robbins, with
    Grover Dale
Premiere: February 26, 1989,
    Imperial Theatre
Cast: Jason Alexander, Richard Amaro,
    Dorothy Benham, Jeffrey Lee
    Broadhurst, Christophe Caballero,
    Mindy Cartwright, Irene Cho, Jamie
    Cohen, Charlotte d'Amboise, Camille
    de Ganon, Donna Di Meo, Donna
    Marie Elio, Mark Esposito, Susann

Fletcher, Scott Fowler, Angelo H. Fraboni, Ramon Galindo, Nicholas Garr, Gregory Garrison, Carolyn Goor, Michael Scott Gregory, Andrew Grose, Alexia Hess, Nancy Hess, Louise Hickey, Eric A. Hoisington, Barbara Hoon, JoAnn M. Hunter, Scott Jovovich, Pamela Khoury, Susan Kikuchi, Michael Kubala, Robert LaFosse, Mary Ann Lamb, Jane Lanier, David Lowenstein, Michael Lynch, Greta Martin, Joey McKneely, Julio Monge, Troy Myers, Maria Neenan, Jack Noseworthy, Steve Ochoa, Kelly Patterson, Luis Perez, Faith Prince, James Rivera, Tom Robbins, George Russell, Greg Schanuel, Debbie Shapiro, Renée Stork, Mary Ellen Stuart, Linda Talcott, Leslie Trayer, Ellen Troy, Andi Tyler, Scott Wise, Elaine Wright, Barbara Yeager, Alice Yearsley

Notes

DANCE FOR A CITY

1. Robert M. Coates, "Friend to the Arts: New York Is Becoming the Capital of Culture," *Holiday*, Apr. 1949, 131, 135.

2. Kirstein to A. Everett Austin, Jr., July 16, 1933, in *I Remember Balanchine: Recollections of the Ballet Master by Those Who Knew Him*, ed. and intro. Francis Mason (New York: Doubleday, 1991), 115.

3. *The Ballet Society, 1946–1947*, vol. 1 (New York: Ballet Society, 1947), [4].

4. More surprisingly, given her long association with Ballet Theatre, Kirstein asked Agnes de Mille to stage a work for NYCB. After much delay, she sent him the scenario for *Rib of Eve*, but in November 1952, just before it was scheduled to go into production, the project was canceled because of a severe financial crisis affecting all the constituents of City Center. De Mille and Kirstein had known each other since the 1930s and met regularly throughout the 1950s, when both served on the ANTA Dance Panel. For Kirstein's correspondence with de Mille, see Agnes de Mille Papers, Folder 650, Dance Collection, The Lincoln Center Library for the Performing Arts.

5. Anatole Chujoy, *The New York City Ballet* (New York: Knopf, 1953), 242.

6. Lincoln Kirstein, *Thirty Years: The New York City Ballet*, rev. ed. (New York: Knopf, 1978), 122. Forty years later, when he resigned from the company, Robbins said: "I joined the New York City Ballet in 1949 for a single purpose: To work for and with George Balanchine" (quoted in Anna Kisselgoff, "Jerome Robbins Is

Resigning as Co-Director of City Ballet," *New York Times* [hereafter *NYT*], Nov. 6, 1989, C13).

7. For the opening of *Picnic at Tintagel*, see John Martin, "Ashton's 'Picnic' Has Its Premiere," *NYT*, Feb. 29, 1952, 19. The cover stories were "Ballet's Fundamentalist," *Time*, Jan. 25, 1954, 66–74; J. Kobler, "Exciting Rise of Ballet in America," *Holiday*, Nov. 1952, 106–13. A photograph published on May 18, 1952 in the *New York World-Telegram and Sun* showed fifteen of the company's women, most in tutus from *Symphony in C*, posing in a lunge fourth around the sundial in Central Park. The caption read: "An outdoor tuneup for the ballerinas of the New York City Ballet Company. The place—Central Park. Note the hands of the dancers and how they draw toward the center girl." *New York World-Telegram and Sun* Collection, Prints and Photographs Division, Library of Congress.

8. Quoted in Nancy Reynolds, *Repertory in Review: Forty Years of the New York City Ballet*, intro. Lincoln Kirstein (New York: Dial, 1977), 109.

9. Ibid., 94.

10. Ibid.

11. Ibid., 109.

12. Daniel Schorr, "Disputed Ballet Wins an Ovation," *NYT*, July 4, 1952, 9.

13. Quoted in Reynolds, *Repertory in Review*, 101.

14. Ibid., 104.

15. Kirstein, *Thirty Years*, 122.

16. Quoted in Reynolds, *Repertory in Review*, 118.

17. Ibid., 209.

18. Kirstein, *Thirty Years*, 113.

19. Suki Schorer, *Balanchine Pointework*, ed. Lynn Garafola, with an afterword by Robert Greskovic, *Studies in Dance History*, No. 11 (1995), ix.

20. "City Center Eyes Move to Project," *NYT*, Oct. 29, 1955, 13; Harold C. Schonberg, "Rockefeller 3d Will Direct Study of a Lincoln Sq. Center for Arts," *NYT*, Dec. 1, 1955, 1.

21. Jennifer Dunning, *"But First a School": The First Fifty Years of the School of American Ballet* (New York: Viking/Elisabeth Sifton Books, 1985), 111.

22. "Tribute to Rockefeller Staged by City Ballet," *NYT*, Jan. 31, 1979, sec. 3, 19. Rockefeller also had a hand in the construction of the Performing Arts Center in Saratoga Springs, a five-thousand-seat auditorium that in 1966 became the company's summer home. In 1960 the company dedicated *Panamerica*, a "program of new choreographies . . . to music by eight Latin American composers," to Rockefeller for "his many past instances of support of artistic interchange between the Americas" (John Martin, "Ballet: Dedicated to the Governor," *NYT*, Jan. 21, 1960, 28).

23. With seven daily newspapers, these events were covered extensively and from many different points of view. The single best collection of clippings, promotional material, and photographs is at the Lincoln Center for the Performing Arts

Archives (hereafter LCPAA). Robert Indiana recalled the neighborhood in "Biography of a Poster," a short essay in the souvenir program for the April 1964 inaugural performances at the New York State Theater.

According to a 1956 memorandum in the Rockefeller Archives, the population of the three square blocks reserved for Lincoln Center was 75 percent white, 2 percent black, and the rest "Spanish-speaking" (Willard Keefe, memo to John D. Rockefeller 3d, Apr. 20, 1956, Rockefeller Family Archives, R.G. 5, Series 1, Box 76, Folder 655).

24. "Report on Survey to Determine Feasibility of Creating and Operating a Performing Arts Center in New York City—To the Exploratory Committee for a Performing Arts Center," 8, LCPAA. This confidential, undated report was prepared by the engineering firm Day & Zimmermann, Inc. On Kirstein's interest in a new theater, see Franz Schulze, *Philip Johnson: Life and Work* (New York: Knopf, 1994), 187; and Martin L. Sokol, *The New York City Opera: An American Adventure* (New York: Macmillan, 1981), 167.

25. Sokol, *New York City Opera*, 169.

26. The letter to Morris is quoted in ibid., 170–71; the letter to Rockefeller on 171–72.

27. Minutes of second Advisory Meeting on [sic] the Dance, Feb. 11, 1958, 3, LCPAA.

28. "What Lincoln Center will mean to you: Progress report on New York City's new 'neighborhood of the immortals,'" *The New Yorker*, Apr. 9, 1960, 139.

29. Allen Hughes, "Centers Collide: Control of New York State Theater Disputed by Culture Combines," *NYT*, Oct. 11, 1964, sec. 2, 13.

30. Allen Hughes, "Ford Fund Allots 7.7 Million to Ballet," *NYT*, Dec. 16, 1963, 1; "Ford Grants Stir Dance Comment," *NYT*, Dec. 17, 1963, 49; Allen Hughes, "Ballet Grants: Ford Foundation Grants Raise Many Questions," *NYT*, Dec. 22, 1963, sec. 2, 11. For an overview of the Ford-NYCB relationship, see Anne Barclay Bennett, "The Management of Philanthropic Funding for Institutional Stabilization: A History of Ford Foundation and New York City Ballet," Ed.D. diss., Harvard University, 1989.

31. Quoted in Kirstein, *Thirty Years*, 183.

32. "House of Balanchine," *Newsweek*, Apr. 8, 1963, 88. According to Johnson, he had only "one boss" on the project—Kirstein. Thus, it was Kirstein, with Johnson, who decided to trade a full stage house for the Promenade. As the architect explained to Sharon Zane, who interviewed him for the Lincoln Center for the Performing Arts Oral History Project: "Backstage was a requirement, but there was no room for a backstage [and] a great reception hall. . . . So . . . Lincoln and I just made that decision." Amazingly, Balanchine was not consulted about the orchestra pit. After it was done, according to Johnson he "took one look at it . . . and said, 'Get those seats out of there and get me a decent orchestra pit!'" As for the so-called "continental seating" (meaning without a center aisle) in the orchestra, a recommendation of seating consultant Ben Schlanger, it was a design "never

. . . done before or since." Finally, on the subject of the hall's much-criticized acoustics: "Lincoln and I, leaning toward the dance, didn't pay too much attention to the opera acoustics. . . . For dance, it doesn't really make that much difference." See 34, 50, 82, 88, 92 of the transcripts, at LCPAA. The interviews took place in August and September 1990.

33. John Martin, "Ballet: Revised Program," *NYT*, Mar. 22, 1961, 38; "Mayor Lauds Balanchine, Kirstein and Ballet Company," *NYT*, Dec. 6, 1962, 55; Nan Robertson, "Ballet a Delight to Slum Children," *NYT*, Feb. 7, 1960, 61; "Free Concerts on L.I. for Schoolchildren," *NYT*, Feb. 2, 1966, 22; "City Ballet Group Appears at Prison," *NYT*, July 26, 1971, 32; "Ballet Talks Begin in 30 City Schools," *NYT*, Feb. 18, 1964, 26.

34. Clive Barnes, "Dance: A Bright Omen," *NYT*, Mar. 26, 1966, 14.

35. Harris Green, "That Subscription Crowd Must Go!" *NYT*, June 7, 1970, sec. 2, 24.

36. Dale Harris, "Balanchine: The End of a Reign," *Saturday Review*, July 15, 1972, 47.

37. Anna Kisselgoff, "City Ballet's 'Arrival' Delights Kirstein," *NYT*, June 17, 1971, 48.

38. Allen Hughes, "New Contracts for Christmas," *NYT*, Dec. 6, 1964, sec. 2, 21; Harold C. Schonberg, "City and Lincoln Centers in Battle Over State Theater," *NYT*, Nov. 8, 1964, sec. 2, 12; Theodore Strongin, "City Center Gets $3.2 Million From Ford Fund," *NYT*, Nov. 18, 1965, 59.

39. For the 1966 strike, see Richard F. Shepard, "Musicians Strike the City Ballet," *NYT*, Nov. 15, 1966, 52, and "Talks Broken Off in Ballet Strike," *NYT*, Nov. 16, 1966, 52; Louis Calta, "Musicians Ratify Pact with Ballet," *NYT*, Nov. 17, 1966, 56. For City Center's 1973 financial crisis and the 1973 dancers' strike, see "Fund Cut Curtails Joffrey's Fall Season" and Mel Gussow, "Ford Fund Lends City Center a Million," *NYT*, Mar. 19, 1973, 46; Emanuel Perlmutter, "On Eve of Its 25th Year, the City Ballet Goes on Strike," *NYT*, Nov. 14, 1973, 47; "Disputes Mar Cultural Season" and Linda Greenhouse, "Center Faces Unending Deficit," *NYT*, Nov. 14, 1973, 47; Clive Barnes, "Dance: One of the Strangest Strikes to Hit the Arts," *NYT*, Nov. 25, 1973, sec. 2, 17–18; Richard Severo, "City Ballet Ends Strike of 25 Days," *NYT*, Dec. 9, 1973, 41. For the 1976–77 strike, see Emanuel Perlmutter, "Current Strike At City Ballet Perils Season," *NYT*, Dec. 29, 1976, 22; "Ballet Cancels Season as Musicians Reject Mediator Plan to End Strike," *NYT*, Jan. 18, 1977, 1; Emanuel Perlmutter, "Musicians End City Ballet Strike; Short Season May Open Tuesday," *NYT*, Jan. 23, 1977, 1. For Jaffe's remarks, see Anna Kisselgoff, "Troubles of the City Ballet—and the Cultural Cost," *NYT*, Jan. 23, 1977, sec. 2, 22; for Kramer, see his article, "The Quest for Funds to Keep the Arts Lively Goes On," *NYT*, Nov. 15, 1973, 54.

40. "'I Cannot Wait,'" *Newsweek*, Oct. 25, 1965, 100.

41. Hubert Saal, "Making Balanchine Happy," *Newsweek*, Jan. 13, 1969, 54.

42. Quoted in Reynolds, *Repertory in Review*, 280.

43. Nancy Goldner, "Dance," *The Nation*, Feb. 16, 1970, 189. Barnes is quoted in Reynolds, *Repertory in Review*, 262.

44. Quoted in ibid.

45. Quoted in Bernard Taper, *Balanchine: A Biography*, rev. ed. (Berkeley: University of California Press, 1996), 100.

46. Sally Moore, "A Ballet Is Born," *People*, July 4, 1978, 74–81.

47. " 'I Cannot Wait,' " 100.

48. Suzanne Gordon, *Off Balance: The Real World of Ballet* (New York: Pantheon, 1983).

49. Toni Bentley, *Winter Season: A Dancer's Journal* (New York: Random House, 1982), 64–65.

50. Quoted in Deborah Weisgall, "The Company He Keeps," *NYT*, Apr. 21, 1996, sec. 6, 28.

51. Taper, *Balanchine*, 402.

52. Ibid., 404–7.

53. Walter Clemons, "Prince of the City Ballet," *Newsweek*, Dec. 26, 1983, 56–63.

54. Quoted in Diane Solway, "City Ballet Moves to an American Beat," *NYT*, Apr. 24, 1988, sec. 2, 1.

55. Quoted in Anna Kisselgoff, "Peter Martins Talks About New Role as City Ballet's 'Daddy,' " *NYT*, Jan. 25, 1984, C17.

56. Kirstein in the entry on "choreography" in *Ballet Alphabet: A Primer for Laymen*, first published in 1939, made a useful distinction between "different levels of creation." "Choreography," he wrote, "may be interpretative or decorative, or more importantly, inventive and creative. To 'interpret' or illustrate music, or to decorate a stage with period revivals, however charming, is less interesting than the creation of lyric drama where dancing may not necessarily be a sole end in itself, but where it can be preeminently an arrangement of ideas particularly suitable to expression in dance terms" (*Ballet Bias and Belief: "Three Pamphlets Collected" and Other Dance Writings of Lincoln Kirstein*, ed. and intro. Nancy Reynolds [New York: Dance Horizons, 1983], 311). Following this distinction, Balanchine was an "inventive" or "creative" choreographer, Martins an "interpretative" or "decorative" one.

57. Quoted in Solway, "City Ballet."

58. Laura Shapiro, "Reviving a Reverie: 'Sleeping Beauty' Bows," *Newsweek*, May 13, 1991, 71.

59. Lynn Garafola, "Ten Years After: Peter Martins on Preserving Balanchine's Legacy," *Dance Magazine*, May 1993, 40.

60. Quoted in Weisgall, "The Company He Keeps."

61. Monique P. Yazigi, "Neighborhood Report: Lincoln Center—Buzz," *NYT*, Nov. 30, 1997, sec. 14, 6.

62. According to the Bureau of Labor Statistics, the consumer price index for New York City was 176.3 in 1976, 288.6 in 1983, and 500.1 in mid-1998.

THE NEW YORK CITY BALLET AND THE WORLDS OF NEW YORK INTELLECT

1. Virgil Thomson, *Virgil Thomson* (London: Weidenfeld and Nicolson, 1967), 313. This division could, in fact, be tracked through the whole of the twentieth century, with the relative weight of each shifting.

2. Irving Howe, "Ballet for the Man Who Enjoys Wallace Stevens," *Harper's Magazine*, May 1971, 102. On Wilson as the "gold standard" for *Partisan Review* critics, see Thomas Bender, *New York Intellect* (New York: Knopf, 1987), 255.

3. On the importance of ballet for Cornell, especially ballet of the romantic era and the ballets of Balanchine, which offered Cornell representations of "female purity" that were safely out of reach, see Deborah Solomon, *Utopia Parkway: The Life and Work of Joseph Cornell* (New York: Farrar, Straus and Giroux, 1997), 110, 112, 155, and passim. Cornell, thanks to an open invitation from Kirstein, regularly dropped by rehearsals.

4. See Clement Greenberg, *The Collected Essays and Criticism*, ed. John O'Brian, 4 vols. (Chicago: University of Chicago Press, 1986), II:288.

5. Ibid., I:124–25.

6. Humphrey Carpenter, *W. H. Auden: A Biography* (Boston: Houghton Mifflin, 1981), 393; Richard Davenport-Hines, *Auden* (London: Heineman, 1995), 219.

7. Quoted in Michael Leja, *Reframing Abstract Expressionism: Subjectivity and Painting in the 1940s* (New Haven: Yale University Press, 1993), 47.

8. Brad Gooch, *City Poet: The Life and Times of Frank O'Hara* (New York: Knopf, 1993), 192.

9. See Daniel Bell, *The Winding Passage* (New York: Basic Books, 1980), 127–28.

10. On Levy, see Russell Lynes, *Good Old Modern: An Intimate Portrait of the Museum of Modern Art* (New York: Atheneum, 1973), 78, 98. For Levy's friendship with Askew, see Solomon, *Utopia Parkway*, 155. For George Platt Lynes's photos of dancers, see his *Ballet* (Pasadena: Twelvetrees Press, 1985) and the souvenir programs for the various Kirstein-Balanchine enterprises from the mid-1930s to the late 1950s.

11. Lincoln Kirstein, *Mosaic: Memoirs* (New York: Farrar, Straus and Giroux, 1994), 177–78; Lincoln Kirstein, *By With To and From: A Lincoln Kirstein Reader*, ed. Nicholas Jenkins (New York: Farrar, Straus and Giroux, 1991), 31, 34.

12. Nicholas Fox Weber, *Patron Saints: Five Rebels Who Opened America to a New Art* (New Haven: Yale University Press, 1995), 179.

13. Virgil Thomson, *Virgil Thomson* (London: Weidenfeld and Nicolson, 1967), 215–16.

14. Nicholas Jenkins, "The Great Impresario," *The New Yorker*, April 13, 1998, 56.

15. Though the phrase is identified with Johnson and Hitchcock, it was Barr who coined it.

16. On the initial importance of MOMA for Cage, see Thomas Hines, "When Not Yet Cage: The Los Angeles Years, 1912–1938," in Marjorie Perloff and Charles

Junkerman, eds., *John Cage* (Chicago: University of Chicago Press, 1994), 65–99.

17. On the way Greenberg's dominance as a critic obscured the persistence of surrealist influences in abstract expressionism, see Leja, *Reframing Abstract Expressionism*; Stephen Polcari, *Abstract Expressionism and the Modern Experience* (New York: Cambridge, 1991); and Martica Sawin, *Surrealism in Exile and the Beginning of the New York School* (Cambridge: MIT Press, 1995).

18. Dan Wakefield, *New York in the Fifties* (Boston: Houghton Mifflin, 1992), 111.

19. Quoted in ibid., 112.

20. "New Stravinsky Ballet," *Time*, Dec. 16, 1957, 67.

21. Gooch, *City Poet*, 427.

22. Amiri Baraka, *The Autobiography of LeRoi Jones* (Chicago: Lawrence Hill Books, 1997), 235.

23. For a revealing sampling from the perspective of MOMA, see Riva Castleman, ed., *Art of the Forties* (New York: MOMA, 1991).

24. Reprinted in Greenberg, *Collected Essays*, I:5–22.

25. Ibid., I:23, 28, 32. For a good brief overview of Greenberg's ideas and role, see Robert Storr, "No Joy in Mudville: Greenberg's Modernism Then and Now," in Kirk Varnedoe and Adam Gopnik, eds., *Modern Art and Popular Culture* (New York: MOMA, 1990), 160–90. The larger context of Greenberg's worry about contamination is developed by Andreas Huyssen, *After the Great Divide: Modernism, Mass Culture, Postmodernism* (Bloomington: Indiana University Press, 1986).

26. Lincoln Kirstein, "The State of Modern Art," *Harper's Magazine*, Oct. 1948, 51.

27. Howe, "Ballet for the Man Who Enjoys Wallace Stevens," 105–6.

28. Guy Davenport, "Civilization and Its Opposite in the Nineteen Forties," in Castleman, ed., *Art of the Forties*, 31.

29. Interesting in this context is the argument of Philip Fisher about the cultural work performed by sentimental novels, another "lower" order artistic form. See Philip Fisher, *Hard Facts: Setting and Form in the American Novel* (New York: Oxford University Press, 1987).

30. Greenberg, "Review of the Ballet *Dim Luster* by Antony Tudor," in *Collected Essays*, II:38.

31. On Duchamp, see Jerrold Seigel, *The Private Worlds of Marcel Duchamp: Desire, Liberation, and the Self in Modern Culture* (Berkeley: University of California Press, 1995).

32. Elisabeth Sussman, "Florine Stettheimer: A 1990s Perspective," in *Florine Stettheimer: Manhattan Fantastica* (New York: Whitney Museum of American Art, 1995), 56. That this is a catalogue for a recent show on Stettheimer at the Whitney Museum reinforces my point.

33. Solomon, *Utopia Parkway*, 98.

34. Stettheimer, incidentally, had her own way of playing with the American flag, particularly in "New York, 1918" (1918), "Fourth of July" (1927), and "Wall Street" (1939).

35. Sussman, "Florine Stettheimer," 62.

36. Kirk Varnedoe, "Philip Johnson as Donor to the Museum Collections: An Overview," in *Philip Johnson and the Museum of Modern Art*, Studies in Modern Art, vol. 6 (New York: MOMA, 1998), 12. Varnedoe points out that Johnson's donations in the 1960s, which included works by Warhol, Donald Judd, Robert Morris, Frank Stella, and Claes Oldenburg, literally created the museum's collection of Pop and Minimal Art.

37. Solomon, *Utopia Parkway*, 269.

38. Sussman, "Florine Stettheimer," 66. I should note that credit for the scholarly rediscovery of Stettheimer belongs to Linda Nochlin's "Florine Stettheimer: Rococo Subversive," *Art in America*, Sept. 1980, 64–83.

39. Sally Banes, *Greenwich Village, 1963* (Durham: Duke University Press, 1993).

40. For a broad survey of twentieth-century performance art, see RoseLee Goldberg, *Performance Art: From Futurism to the Present*, rev. ed. (New York: Abrams, 1988). For an account more sharply focused on New York in the 1960s, see Banes, *Greenwich Village*.

41. See ibid., 54, 10.

42. William Mackay, "Edwin Denby, 1903–1983," in Edwin Denby, *Dance Writings*, eds. Robert Cornfield and William Mackay (New York: Knopf, 1986), 32; Banes, *Greenwich Village*, 55.

SIBLING RIVALRY: THE NEW YORK CITY BALLET AND MODERN DANCE

I am deeply grateful to Barbara Barker, Jim Sutton, and Noël Carroll for their help with and advice on this essay, and especially to Lynn Garafola and Eric Foner for commissioning it and guiding it to fruition.

1. Isadora Duncan, *Isadora Speaks*, ed. and intro. Franklin Rosemont (San Francisco: City Lights, 1981), 33–34.

2. Quoted in Bernard Taper, *Balanchine: A Biography* (Berkeley: University of California Press, 1996), 59.

3. Agnes de Mille, *Martha: The Life and Work of Martha Graham* (New York: Random House, 1991), 161.

4. Lincoln Kirstein, *Movement and Metaphor: Four Centuries of Ballet* (New York: Praeger, 1970), 4.

5. Quoted in Diane Solway, "City Ballet Moves to an American Beat," *The New York Times*, Apr. 24, 1988, sec. 2, p. 1.

6. Dorothy Bird and Joyce Greenberg, *Bird's Eye View: Dancing with Martha Graham and on Broadway* (Pittsburgh: University of Pittsburgh Press, 1997), 154.

7. Ibid., 189. Also see "Anna Sokolow" in Robert Tracy, *Goddess: Martha Graham's Dancers Remember* (New York: Limelight Editions, 1997), 24.

8. See, for example, the photograph on page 37 of Nancy Reynolds, *Repertory in*

Review: Forty Years of the New York City Ballet, intro. Lincoln Kirstein (New York: Dial, 1977). Though their line is more refined and lyrical, the dancers still show muscular strength in the 1950s, but less so by the mid-1960s (see 38).

9. Marcia B. Siegel, *The Shapes of Change: Images of American Dance* (Boston: Houghton Mifflin, 1979), 72.

10. Quoted in Sali Ann Kriegsman, *Modern Dance in America: The Bennington Years* (Boston: G. K. Hall, 1981), 58. Boris's article, "The Ballet Caravan," was published in October 1937 in the banner issue of *Dance Herald*.

11. Yuri Slonimsky, *The Bolshoi Theatre Ballet: Notes* (Moscow: Foreign Languages Publishing House, 1956), [21].

12. See Elizabeth Souritz, *Soviet Choreographers in the 1920s*, trans. Lynn Visson, ed. with additional trans. Sally Banes (Durham: Duke University Press, 1990), 73–78.

13. Lincoln Kirstein, *Thirty Years: The New York City Ballet* (New York: Knopf, 1978), 244. This was a revised and expanded version of Kirstein's *New York City Ballet*, published in 1973.

14. Quoted in Reynolds, *Repertory*, 102. De Mille's article, "Acrobatics and the New Choreography," was published in the January 1930 issue of *Theatre Guild Magazine*.

15. All quoted in Reynolds, *Repertory*, 152.

16. Letter to A. Everett Austin, Jr., July 16, 1933. This letter, now in the Wadsworth Atheneum archives, is reprinted in Francis Mason, *I Remember Balanchine* (New York: Doubleday/Anchor Books, 1992), 118.

17. Lincoln Kirstein, *Three Pamphlets Collected* (New York: Dance Horizons, 1967), 45.

18. Kirstein, *Thirty Years*, 69.

19. Kirstein, *Three Pamphlets*, 110–11.

20. Kirstein, *Thirty Years*, 69.

21. Ibid., 72.

22. Lincoln Kirstein, *Paul Cadmus* (New York: Rizzoli, 1984), 21.

23. See, for instance, the videotape *The Men Who Danced*, produced and directed by Ron Honsa in 1985.

24. Edwin Denby, *Dance Writings*, ed. Robert Cornfield and William MacKay (New York: Knopf, 1986), 219.

25. See *Choreography by Jerome Robbins with the New York City Ballet*, produced by Judy Kinberg and directed by Emile Ardolino for the PBS series *Dance in America: Great Performances* and aired on WNET-13 on May 2, 1986.

26. Kirstein, *Three Pamphlets*, 92.

27. Quoted in Kriegsman, *Modern Dance*, 196. Kirstein's article, "Martha Graham at Bennington," was published in *The Nation* on September 3, 1938.

28. De Mille, *Martha*, 229.

29. Ibid., 239–40.

30. Quoted in Reynolds, *Repertory*, 46. This was published as a letter to the editor of *Time* magazine on May 30, 1936.

31. See *Stravinsky and Balanchine: Genius Has a Birthday*, produced by John Goberman for PBS and aired on WNET-13, October 4, 1982.

32. Siegel, *Shapes*, 223.

33. Reynolds, *Repertory*, 225.

34. Edwin Denby, *Dancers, Buildings, and People in the Streets* (New York: Horizon, 1965), 121.

35. See Sally Banes, *Terpsichore in Sneakers: Post-Modern Dance* (1980; rev. ed. Middletown: Wesleyan University Press, 1987).

36. Quoted in Reynolds, *Repertory*, 259.

37. Quoted in ibid., 260.

38. See Sally Banes, "Pointe of Departure," *Boston Review* (Oct. 1986), reprinted in *Writing Dancing in the Age of Postmodernism* (Hanover: Wesleyan University Press/University Press of New England, 1994), 290–97.

39. Quoted in Solway, "City Ballet."

40. When I say modern dance declined, I do not mean that people stopped taking modern dance classes or using modern dance technique or choreographic methods. Work in that idiom continues, just as, long after the age of realism, many people continued to paint in a realist mode. But with the advent of postmodern dance, modern dance has ceased to be the arena where new discoveries in dance take place, nor has it (or postmodern dance) sustained the general cultural weight it had in its heyday.

THE MAKING OF *AGON*

1. Denby's remarks are from his well-known article, "Three Sides of *Agon*," reprinted in *Dancers, Buildings and People in the Streets* (New York: Horizon Press, 1965), 119–27. A. V. Coton's review of *Agon* is reprinted in *Writings on Dance, 1938–68* (London: Dance Books), 126. Balanchine's reference to *Agon* as a thinking machine was first mentioned in an introduction to the ballet, entitled "A Note from George Balanchine," included in the opening night program booklet. Stravinsky retained a copy of this in his archives.

2. Of the many studies of the ballet, a few deserve particular mention. Irene Alm, "Stravinsky, Balanchine, and *Agon*: An Analysis Based on the Collaborative Process," *The Journal of Musicology* 7 (2) (Spring 1989): 254–69 is useful in its facsimile reprinting of an early "mapping out" of the ballet's sections. The author's claim that it is the first draft, however, is not quite accurate. An earlier version was sketched by Stravinsky and Balanchine, but actually ripped from the yellow legal pad paper that Alm confuses with the original draft. The details of the earlier draft—showing a different ordering of *Agon*'s dances, for example—confirms that the final divisions of the ballet were not the first ones imagined, and that adjustments were made by both composer and choreographer during the summer of 1954. For a more recent and especially perceptive essay addressing various dance aspects of the ballet, see Sally Banes, *Dancing Women: Female Bodies on Stage*

(London: Routledge, 1998), 194–211. Arlene Croce's well-known article, "The Spelling of *Agon*," *The New Yorker*, June 12, 1993, 84–92, offers some intriguing theories about the evolution of the ballet. However, when examined in light of Stravinsky's archival source materials, some of the conclusions appear questionable. For a detailed response to Croce's essay, see Robert Craft's *The Moment of Existence* (Nashville: Vanderbilt University Press, 1996), 278–82; see also Stephanie Jordan, "*Agon*: A Musical/Choreographic Analysis," *Dance Research Journal* 25 (2) (Fall 1993): 1–12. Jordan's careful study is based upon a clear understanding not only of the dance, but also of Stravinsky's music. Finally, see Glenn Watkins, *Pyramids at the Louvre* (Cambridge: The Belknap Press of Harvard University Press, 1994), 360–74. Watkins' discussion of *Agon*'s "mask" as a component of ritual is richly informative and provocative in its at times far-ranging implications.

3. The edited letter is reprinted in Robert Craft's *Stravinsky: Selected Correspondence*, vol. 1 (New York: Knopf, 1982), 284–85. The original is held by the Paul Sacher Stiftung, Basel. In this "draft" sketch, Kirstein imagined the setting as a "vast ballroom in space" for a "reception of the gods" with Apollo and Terpsichore (André Eglevsky and Maria Tallchief), Cupid (Janet Reed), Pegasus (Patricia Wilde), Prometheus (Francisco Moncion), Orpheus and the Bacchante (Nicolas Magallanes and Tanaquil LeClercq), Venus and Mars (Diana Adams and Herbert Bliss), Zeus (Hugh Laing), and Jerome Robbins (Mercury), who was to lead the "big jazz finale."

4. Although Eliot and Stravinsky did not meet until December 1956, they shared a mutual admiration. Stravinsky was well aware of Eliot's considerable knowledge of dance as early as the 1920s, and he often quoted Eliot in his articles and lectures during the 1940s. Eliot made his first acquaintance with the composer's *Rite of Spring* through Léonide Massine's 1920 restaging of the ballet, which had a powerful impact on him. The connection between Stravinsky's *Rite* and Eliot's 1922 *The Waste Land* has been noted by many. See Nancy Hargrove, "The Great Parade: Cocteau, Picasso, Satie, Massine, Diaghilev—and T. S. Eliot," *Mosaic* 31 (1) (March 1998): 83–106; also Lynn Garafola, *Diaghilev's Ballets Russes* (New York: Oxford University Press, 1989). The composer and poet discussed another possible collaboration in the late 1950s (leading eventually to Stravinsky and Craft's 1962 *The Flood*), but Eliot's interest waned as he turned to other projects. Also in 1962, Stravinsky, at Eliot's suggestion, composed a twelve-tone musical anthem set to the words of Part IV of Eliot's *Four Quartets*. The composer dedicated the piece to the poet.

5. Terrence Diggory, *Yeats and American Poetry: The Tradition of the Self* (Princeton: Princeton University Press, 1983), 106–7.

6. See Eliot's now classic article, "The Beating of a Drum," *The Nation and the Athenaeum*, Oct. 1923, 11–12.

7. See Craft's *Present Perspectives* (New York: Knopf, 1984), 253. Coincidentally, Eliot felt that with the failure of *Sweeney*, he had reached the end of his career as a poet.

He confessed his disillusion in a 1952 article that appeared in *The New York Times* only a few months after Stravinsky faced his own crisis, and it is likely that the composer read Eliot's disclosure with a considerable measure of empathy.

8. The reprint was published in 1952 by Frederick Muller Ltd., London. Unless otherwise noted, the illustrations accompanying this essay are from Stravinsky's copy, courtesy of the Paul Sacher Stiftung, Basel.

9. Stravinsky's letter appears in Robert Craft's *Stravinsky: Selected Correspondence*, 253, but the letter (like much of the correspondence between Kirstein and Stravinsky) has been edited.

10. Stravinsky and Balanchine—just as they had done in their preliminary discussions of *Orpheus* in 1946, and for that matter even in 1927 when the two discussed *Apollo* (often in the presence of Diaghilev and Lifar)—first determined very precise durations for each portion of the ballet. These calibrations are marked every few measures in the composer's sketches. The actual divisions of the ballet were decided over a six-week period during the summer of 1954 while Balanchine's New York City Ballet was performing at the Greek Theater in Los Angeles. Of course, by this juncture, Stravinsky was thoroughly familiar with the de Lauze manual. Vera Stravinsky remembers her husband and Balanchine secluding themselves in the composer's study, where they drafted the timings and broad architectural plan of the ballet, although the composer did not formally reveal the choreographic structure for another year. In the earliest known draft of the ballet's plan (earlier than the facsimile that Alm reprints in her article), Stravinsky and Balanchine planned a "Quartet of girls," just after the Pas de Deux, perhaps to balance the male Pas de Quatre that opens and closes the ballet. In the fall of 1956, when Stravinsky was in Venice, the New York City Ballet performed there on tour, affording Balanchine the opportunity to meet with the composer and hear parts of the score for the first time. The choreographer procured a tape of the performance and used it to prepare the final choreography during the fall of 1957. By the next summer, the work was completed and performed in Los Angeles as an orchestral work, with Balanchine in attendance.

11. The remark, made in an interview for the *Syracuse Post Standard* on September 19, is cited by Nancy Reynolds in *Repertory in Review*, intro. Lincoln Kirstein (New York: Dial Press, 1977), 182. Reynolds reprints several statements about the ballet by both Stravinsky and Balanchine, as well as excerpts from the reviews of John Martin, Walter Terry, and other critics who attended early performances.

WATCHING MUSIC

1. Igor Stravinsky, *An Autobiography* (New York: Simon and Schuster, 1936), 99–100.

2. Ibid, 99.

3. Arlene Croce, "Apollo," in *Going to the Dance* (New York: Knopf, 1984), 114.

4. George Balanchine, "The Dance Element in Stravinsky's Music," in Minna

Lederman, ed., *Stravinsky in the Theatre* (New York: Da Capo, 1975), 81.

5. Ibid.

6. Robert Garis, "Balanchine-Stravinsky; Facts and Problems," *Ballet Review* 10 (3) (Fall 1982): 16.

7. Quoted in Richard Buckle, in collaboration with John Taras, *George Balanchine, Ballet-Master* (New York: Random House, 1988), 327.

SUBSTITUTE AND CONSOLATION: THE BALLET PHOTOGRAPHS OF GEORGE PLATT LYNES

I would like to thank Lynn Garafola for her patient explanations about ballet and its history. This essay could not have been written without the invaluable work of Jack Woody and James Crump in resurrecting the work and career of George Platt Lynes. I would also like to thank Richard Martin for sharing with me his crucial essay "Identity: George Platt Lynes' Photograph of Carl Carlsen," *Dress* 22 (1995): 78–84, in which he discusses Lynes's work in relationship to clothing and queer identity.

1. George Platt Lynes, untitled statement, in Jack Woody, *George Platt Lynes: Ballet* (Pasadena: Twelvetrees Press, 1985), n.p. This was originally published in *Dance Index* 3 (12) (Dec. 1944).

2. George Balanchine, untitled statement, in Woody, *George Platt Lynes*, n.p. This was originally published in 1957, after Lynes's death, in *New York City Ballet Photographs from 1935 through 1955 Taken by George Platt Lynes, 1907–56*, a company souvenir program.

3. Lynes, in Woody, *George Platt Lynes*.

4. Roland Barthes, *Camera Lucida*, trans. Richard Howard (New York: Hill and Wang, 1995), 82.

5. Ibid., 47.

6. Lynes, in Woody, *George Platt Lynes*.

7. Balanchine, in Woody, *George Platt Lynes*.

8. James Crump, *George Platt Lynes: Photographs from the Kinsey Institute* (Boston: Bullfinch Press, 1993), 142.

9. Ibid., 143–44.

10. Glenway Wescott, "Illustrations of Mythology," *U.S. Camera* 2 (Jan.–Feb. 1939) reprinted in Jack Woody, *George Platt Lynes Photographs 1931–1955* (Los Angeles: Twelvetrees Press, 1980), n.p.

11. For a short discussion of the series of some thirty photographs see David Leddick, *Naked Men: Pioneering Male Nudes* (New York: Universe Publishing, 1997), 20–21.

12. Lincoln Kirstein, *Nijinsky Dancing* (New York: Knopf, 1975), 13.

13. For a discussion of homophobia and the stereotype of the effeminate male dancer in the United States, see Ramsay Burt, *The Male Dancer: Bodies, Spectacle, Sexualities* (London: Routledge, 1995).

14. Lynes, in Woody, *George Platt Lynes*.
15. Balanchine, in Woody, *George Platt Lynes*.

LISTENING TO BALANCHINE

1. Gould composed *American Concertette*, which became the score for Jerome Robbins's *Interplay* (1945); *Rag Waltz*, used by Peter Martins for a section of *The Waltz Project* (1988); and variations on "You Were Never Lovelier" (Jerome Kern) for Robbins's *I'm Old Fashioned (The Astaire Variations)* (1983). Starting in the 1950s, Gould also worked off and on for some thirty years on the score for a full-length ballet by Balanchine, tentatively entitled *Birds of America* (inspired by the artist John James Audubon), which was never choreographed.

2. Satie died in 1925 and was active with the Ballets Russes at least through 1924, the same year Balanchine was engaged by Diaghilev. The score for *Jack in the Box* was orchestrated by Milhaud from Satie's piano original after his death.

3. The Ravel Festival version received its New York City Ballet premiere on May 15, 1975. Balanchine also created a version for the PBS series *Dance in America* in 1981.

4. Boris Kochno was hired in 1921 as Diaghilev's secretary. In addition to acting as general factotum to the company, he provided librettos for five of Balanchine's ballets, including *Le Fils Prodigue (Prodigal Son)*.

5. The Derain costumes and scenery were subsequently used for *Mother Goose Suite* (1948), choreographed by Todd Bolender.

6. Warburg was a friend of Lincoln Kirstein as well as director and chief patron of the American Ballet (1935–37).

7. Nabokov also orchestrated several Beethoven waltzes for Balanchine's *Les Valses de Beethoven* (1933) and wrote the score for Balanchine's *Don Quixote* (1965).

8. John Colman's cadenza has been used in Balanchine's *Divertimento No. 15* since the late 1960s. On commission from Ballet Society, he composed the score for *The Filly* (1953), choreographed by Todd Bolender.

9. Morton Baum was Chairman of the Executive Committee of the City Center of Music and Drama—and thus de facto director of the organization.

10. The new production premiered on May 28, 1970 at the New York State Theater.

11. Balanchine's *Coppélia* (co-choreographed with Alexandra Danilova) premiered on July 17, 1974, in Saratoga Springs, New York, and was thus brand-new at the time of this interview.

12. When the ballet premiered in Paris in 1870, the male dancer was held in low esteem. The role of Frantz, the hero, was originally danced by a woman *en travesti*.

WORKS CHOREOGRAPHED AND STAGED BY JEROME ROBBINS

1. Although *Fancy Free* was Robbins's first major piece of work, it was not his first original choreography. As Dorothy Bird recounts in her memoir (with Joyce Greenberg), *Bird's Eye View: Dancing with Martha Graham and on Broadway*

(Pittsburgh: University of Pittsburgh Press, 1997), he choreographed many dance numbers for the weekly revues produced at Camp Tamiment, the Pennsylvania resort where he spent the summer of 1939. The company of ten consisted of modern dancers as well as ballet people. Among the first group were Bird, Anita Alvarez, and William Bales; the second group included Ruthanna Boris and Albia Kavan, both members of Ballet Caravan. Robbins, who began his dance studies with Gluck-Sandor, a maverick who worked in many genres, choreographed for both groups.

2. In September 1953 the New York City Ballet made its debut at La Scala with a repertory that included five works by Robbins—*The Cage*, *The Age of Anxiety*, *Afternoon of a Faun*, *Fanfare*, and *The Pied Piper*. The Milan theater already had Balanchine's *Ballet Imperial* in its repertory. Now, for the 1953–54 season, it announced the Italian premiere of a ballet by Robbins—*Appalachian Spring*, to the music of Aaron Copland. The work, which was not produced, was apparently never choreographed.

Index

Page numbers in *italics* indicate illustrations.

This book was set in 11/15 Bembo, licensed from Mono-
type/Adobe, a facsimile of a typeface cut in 1495 by
Francesco Griffo (1450-1518) for the Venetian printer
Aldus Manutius (1450-1515). The face was named for
Pietro Bembo, the author of the small treatise *De Ætna*, in
which it first appeared. The companion italic is based on
the handwriting of the Venetian scribe Giovanni Tagliente
from the 1520s. The present-day version of Bembo was
first introduced by the Monotype Corporation in 1929,
under Stanley Morison's supervision. Serene and versatile,
it is a typeface of classical beauty and high legibility.

This book was designed by Linda Secondari.
Composed by Danielle DeLucia
at Columbia University Press.
Printed and bound at Book Crafters.